Cy Young

The Baseball Life and Career

LEW FREEDMAN

McFarland & Company, Inc., Publishers

Jefferson, North Carolina

All photographs courtesy National Baseball Hall of Fame

LIBRARY OF CONGRESS CATALOGUING-IN-PUBLICATION DATA

Names: Freedman, Lew, author.
Title: Cy Young : the baseball life and career / Lew Freedman.
Description: Jefferson, North Carolina : McFarland & Company, Inc.,
Publishers, 2020. | Includes bibliographical references and index.
Identifiers: LCCN 2020026132 | ISBN 9781476676821
(paperback : acid free paper) ∞
ISBN 9781476637808 (ebook)
Subjects: LCSH: Young, Cy, 1867-1955. |
Baseball players—United States—Biography. |
Pitchers (Baseball)—United States—Biography.
Classification: LCC GV865.Y58 F74 2020 | DDC 796.357092 [B]—dc23
LC record available at https://lccn.loc.gov/2020026132

BRITISH LIBRARY CATALOGUING DATA ARE AVAILABLE

ISBN (print) 978-1-4766-7682-1
ISBN (ebook) 978-1-4766-3780-8

Front cover: Red Sox pitcher Cy Young warming up
in the Huntington Avenue Baseball Grounds
in Boston on July 23, 1908 (Library of Congress)

Printed in the United States of America

McFarland & Company, Inc., Publishers
Box 611, Jefferson, North Carolina 28640
www.mcfarlandpub.com

Table of Contents

Introduction

By November 4, 1955, the man born Denton True Young in Gilmore, Ohio, had been retired from Major League Baseball for 44 years. His career marks had stood the test of time. The same numbers remain all-time records more than 60 years later. By 1955, baseball officials seemed to realize that while very little in their game or in this world is forever, Young's statistics were going to be unimpeachable, and for that matter, unapproachable, forever.

To honor the greatest pitcher of all, the sport's authorities decreed that beginning in 1956, a new award would be created honoring the best big-league pitcher of each season. For a decade, the best single pitcher in the game was presented with the Cy Young Award. However, starting in 1967, the award was expanded and given to the finest pitcher in the American League and the finest pitcher in the National League. The Cy Young Award is still regarded as the most prestigious honor a pitcher can claim.

Young was born in Ohio farm country in 1867, just after the conclusion of the Civil War, when baseball itself was in its infancy and no professional games had yet been contested. The first paid professional team was the Cincinnati Red Stockings, when they began touring in 1869. Yet even in his youth, Young was passionate about the sport.

It is ironic that only a small percentage of baseball fans are even aware of what Young's real name was. Mentioned in passing to a casual fan just recently, someone supposed Cy must have been short for Cyrus. Not so. Cy was the diminutive of a nickname, Cyclone. That appendage was placed next to Young's name when he impressed in an early-in-life tryout. His fastball was so swift it was likened to the speed of a cyclone. Before that his friends called Young "Dent."

Young made his debut in Major League ball in 1890 and retired before the start of the 1912 season. In between, the right-hander pitched for five clubs, the Cleveland National League club known as the Spiders, the Boston Americans, who eventually became known as the Red Sox, the

St. Louis Perfectos, who were never well-known at all, back in Cleveland when the team was called the Naps, and in 1911 for the Boston Rustlers. The Spiders and Naps are part of Cleveland Indians history. The Rustlers, founded in 1871, are part of the Atlanta Braves' lineage.

Just about wherever he went during his 22 big-league years, Young was a winner. When he laid his glove and spikes aside in 1912, he had amassed 511 regular-season victories. No pitcher has ever come close. Young also holds the record for the most losses, with 316 (although some recent studies indicate it may have been only 315), most games started with 815, most complete games with 749, and most innings pitched with 7,356. As an indicator of the stats somewhat common in the 1890s, five times Young threw more than 400 innings in a single campaign. In today's baseball, it is considered an achievement if a starting pitcher tops 200 innings.

The next closest career winner was Walter Johnson with 417. No other pitcher has won 400 games. Christy Mathewson and Grover Cleveland Alexander each won 373 contests. The only hurler who pitched past 1930 to come close to the old, venerable pitchers' totals was Warren Spahn. His 363 wins rank fifth all-time. Spahn retired in 1965. More than a century after Young's retirement, he still owns a share of the record for most victories by a Red Sox pitcher. He shares the record of 192 with Roger Clemens.

Young cracked the 30-win barrier five times during his career, actually collecting at least 32 victories in each of those seasons. One season his earned run average was 1.26. On five other occasions, his ERA was below 2.00 for a season. Young's lifetime earned run average was 2.63.

Baseball Reference lists Young's personal dimensions as 6-foot-2 and 210 pounds. That was probably his playing weight at the peak of his game. Near the end of his career, Young referred to himself as being too fat to continue pitching, partially because he could no longer (in his mind) adequately field bunts. So chances are that when he visited the scale in his late 30s or early 40s, his weight registered well north of 210.

Those early manhood measurements made Young a large player for his time and no doubt aided the power in his arm. Uniforms, the flannels, which players wore in those years were hardly as flattering as the modern uniforms, which better show off muscle. Young's uniforms were bulky and loose-hanging, and in many photographs of him as a player, his uniform pants seem as if they would flap in the breeze. They would receive an "F" in fashion ratings today. They also were high-waisted. One could almost imagine those 1890–1911 uniform pants being held up by suspenders. Apparently, though, the uniforms were never a hindrance to Young's athleticism on the field.

During his playing days—and after—Young was regarded as a gentleman. He was not viewed as someone who unnecessarily threw at batters with brushback pitches, and he was considered a good locker room companion and traveling teammate.

Besides the bold-faced statistics next to Young's name in the record books, he holds other distinctions. When he signed with Boston in 1901, it helped make the upstart challenger American League viable in its fight for survival against the skeptical National League. When the first World Series was played in 1903, Young was on the mound for the first game. He won twice in that Series to help lift the AL champs to the world championship. Young pitched for a salary of $3,500 that season. The Los Angeles Dodgers' Clayton Kershaw, one of the kings of the mound two decades into the 21st century, earned $30 million in 2019. Being paid those kinds of dollars for throwing a baseball would be unimaginable to Cy Young.

A hint of Young's thinking on that topic comes from a comment he made in 1948, when he delivered a speech at a luncheon in Philadelphia. At that time, he said, "Gosh, all a kid has to do these days is spit straight and he gets $40,000 to sign."[1] He was blown away by a $40,000 signing bonus, never mind by multi-million-dollar contracts, which he did not live to see.

What would Cy Young say? That is unknown. What would he say about the state of the game today? Again, unknown. He was of another time, and yet he also saw—and lived through—a large amount of change during the years he played in the majors. Whether it was innings pitched, salaries or other matters, Denton True Young was definitely a pitcher from another era. Yet his most magnificent diamond accomplishments endure.

1

Perfect

When Cy Young collected the final out of his 3–0 victory over the Philadelphia Athletics on May 5, 1904, he was a satisfied pitcher. Not only did the "W" accrue to his record, not only did his Boston Americans (soon to be known as the Red Sox) trump Connie Mack's visitors at Boston's Huntington Avenue Grounds, but his wicked right-handed fastballs had shut the mouth of needling, talkative mound foe Rube Waddell.

It was only after the last pitch was thrown—and Waddell himself flied out to Chick Stahl—that Young truly relished what he had accomplished. When the contest ended, he was unaware he had done something remarkable. On that day, Young pitched a perfect game.

Perfection is something rarely attained in daily life and only rarely achieved in the sporting world. Bowlers who roll 300 games, 12 straight strikes, at times do put the word perfect on their resumes. Every time they walk to the mound to start a ballgame, Major League hurlers have a chance to throw a perfect game. But they hardly ever do. A perfect game means the starter has faced three batters per inning and induced the 27 batsmen to make outs without a man reaching base. Sometimes perfection is lost with the first batter, who may walk, reach base on an error, stroke a single to the outfield, or even smash a home run.

Later on, Young said he did not realize he had thrown a perfect game until he left the ballpark. At least one account suggests that he did not find that out until he was approaching bed-time that evening. In modern baseball, scoreboards are more detailed and efficient, and fans are interacting with technology even while seated in the stands. Even in 1904, with slow-motion communication, could this be possible? It sounds iffy. If Young was slow on the uptake, sports writers were not. The *Boston Post* splashed the story of Young's perfect game on its front page the next day, not the front page of the sports section.

On the day in question, Young faced Waddell for the second time in a week. Waddell, who was born in Bradford, Pennsylvania, in 1876, was a fireballing left-hander who was regarded as a screwball for his behavior. Connie Mack loved the guy's abilities, but his antics drove the manager mad. Waddell was known for jumping the team on a whim to go fishing, and stories indicate he even ran out of ballparks to chase fire engines at the lure of their sirens. Decades later, when Waddell was written about, some of the spice and humor was drained from his offbeat exploits when some suggested he may have been mentally ill, not merely a jokester.

Waddell won 193 games in a 13-year career with a lifetime 2.16 earned run average, statistics good enough to gain him entry into the Baseball Hall of Fame in 1946. Waddell was definitely a strikeout artist, more so than his contemporaries, including Young, who led the AL in strikeouts just twice.

Six times Waddell led the American League in strikeouts, including 1904, when he fanned 349 batters. That record held up as a Major League best until Sandy Koufax struck out 382 men in 1965. Along the way, in 1946, Bob Feller came within one K of Waddell's standard. In 1904, Waddell won 25 games and finished with a 1.62 earned run average, one of his finest years.

Waddell, whose real name was George Edward, faced Young on the mound for the first time that season on April 25. The A's reached Young for two runs early, and Waddell made them hold up for a 2–0 Philadelphia victory. Proud of his smooth throwing, and with no governor on his tongue, Waddell boasted of besting the accomplished star. Young was 37 years old, though his performance did not indicate he was nearly at the end of the line as a top-flight pitcher.

Given his natural inclination to show off, when the two men found themselves as opponents again in early May, Waddell did much to hype the gate verbally. In that manner, he was a Muhammad Ali type decades prior to the heavyweight champ's emergence on the sporting scene. It did no harm to Waddell's ego that three days before this rematch, he pitched one-hit ball, besting Boston again, although Young was not his mound foe.

Even in his quietest of times—if there were such occasions—it was not in Waddell to be discreet. Shortly before the May 5 encounter began, Waddell strutted back and forth in front of the Boston dugout, informing the players that they were in for more of the same from his brilliant arm. "I'm going to give you the same thing I gave [you] the other day," he said.[1]

Young was much less temperamental than Waddell and was not the type to make proclamations about what he was going to do. His showing off consisted of what he did do. This was one time, however, when Young took notice of Waddell's disrespectful attitude. Young was not one to hold major grudges or to talk about seeking revenge. This time, he felt strongly that he must do something to tame this whippersnapper. Really, Waddell was no kid, being 27 at the time of the game, but he was acting childish. Rather than causing Young to chuckle, the big-mouth claims pricked his competitive nature. "I'd been watching him," Young said. "He was a damned fine pitcher, but he ran his mouth quite a bit. I figured he was calling me out and I had better do something about it."[2]

Waddell was definitely calling Young out, suggesting that he was over the hill and maybe should give up the game. Over the following one hour, 23 minutes (a pretty fast game even by early 1900s standards), Young showed Waddell, the A's, and the 10,267 Boston spectators who was still king.

It was a day game, as they all were during that era, and Young did not keep the fans around very long. He struck out eight men. Waddell was sharp in the early going, shutting out Boston through five innings. The Americans touched him for a single run in the bottom of the sixth inning and added two more runs in the seventh.

Young received good support from his teammates, who clouted 10 hits that day. Future Hall of Famer Jimmy Collins smacked a double and single. Lou Criger, Young's favorite catcher, also doubled. Buck Freeman, Hobe Ferris, and Chick Stahl each tripled. Shortstop Freddy Parent knocked out two singles. Young went hitless in three at-bats. So did the entire Athletics lineup.

Actually, Philadelphia played 10 men that day, Topsy Hartsel pinch-hitting for Danny Hoffman. Everyone else in the lineup went 0-for-3 against Young, including Waddell, who made the final out on a high fly to Stahl.

The perfect game was significant for several reasons other than quieting Waddell's mouth. This was the first perfect game in the history of the American League, which was founded in 1901. It was also the first perfect game thrown from the now-traditional distance between the pitching rubber and home plate of 60 feet, 6 inches, which dated to 1893.

Including the post-season, there have been 23 perfect games pitched since the founding of the National League in 1876. More than 210,000 big-league games have been played. On June 12, 1880, Lee Richmond, throwing for the Worcester Worcesters of Massachusetts, pitched the first perfect game, beating Cleveland, 1–0. His was a somewhat bizarre story. Richmond attended Brown University, and he kept very busy the night before his scheduled start at pre-graduation parties back at the school in Rhode Island. He stayed up all night partying, till 6:30 a.m., and then took the short train ride to rejoin his team in time for the game.

The southpaw had a somewhat peculiar career. While pitching the first-ever perfect game, Richmond's big-league stay amounted to parts of six seasons with a 75–100 overall record. Contained within that mark was a 32–32 season.

Soon after, on June 17, the second big-league perfect game was recorded, this one authored by John Montgomery Ward. Ward's masterpiece was a 5–0 win for the Providence Grays over Buffalo. The best-known player on the opposition was future Hall of Fame pitcher Pud Galvin, winner of 365 games in his career.

Ward, also a future Hall of Famer, was a versatile man, pitching, playing the infield, and managing. He was a very early proponent of players' rights and started a union to force owners to pay higher salaries. He graduated from Columbia Law School and put his expertise into founding the Brotherhood of Professional Base Ball Players. He helped jump-start the renegade, short-lived Players' League to compete with the National League.

Richmond's and Ward's perfectos were the only perfect games thrown in the 1800s. When Young recorded his perfect game, 24 years had passed and ironically, he was pitching in the league that survived National League competition instead of the Players' League. The modern era of baseball is considered to have begun in 1901, and Young's perfect game is listed as the first following the turn of that century, after new rules were promulgated that gave the sport more in common with today's game.

The next perfect game was not recorded until 1908, when Addie Joss of Cleveland hurled one during a season when he compiled a 1.16 earned run average. The specialness and rarity of the achievement became clearer with the passage of time. Charlie Robertson of the Chicago White Sox next hurled one in 1922. One thing made clear by Richmond's and Robertson's perfect games was that it did not take a great pitcher to throw one. Sometimes, such as in the case of Young, there was a match between career greatness and the perfect showing. But almost as often, the pitcher who caught lightning in a bottle, or was tapped on his shoulder by God's fingertips for one given game, was an average player. Robertson finished 49–80 in his career and never once had a winning season in his parts of eight years in the big leagues. There is no doubt that the greatest day of his career was April 30, 1922.

Some 34 years passed before there was another perfect game. Don Larsen of the New York Yankees blanked the Brooklyn Dodgers, 2–0, in Yankee Stadium on October 8, 1956, the only perfect game in World Series history. Larsen's lifetime regular-season record was 81–91.

Other perfect games: Jim Bunning, Philadelphia Phillies Hall of Famer in 1964; Sandy Koufax, Los Angeles Dodgers Hall of Famer in 1965; Jim Hunter, Oakland A's Hall of Famer in 1968; Len Barker, Cleveland Indians, 1981; Mike Witt, California Angels, 1984; Tom Browning, Cincinnati Reds,

1988; Dennis Martinez, Montreal Expos, 1991; Kenny Rogers, Texas Rangers, 1994; David Wells, New York Yankees, 1998; David Cone, New York Yankees, 1999; Randy Johnson, Arizona Diamondbacks Hall of Famer, 2004; Mark Buerhle, Chicago White Sox, 2009; Dallas Braden, Oakland A's, 2010; Roy Halladay, Philadelphia Phillies Hall of Famer, 2010 (also pitched a no-hitter in the playoffs, the only one besides Larsen's); Philip Humber, Chicago White Sox (career 16–23), 2012; Matt Cain, San Francisco Giants, 2012; Felix Hernandez, Seattle Mariners, 2012.

As the 2019 Major League Baseball season was poised to begin, there had not been a perfect game thrown in nearly seven years, that streak immediately following 2012, when three were hurled during one season. No team in MLB history has won more than two perfect games.

The most famous almost-perfect game, considered to be a perfect one for decades before it was retroactively removed from the list, was tossed by Pittsburgh Pirates lefty Harvey Haddix. On May 26, 1959, Haddix faced the Milwaukee Braves on a drizzly night in Wisconsin. Haddix pitched 12 perfect innings before losing the game on a Braves rally in the 13th inning. Some call Haddix's fabulous effort "The Imperfect Game."

Cy Young's initial public reaction to his perfect game was low-key, nothing like Waddell's would have been. "I had good speed and stuff," Young said.[3]

However, he had already let Waddell know what he thought on the field, being uncommonly terse and sarcastic to the flamboyant hurler. "How did you like that one, you hayseed?" Young said.[4]

Back to Young's jewel of a game. He was aided by some nifty fielding, though few swipes of the bat produced real danger for the Boston fielders. Buck Freeman and Chick Stahl each made good outfield catches, and Freddy Parent took care of a somewhat difficult grounder at short. When he grabbed the ball for the last out, Stahl remarked on how high Waddell hit it, "Ya know, I thought that ball would never come down."[5]

Young knew his pitches were clicking that day against Philadelphia, right from game's start, when he told himself, "I should be able to put the ball exactly where I want to."[6] But the park's scoreboard did not contain the critical information about how many hits he had allowed. When the game concluded, Young knew he was the winner and had pitched a shutout. As the age-old habit of teammates being superstitious and not speaking to a pitcher while he has a no-hitter going was adhered to by the Bostons, Young, as he said, was probably unaware he had just thrown one. He had no idea he had tossed the first Major League perfect game in nearly a quarter-century.

Other people were keeping track, though. Fans poured out of the stadium to surround Young on the field. Teammates rushed and hugged him.

He wasn't sure exactly why initially. Actually, not all of Young's teammates had kept silent while observing what was going on as Young set down batter after batter. It was fairly late in the game—some said around the seventh inning—when Boston's first baseman, Candy LaChance, risked a low-throated whisper to Young. It was somewhat abstract, but the meaning was clear if Young heard it (apparently he did not) or took time to digest it. LaChance said, "No one has been by here yet."[7] As in no opposing player had reached first base.

One thing Young did with his sterling outing was put to rest any suggestions that he was getting too old to stick in the bigs. Teammate Duke Ferrell chewed on the fact of the perfect game and issued the type of I-told-you-so Young might well have uttered if he was a different type of person. "And they said Uncle Cy was all in, did they?" Ferrell noted. "He fooled them, didn't he?"[8]

Although overshadowed by the perfect game, Young was in the middle of throwing 24 straight innings without a hit, spread over three games. That was a record.

Despite the apparent pre-game testiness provoked by Waddell, when the game ended and Young's superiority was acknowledged for the day, both Waddell and manager Mack were gracious. "[Waddell] and Connie Mack were the first to congratulate me," Young said.[9]

Long into retirement, Young periodically entertained sports writers at his Ohio home. One of those was a well-known writer named Francis J. Powers, who helped supplement a famous baseball book of the 1940s called "My Greatest Day In Baseball." As his greatest single day in the sport, Young chose his perfect game. After all, how can one improve on perfection? "A pitcher's got to be good and he's got to be lucky to get a no-hit game," Young told Powers during a visit at his Peoli, Ohio, farm. "But to get a perfect game, no hit, no man reach first base, he's got to have everything his way. I certainly had my share of luck in the 23 years I pitched in the two big leagues because I threw three no-hitters and one of them was perfect. So it's no job for me to pick out my greatest day in baseball."[10]

Speaking when he was 78 years old, long before Nolan Ryan threw seven no-hitters in his Hall of Fame career and prior to Sandy Koufax tossing four no-hitters, Young brought to the conversation Larry Corcoran, a 19th-century hurler who pitched three no-hitters, none of which were perfect games.

Corcoran, who was a diminutive 5-foot-3 and 127 pounds, had a peculiar career. In 1880 he won 43 games, and in five seasons he won no fewer than 27 games. At times he threw lefty and righty, and he was credited with being the first pitcher to exchange signals with his catcher. Then he dropped off sharply with a dead arm. He was out of big-league ball by the time he was 27 and died from Bright's Disease, a kidney illness, at 32.

"As I said," Young said, calling the perfect game easily his finest hour, "my greatest game was against the Athletics, who were building up to win the 1905 pennant, and Rube Waddell was their pitcher. And I'd like to say that beating Rube anytime was a big job. I never saw many who were better pitchers."[11]

Young called himself a pretty fast thrower in those days, but he also had some tricks in his repertoire that fooled batters. "But what very few batters knew was that I had two curves," Young said. "One of them sailed in there as hard as my fastball and broke in reverse. It was a narrow curve that broke away from the batter and went in just like a fastball. And the other was a wide break. I never said much about them until I was through with the game. I don't think I ever had more stuff and I fanned eight."[12]

Whatever he called those pitches and however Young described them, none of the A's could hit them that day. Much later in life, when Young was in his 70s and 80s, and had decades to reflect on his career and his accomplishments, he was more effusive in explaining what the perfect game meant to him, if not right when it occurred, but in the big picture. "I think the hullabaloo that broke loose after that game was probably the biggest thrill I had in my career," Young said. "That always has to be my biggest thrill."[13]

Since no one has ever pitched more than one perfect game, it is not surprising for any pitcher to categorize the achievement as his biggest thrill. By the time Young died in 1955, some 44 years had passed since he retired as an active player. By then it had to be apparent to him that no player over the next 44 years, or even 100 years, would ever eclipse his all-time record of 511 victories. But that mark was 22 seasons in the making. Certainly, the perfect game had to be the absolute best hour and a half of his baseball career.

2

Ohio

Denton True Young was always an Ohio farm guy. He was born there, died there, resided there in the off-season of his playing days, and when he retired he returned to rural Ohio permanently. He was a homebody, someone who did most of his life's traveling for work-related business reasons—baseball.

Ohio was not one of the original 13 colonies that became the United States after the Revolutionary War, but it was approved for statehood in 1803, its borders ranging from the Ohio River to Lake Erie, a state that was aligned with the Union Army, the North, during the Civil War, serving as a supply conduit for the blue-coated troops.

Some in the southern portions of the state, however, were either indifferent to the war or sympathized with the separated Confederate states. Ohio did share part of its border with West Virginia and Kentucky, but one of its main roles during the nation's ugliest conflict was sending hundreds of thousands of men for enlistment on the Union side. Fortunately for the growing state, it also avoided being the site of bloody battles as the Northerners repressed the Southern rebellion and conquered the South.

Young was born on March 29, 1867, in Gilmore, Ohio, 105 miles south of Cleveland and 208 miles northeast of Cincinnati. The wounds of the Civil War were raw, but nothing reported about his childhood indicates that Young was much affected by the recently concluded conflict. Young's father was McKinzie Young, Jr., and his mother Nancy Mottmiller (later apparently Americanized to Miller). He was the first-born of five children in the family. Denton's siblings were named Jesse, Alonzo, Ella, and Anthony. None of their names show up in *The Baseball Encyclopedia*. While his mother was German-American, the Young side of his family was of Scottish-Irish heritage.

McKinzie Young was gifted a 54-acre farm by his own father, located in Tuscarawas County. As a youngster, relatives and friends called the future pitcher "Dent," short for his given first name. McKinzie, who was one of 12 children, did serve in the Civil War as a medical aide. This Young was not the first in the clan to be named Denton, although there was no antecedent for anyone who floated to the United States from Great Britain in the Young family called "Cyclone," before or after settling in Baltimore. Family westward migration to Ohio followed.

While his parents raised a respectful and well-behaved son, they did not put undue emphasis on formal education, and Young dropped out of school in the sixth grade to focus on helping out on the family farm. When he was about eight years old, Dent joined McKinzie Jr., on a speculative trip to Nebraska. They were exploring whether the farmland was greener. Leaving behind the rest of the immediate family, Young father and son spent two years in Nebraska. In 1887, they returned to Ohio, having given up the experiment. Ohio would remain their home.

McKinzie was devoted to helping his own father, McKinzie Sr., and mother Sarah, with their farm. This property was 140 acres in size, and eventually he was supervising more than 200 acres. The soil was good in this region.

As the United States began to slowly heal in the late 1860s and early 1870s, and as the Reconstruction period began in the South, the sport of baseball also burgeoned. It was long at least loosely believed and claimed that baseball was invented in Cooperstown, New York, by a future Union general named Abner Doubleday in 1839. Such mythology was long ago disproved. Over time, further investigation revealed no eureka moment that everyone can point to with firmness and clarity and shout, "This was it!" Instead, gradually it was concluded that baseball's origins were not purebred, but of mixed breed, the outgrowth of such predecessor games as rounders and cricket.

When the Civil War ended and men dispersed, both back to their homes, and as family men, miners, gold seekers, and cattle ranchers in the west, the gospel of baseball spread with them. This was how baseball became "The National Pastime." The birth of the professional game was not far off.

Denton Young was infected by baseball fever at a young age. In an era long before mass media, his only exposure to the sport had to be first-hand. He apparently saw the game played, wanted to give it a try, and loved it from the start. By the time Young was in his late teens, he had grown to 6-foot-2, quite tall for the time period. His weight was estimated at 170 pounds, which was also notable for the times. However, Young was still growing. By the time he became a major leaguer, his weight was probably about 210 pounds. At the time, it would have been firm muscle from his labor in the fields and his eventual athletic workouts.

Among other great, Hall of Fame pitchers of the 19th century, Tim

Keefe and John Clarkson stood 5–10, and Pud Galvin, 5–8. Of renowned position players of the time, Buck Freeman was 5–9 and John J. McGraw 5–7. Among those characters, Young loomed as a veritable center for a basketball team.

Young was infected with baseball fever at a young age. His brothers shared his passion for the sport, but they were not nearly as good as he was at playing it. There was no Dent-Lonzo or Dent-Jesse tandem that extended beyond local play. Dizzy Dean's brother Daffy was pretty darned good, but the other Young boys' skills went only so far, not translating beyond the neighborhood. "All us Youngs could throw," Dent said. "I used to kill squirrels with a stone when I was a kid and my granddad once killed a turkey buzzard on the fly with a rock."[1] That had to be a challenge, but such stories were told by others over the years, especially if they grew up rural or poor where proper equipment was scarce.

The Youngs did own a baseball to practice with, and Dent practiced hard. There was not much to aspire to beyond representing a local area team, but he was self-motivated. He was kept busy, as were all members of the family, by making the farm a going concern. But whenever he had a chance, Young threw, played catch, or was motivated to build his arm strength by throwing against a barn door. At times, he substituted walnuts in place of the balls. At least once a curious passer-by couple watched Young throw green apples at the barn and wondered what the heck he was up to. He told them he was engaging in his throwing practice. "As a boy I threw anything that could be thrown," Young said years later.[2]

As Young improved and aged into his teens, he was chosen to pitch for the local Gilmore team. He was good enough to be noticed by those who scouted talent for other squads in the vicinity, representing bigger towns, and by the age he would have graduated from high school, he was catching the eye of regional semi-pro teams. His right arm could get people out. Some of those teams shelled out the cost of Young's travel expenses and paid him some small renumeration to make appearances for them. Young was already on this track when he and his father uprooted for their two-year stay in Nebraska. Young kept up his pitching work in the new state, and he was better than ever when he returned to Ohio.

Young pretty much had only one girlfriend in his life. His childhood friend and sweetheart was named Robba Miller, and she was back in Ohio. He figured he belonged with her, and they did marry and spend decades together.

If Young began thinking of baseball as a professional career, he could not have held out much hope for one originally. There didn't seem to be much prospect that he would be noticed, and beyond that his family frowned on playing the game for anything beyond amusement. The

Youngs were a farm family, and Young's father McKinzie was not disposed to allowing one of his key laborers to waltz away on some silly quest. By the late 1880s, there were definitely ballplayers making a living at the game, but they were not getting rich and there was little mainstream publicity about their exploits outside of the big cities of the east and perhaps only as far away as St. Louis.

Young was family-oriented and did not really want to leave his family behind. He was also an obedient son and respected his father's word as law. At the same time, he felt an inner tug to take a risk and see if he could make it as a pro in baseball though his dad was saying no way. When a man named George Moreland made his way to Gilmore to recruit Young, then turning 23 years old, for the Canton, Ohio, team he managed, McKinzie Young Jr.'s. first reaction was, "No future in it."[3]

At the time Young was being paid $10 a month, plus his room and board at home. Moreland's pitch called for $40 a month during the season. Father still said no, and Dent was not willing to take a step against his father's wishes. It should be noted that in the 1880s, and for years beyond that, baseball players did not have the best images. For the most part, they were seen as hard-knocks guys of low moral fiber. That could have influenced Young's father, too.

Moreland returned to Canton, 47 miles distant, without his player. But he left behind a promise that just because Young's answer was no on that day, the offer would not be immediately withdrawn either. "Think it over," Moreland said. "The offer will stand in case you change your decision."[4] Some say he also raised the offer to Young to $60 a month, a whole $2 a day.

Two weeks passed, but Young was given permission to take his chances in the wide world. Whether Young cajoled and begged, his intense love for the game convincing his father, or McKinzie deciding he had best allow his son to find out how good he really was, dad relented, and Young set off to join the Canton club. It was not as if Young was going off to the great unknown or being loosed in some sinful major city. Canton was a reasonable, if half-day hop by horse and buggy and train, with a layover in between. Canton was the birthplace of future President William McKinley, but hardly a major metropolis. Even in the second decade of the 21st century, Canton is a medium-sized city of 70,000, best known as the home of the Pro Football Hall of Fame.

The league Moreland recruited Young for was the Tri-State League, with teams in Ohio, Michigan, and West Virginia. That version of the league was founded in 1887 as the Ohio State League.

Denton True Young was the player recruited, but it took only a few days after reporting to the team in April of 1890 at home Pastime Park, for the first and middle names to become lost in time. Often, in those days, if a young man was setting out to make his fortune, his family dressed him to the nines to make a good first impression. It is not known if Young owned a suit at the time, but when he appeared to meet his new teammates, he was apparently wearing blue overalls, the stereotype of a farmer's outfit.

Only Moreland could vouch for Young's talents, and he sought to make a different kind of first impression on the other players. Not surprisingly, they lined up with a let's-see-what-he's-got attitude when Young began throwing. It was not an audition because Young already had a deal in hand. If someone wants to call it showing off, no one could blame Young. The legend of the winningest pitcher of all time began right there.

This was more than a half a century before the use of the most rudimentary radar guns to measure pitch speed (Bob Feller never got an accurate reading in the 1940s), so no one ever knew how fast Young's fastball traveled.

Young was first matched with a skeptical catcher, whose attitude adjusted swiftly after Young burned his hand through the glove with his hard ones. Moreland stepped in upon seeing that his catcher was actually frightened and urged Young to direct his next throws at the park's wooden fencing. Young reared back and threw one of his speedy heaves at a fence in the park. Crack. The wood snapped. He repeated the throwing and after several pitches, there was no longer enough kindling to build a fire on a cold night. None of the witnesses had seen anything like it. "I threw the ball so hard, I tore a couple of boards off the grandstand," Young said. "One of the fellows said it looked like a cyclone struck it."[5]

The players could not quantify what they saw with a number, but they knew what they saw. A man threw a pitched ball so hard it broke the fence. How fast was fast? They quickly determined that this young man named Young threw as hard as a cyclone blew. Forget Denton True Young, welcome Cyclone Young. It was an intimidating nickname, guaranteed to toy with the psyches of opposing batsmen. A terrific one, too, to stand the test of time when matched with the explosive energy that erupted from his right arm.

Cyclones roar with winds clocked at a minimum of 74 mph, but also register at more than 120 mph. It is enough to say that the onlookers were impressed no matter what projected speed lodged in their heads. Eventually, for convenience, it became unwieldy to call Young Cyclone, and his new nickname was shortened to Cy within a couple of years. By then, Young was fulfilling his dream of pitching in the major leagues.

After a short spring exhibition season, Canton opened its season on the road April 30, at Wheeling, West Virginia. Starting the opener was the freshly christened Cyclone Young. If his family members were even aware of this moniker at the time, they would have laughed. Canton won the game, 4–2, giving Young his first professional victory. The contest took one hour, 45 minutes to complete. Young surrendered three hits and struck out six, those men presumably whiffing at the high winds stirred by his fastball.

Canton was not a particularly good team that year. Young was its stalwart twirler. Most of the time he kept his club in the game, or ahead, although on one occasion he lost after allowing 10 unearned runs, that onslaught provoked by errors.

Young had to rely on his own pitching more than his teammates' slugging and fielding, and in a late July game he fulfilled that role to the extreme. When he was warming up, Young told teammates he felt particularly good, saying he was prepared to throw his best game ever. He did so, turning the good vibes into reality by besting McKeesport (Pennsylvania), 4–1. Young hurled a no-hitter, struck out an awesome 18 batters, and only lost his shutout when an unearned run followed a Canton error. No one on the Canton club commented on the progress of the no-hitter as Young retired the hitters, though Moreland offered some oblique encouragement. He said, "Good going, Young. Keep it up."[6]

Despite being an outstanding pitcher day in and day out, Young's record was just 15–15, though his strikeouts to walks ratio was 201:33. Still, it is difficult to be a winner on a loser. Word spread of his talents, and big-league teams on the prowl for new faces got wind of his achievements. Young was lucky he made his pro leap in 1890, because that season three major leagues competed for players—the National League, John Montgomery Ward's Players' League, and the American Association. Rosters were thin and scouts were hungry to discover fresh faces. Young had been drawing interest, but the no-hitter clinched his prospects.

The closest major league club was situated in Cleveland, just 60 miles from Canton. The Cleveland Spiders of the National League (only recently moved over from the American Association) were looking for help and approached Canton's management about a deal. This was after the famous Adrian "Cap" Anson came to town to give Young a look-see on behalf of the Chicago White Stockings, but left Canton dismissive of Young's ability, a fatal scouting mistake. Perhaps he caught him when he gave up those 10 unearned runs, but Anson said, "Just another big farmer."[7]

At first Canton sought $1,000 for Young's contract, but Cyclone or no Cyclone, the Spiders weren't buying at that price. The negotiations didn't tilt Canton's way. Finally, probably realizing that after the final few months of the season, Young was bound for bigger things, Canton sold him for $300. Young got a raise out of the transaction, too, his monthly wages upped to $75. Cleveland officials threw in a new suit, so he didn't have to wear those overalls to his player introduction at National League Park. He could dress up instead.

Young, only months removed from farm life, with only a few months of professional pitching on his resume, was nervous about taking the mound for his Major League debut in a Spiders uniform. "Well, I'll pitch a game," Young said, "and if I win, I'll stay. If I lose, I'll go home this evening."[8]

Young not only got to stick around longer than a single game, from then on, it was his choice whether he returned to Gilmore.

3

The Majors

The 1890 season was a momentous one in Cy Young's baseball career. It was in some ways a blur. Beginning with George Moreland's on-scene visit to the family farm in the spring, fast-forwarding through a few months representing Canton in the Tri-State League, then his sale to the Major League Cleveland Spiders and finally his early success, or at least promise shown, at the highest level of the sport, all of that took place over a period of less than six months.

By fall, Young was back on the farm, milking cows, pitching hay, and regaling his family and friends about his whirlwind beginnings in pro ball. His head had to be spinning, especially if he told someone not to call him Dent anymore because his new name was Cyclone. That probably didn't happen, but it was definitely a wow segment of his life.

Once Young's contract was bought by the Cleveland Spiders, he spent the rest of the season with the big-league club. His pitching mark as a rookie was 9–7, and he posted a 3.47 earned run average. At 23, he was not the finest pitcher in the world, but he did show potential. He did not pitch a shutout, but he did throw 16 complete games among the 17 he appeared in. One of his games was in relief.

Pitching staffs were small in the 1800s, and starters were pretty much counted on to go all the way if they were given the start. They either had to be phenomenally shelled to the point of near-humiliation or injured to be taken out of a game.

It wasn't as if Young was hired by the best team in baseball. The Spiders had needs, and that's why they undertook a search for new arms. They were not the most stable of franchises, either. The Cleveland team was founded in 1887 as a member of the American Association. In their first two seasons of existence, they were affiliated with that league. In 1889, the Spiders shifted to the National League. They remained in that league through the 1899 season, and Young was with them through the 1898 campaign.

Young's first game for the Spiders took place on August 9, 1890, against the Chicago Colts. Young won the game, 8–1. Playing for that club was Adrian "Cap" Anson, who had briefly scouted him and did not go away with any interest in the person labeled "just another big farmer." One of the newspapers that covered the game was clearly caught up in Young's nickname, referring to him as a "cyclonic" pitcher. Anson, who did not garner any base hits that day, reportedly realized his error and supposedly made a proposal to buy Young on the spot for $1,000. Nothing came of that offer.

Young knew well that he had been snubbed by Anson when in Canton, and in an interview many years later recalled how he felt after his first Cleveland game when he sent Anson back to the bench hitless several times. "I've won many important games since then, but none that gave me half the satisfaction that victory did," Young said.[1]

One of Young's accomplishments—something never attempted today—was starting both games of a doubleheader. On October 4, 1890, he took down the Philadelphia Phillies twice in one day, 5–1 and 7–3. That was the only time in Young's career he attempted the feat. Others have

John L. Sullivan (left), the first heavyweight boxing champion of the world, was a Boston baseball fan. Here he sits with Americans player-manager Jimmy Collins, a future Hall of Famer.

equaled it, but such a challenge has been unheard-of in the big leagues for at least 40 years. In the most recent attempt, the Chicago White Sox's Wilbur Wood gave it a shot in the 1970s, but he was not successful.

The Spiders were no powerhouse that season. They finished 44–88, seventh in an eight-team National League, 43½ games behind first-place Brooklyn, known as the Bridegrooms that season. They were not the worst team in the league. The Pittsburgh Alleghenys were a stunningly bad 23–113 and finished 66½ games out of first.

Cleveland did not hit much. The squad had just one .300 hitter, and it was a back-up, Jake Virtue, a first-baseman who appeared in 62 games and hit .305. There was not a large number of household names, or enduring ones in the history of the sport, either, who shared the roster with Young that year.

One player of some significance was Young's catcher. Born Charles Louis Zimmer, seven years before Young, Zimmer was regarded as a first-rate receiver who was in the midst of a 19-year, Major League career. Nicknamed "Chief," Zimmer was in his fourth season with Cleveland and would stick with the club into the 1899 season, when he was traded. In 1890, Zimmer batted just .214, not high for a catcher who batted .269 life-time. But Zimmer and Young cemented a life-long friendship after serving together as Spiders.

In the early days of Major League ball, just about every player of Native American heritage was anointed with the nickname of "Chief." However, Zimmer acquired the nickname despite not being a Native American. He explained that his 1886 team in Poughkeepsie, New York, was known for its foot speed and were called Indians. He was viewed as the leader of the team and thus was dubbed Chief. Zimmer was an energetic and creative fellow away from the dugout. He started a cigar business while still playing, and he invented a game called "Zimmer's Baseball Game."

A better catcher than slugger, he led leagues in various fielding statistics and was well-known for inserting a beefsteak into his mitt to ease the pain of catching fast throwers like Young. In those days, the leather gloves were much thinner with less padding. Even during the early days of pro baseball, the catcher's job was perceived to be the most rigorous on the field. When Zimmer caught 125 games in 1890, a record, it was considered a big deal. Up until then, catchers were as interchangeable as pitchers, often specialists taking the field when a preferred batterymate did so. Zimmer turned the role into closer to a full-time job.

The pitching distance was just 45 feet when Zimmer broke in. Young, who made his throws sizzle enough to frighten his Canton catcher and thus gain his appendage of Cyclone for wounding a fence, was taken aback at first when Zimmer could handle his fast ones. "I've lost some speed up here," Young told a friend when he reached the majors. Asked why, he said, "That fellow Zimmer caught every one of my pitches It's the first time that ever happened. Must be slowing up."[2]

Young just couldn't get over Zimmer's wizardry and blamed himself for what must have been a drop-off in speed. When team executive Davis Hawley, who made the purchase of Young from Canton, congratulated him on a good outing, Young repeated his worry. Hawley laughed because he didn't believe what he was hearing. "There is nothing wrong at all," Hawley said. "Zimmer is one of the best catchers in the business. I doubt if there is a pitcher anywhere he can't hold. Lots of difference between his catching and that of the average backstop. Don't you worry about that, son." Zimmer was impressed by Young's ability from the start and praised the way he controlled his pitches. What made Young special, he said, was "perfect command of the ball."[3] Putting the ball where you want it to go is always an advantage for a pitcher over a hitter.

There were about 63 million Americans in 1890, about 20 percent of what the nation's population is two decades into the 21st century. The professional baseball league Young joined had teams in Brooklyn, Chicago, Philadelphia, Cincinnati, Boston, New York City, Cleveland, and Pittsburgh. The American Association fielded teams in Louisville, Columbus (Ohio), St. Louis, Toledo, Rochester (New York), Baltimore, Syracuse, Philadelphia, and Brooklyn. The Association fizzled out after the 1891 season. The Players' League, in its only season of activity, had teams in Boston, Brooklyn, New York City, Chicago, Philadelphia, Pittsburgh, Cleveland, and Buffalo. The Cleveland competition to Young's Spiders was called the Infants. They did not grow to adulthood.

Even with three professional circuits, baseball was not truly a national game. There were no big-league clubs in the south or the west. That season it was definitely a players' market. It was a good year for Young to be noticed and prove himself. The next year there were two leagues, and by 1892 just one. Competition for jobs was fierce. Salaries were suppressed after that, too, since players had to work at the wages owners were willing to pay.

Some of the best players in baseball history were in the game in 1890, although they were scattered. One notable slugger was Roger Connor in the Players' League. He was a 10-year veteran by 1890. Then playing in New York, Connor was influential in the New York franchise's nickname change from the Gothams to the Giants.

Connor, who was 6-foot-3 and 220 pounds, most assuredly a giant himself for the times, was from Waterbury, Connecticut. His lifetime average was .316, and he was elected to the Baseball Hall of Fame 45 years after his death, in 1976. His No. 1 claim to fame was holding the career home record of 138 until Babe Ruth came along and made the weapon famous.

The league Young joined remained pre-eminent, despite the siphoning off of some good players. One of the National League's great pitchers of the time—and considered an all-time great—was right-hander John Clarkson. He stood just 5–10 and weighed 155 pounds but owned a disproportionately powerful arm. Six years older than Young, Clarkson broke into the majors in 1882, and some astonishing statistics reside next to his name in the record books.

In a 12-year career, Clarkson won 328 games, including an insane high of 53 victories in 1885, when he started 70 games. He threw 623 innings that season and in 1889 came back with a 620-inning season. With a workload like that, it was no shock that Clarkson was out of the sport by the time he was 32. This was the world Cy Young had signed up for. Some pitchers threw every other day.

Clarkson excelled, and he and Young had their share of showdowns, not all of them won by Young. Until 1890, the pitching distance was 45 feet from home plate. In 1892 it was moved back to 50 feet. In 1893, rules makers tinkered with the distance again, moving it to 60 feet, 6 inches away, where it has remained since. It was Clarkson who predicted that the longer distance would have a major impact on hurlers. "The new rule will revolutionize the base ball world," Clarkson said.[4]

Whether it was arm fatigue or Clarkson's failure to adjust to the critical change, he was never the same level of pitcher again, concluding his career with two losing seasons. However, the shift in the distance he had to throw to fool batters with his assortment of curveballs and other pitches besides a fastball, may not have been the main reason for his departure from the sport and his failings at the end of his career.

As all of these changes were taking place, Clarkson joined the Spiders and was a teammate rather than a rival of Young's in 1892 and 1893; by then, Young was clearly the staff leader. It was suggested by some that Clarkson, who was high-strung, was mentally demoralized upon witnessing a close friend fall from a train and lose his legs when they were on a hunting trip. He retired soon after. In about 1905, Clarkson suffered a mental breakdown and was committed to a psychiatric hospital in his home state of Massachusetts. He died there of pneumonia at 47. Young and Clarkson never had the chance to perform as Spiders when they were both at the peak of their forms.

Once he showed his stuff in 1890, Young was no longer considered a fringe player for Cleveland. When he returned to the family farm at season's end, he had already been presented with a new contract for 1891, one that would pay him $1,430. However, when the established Clarkson joined the team in 1892 and 1893 and did not contribute as much to the team as Young, the younger player got wind that the veteran was being paid far more than he was. He resented that. He approached management and demanded a big raise. Clarkson was making $2,400 a season, and Young may have had his wages jumped to equal the passing-through newcomer.

During his earliest starts with the Spiders, Young was a highly praised fresh face. He won his first three games, and the baseball writers began predicting stardom. When he eventually lost, as all pitchers do, he was able to read the flip side of the analysis. "No Longer a Phenom!" one Cleveland newspaper headline writer decided.[5]

On the last day of the regular season, October 4, Young, in conspiracy with Hawley, was determined to leave the Cleveland fans gasping, to leave them with something special to remember him by over the winter. In those days, before artificial lights were installed at ballparks, doubleheaders were played early in the day to maximize daylight. The first game was scheduled for the morning, and the nightcap was really an afternoon-cap.

This was the day Young stifled the Philadelphia Athletics twice. After the first game, Young's record was 8–7 for the season. He most assuredly wanted to finish above .500. Before Cyclone took the mound for the second game, he had a talk with Hawley.

"It's a risk, Young," Hawley said. "I know," the pitcher replied. "I'm willing to go along."[6] Everything worked out fine. Young claimed victory for the second time that day and completed his rookie big-league season with a 9–7 record. After sorting out his immediate future with the contract for the next summer, Young, who had experienced so much since leaving home in April, returned to Gilmore. In no time he was back in the fields, harvesting corn.

One of his neighbors, who hadn't assimilated Young's new name Cyclone and was still calling him Dent, talked about the improving technology and the likelihood he would buy a reaper before the next year. Instead of being bound to his farm sunup-to-sundown, he said, he might have more free time, perhaps even enough time to make a journey to Cleveland to watch Young pitch a game.

Young dove right into his old life. That included attending a husking bee, which called for finding a red ear of corn in the mix of the regular stuff, with his girl, Robba. Young was a celebrity among the farmers, who peppered him with questions about his new life and especially about the major leagues.

When his parents realized their son was going to be paid about $200 a month to play ball the next season, they were astonished. McKinzie, his father, had told Dent there was no future in it. Well, Young's immediate future was looking pretty bright, and it also promised far more money than he ever made farming in Ohio or Nebraska. The sport was no more than a toddler, but it was becoming more obvious all the time that it did indeed have a future, and Dent was going to be part of it.

Young was like a soldier back on leave to the world he had known growing up, having established a likely future, still very much unknown, but having proved that entering professional baseball was a risk worth taking. One thing the big-league pitcher wouldn't be doing that off-season was staying in shape by throwing apples or walnuts at a barn door.

Spring training for the Spiders was scheduled for Jacksonville, Florida, another new experience for Young. As the winter passed, all of his old friends seemed proud of Young. In second-hand conversation, they even began referring to him as Cyclone, although they stuck with his real name when they passed him. It was if Cyclone was an alter ego. Nobody could blame Young if he felt that way himself. The speed of his ascension to the majors had to be dizzying. Neither Young nor his family and friends realized that this was just the beginning. The boy they knew was just emerging as a star in the sport, and his name would soon be known all across the land.

4

Back to Cleveland

At 24, Cy Young was more strapping than portly, as he became near the end of his career. He was a more savvy player in 1891 when he rejoined the Cleveland Spiders after his first partial season in the National League. He was a young man on the rise in his profession, having absorbed the rudiments of the pro game the year before.

Young's future was not quite established yet, but those experts who watched him throw in 1890 sensed he was going to be a good one. The Spiders' future in Cleveland was iffier. There was talk that the Spiders were no longer on sound financial ground, and owner brothers Stan and Frank Robison kept worrying about that. At least there was suspicion that they might not keep the franchise in Cleveland. Such speculation was premature, but catcher Chief Zimmer raised the topic with Young when the season was getting underway.

Opening Day for the Spiders was in Cincinnati on April 22, and the first home game was slated for May 1, again with Cincinnati as the opponent. What constituted a good crowd in 1891 would be equated with a bottom-of-the-barrel crowd in the 2000s. Zimmer and Young thought attendance of between 3,000 and 4,000 would indicate the fans were still with them. "If the weather is good there should be that many," Zimmer said.[1]

Young was scheduled as Cleveland's starter, and that was worth noting since he had left the city on a high the previous autumn. If there were concerns about support, they were allayed at least for that day, when about 9,000 people came out to cheer the Spiders. The fans were in a good mood when they arrived, and they were probably in a better mood when they filed out. Cleveland—and Young—won, 12–3. "I wouldn't have lost that game for $100," Young insisted afterwards.[2] Although it is not 100 percent clear what he meant, it does indicate that he was pretty confident of the result.

The Spiders as a bunch were improved. Though not pennant contenders, their roster was beefed up and Young was surrounded by some additional solid ballplayers. Cleveland wasn't a threat to do anything special, but the club won 21 more games than the previous season, finishing 65–74.

Young showed signs of maturity. For one thing, he grew a mustache, quite the popular facial hair addition during that era. Otherwise, playing a full season in the majors, his numerous extra appearances paid off. That season, Young won 27 games, the first of 16 times he won at least 20 games in a season and the first of 14 years in a row. He appeared in 55 games, 46 as a starter, and his earned run average was 2.85, a significant drop from the preceding season. Young completed 43 starts, and his workload was a stupendous 423⅔ innings.

There was no doubt Young was the main man on the mound for the Spiders. Cleveland used only three starters with regularity. Young's partners in the front line were Lee Viau, who went 18–17, and Henry Gruber, who finished 17–22. No one else on the pitching staff won more than two games. This was a particularly important year for Viau. The right-hander was just 5 feet, 4 inches tall and weighed about 160 pounds. Viau began his career with Cincinnati of the American Association and in his first two seasons won 27 and 22 games. Abruptly, however, he seemed washed up and staggered through the next several seasons, only once capturing as many as 11 wins, until 1891.

A sidearmer originally from Vermont, Viau attended Dartmouth College in New Hampshire and did a little bit of pitching for the Ivy League school. It was not until he got the chance to play in the minors that Viau showed enough quality to gain major league interest. It was said that Viau was heavily courted by the Players' League and that played a role in his poor follow-up seasons, or maybe it was a case of too many innings too soon. The Spiders grew excited when Viau seemed to re-flower with his 18-win campaign, but he had nothing left after that and was soon out of baseball. He was no long-term solution for helping Young in the rotation.

The Spiders did muster a little bit more offense in 1891. Clarence "Cupid" Childs took over second base in his first season with Cleveland and hit .281. He played in a league-leading 141 games, and his on-base percentage was .395. Childs was a long-time Spiders teammate of Young's and six times batted more than .300 when they were teamed together, once reaching .355. While he adopted Baltimore as his home, Childs was much like Young and so many other big-league players of the time, growing up in a rural area of Virginia.

Childs got better and better for much his career, and his final marks included a .306 batting average and a .416 on-base percentage. The left-handed swinger was sometimes described as possessing surprising power for an infielder, but in days featuring spacious stadiums, home runs came dearly. Childs collected just 20 of them, although he did smack 101 triples. He accumulated a high share of bases on balls and doubles. At 5–8, Childs was not particularly tall, but he was strong at 185 pounds, even though his figure was not categorized as muscular.

George Davis made his debut in 1890 with Cleveland, the first of 20 seasons in the majors that led to election to the Baseball Hall of Fame. He played some outfield but quite a bit of shortstop and third base, and he scored an impressive 1,545 runs with 2,665 hits. He was very much a Spiders spark who got on base and helped jump-start rallies. As was shown the preceding season when Young only managed to finish above .500 on the last day of the season by winning a doubleheader, he needed more assistance from the batter's box. The bulk of Davis' career was spent elsewhere—1892 was his last year with Cleveland—but he was an important cog in 1891.

Although it was not readily apparent just how big a star 22-year-old outfielder Jesse Burkett was going to become in 1891, he had shown well for New York in his rookie season of 1890. Burkett batted .309, but he was not a full-time regular for Cleveland the next campaign, used in just 40 games with 167 at-bats. He hit .269.

Born in Wheeling, West Virginia, Burkett soon blossomed into one of the best hitters in the league and one of the highest average hitters of all-time with a .338 mark. This was the guy, not yet in 1891, but in the coming years, for the length of Young's stay in Cleveland, who could make things happen on offense. Burkett, who was selected for the Hall of Fame in 1946, won three batting titles and twice batted higher than .400. But he was not always Mr. Personality, the man of a thousand smiles. Rather, he was more likely to be frowning as part of his overall serious demeanor, and he was not one to be pushed around. More often he pushed to gain every inch. Some thought of him as cantankerous, a dark cloud moving around on two legs. His nickname, bestowed due to such viewpoints, was "Crab." This was the same nickname given to another Hall of Famer, second baseman Johnny Evers, who came later. Evers received a longer version of the moniker: The Human Crab. There was one Crab for each century of baseball, though the 21st century has failed to yield one to date. Evers once said he believed the only good umpire was a dead umpire, so it stands to reason he was afforded the nickname by umpires.

Neither was Burkett likely to have many umpires on his Christmas card list. During a Cleveland doubleheader versus Louisville in 1897, Burkett was ejected from both games after irritating umpire Chicken Wolf. When Burkett read the *Louisville Courier-Journal*'s report that there had been incidents during play, he said, "Truer words were never written."[3]

Burkett, whose skill and personality were well-established by 1897, did not last long in the opener, ousted in the second inning. He questioned two strike calls by the home plate umpire (never a fruitful strategy) and used some ill-advised words mixed in with an accusation of "You're a [blank] robber." Wolf followed up with a phrase similar to "You're outta here!" Burkett ignored the command and made as if to continue hitting. That was not to be. Lasting until the ninth inning of the second game with the same umpire was probably a long-shot success story for Burkett, but he was heaved before the end of the game in another incident.

Burkett began developing his reputation for toughness, hard play, and verbal assault early in his career with Cleveland. He did not take kindly, or turn the other cheek, if fans cursed him out or taunted him. Rather than ignore them, Burkett gave it right back with smart talk.

These were some of the men the young version of Cy Young found himself surrounded by. He had been raised right by his parents and, while competitive, was not inclined to mix it up either with opposing players or fans. He was also not a headhunter. While some pitchers welcomed the concept of brushing top hitters back from the plate to disrupt their stances, Young's approach was to come right at them with his best stuff, not try to deck them. Whether it was merely the philosophy of a gentlemanly hurler or Young carried in his mind the image of his fastball breaking boards in a fence, he was not keen on employing the high hard one as a discouragement weapon due to the risk of hurting someone seriously.

The Spiders' manager at the start of the 1891 season was Bob Leadley, and based on Young's strong finish as a rookie and good showing in spring training, he was handed the ball for the season opener on April 22. Young was a 6–3 winner on the road over Cincinnati.

Young fared well in 1891, winning most of the time, but also losing some games. In August, the Spiders, who had been playing very well, went into a serious tailspin. If Cleveland had been a prop plane, it would have corkscrewed into the earth. The slump led to a change of managers by team management. Leadley was out, his replacement Oliver "Patsy" Tebeau, already with the team as an infielder. Tebeau was just three years older than Young but a fiery on-field leader. Now he was expected to be a fiery on-and-off-the-field leader. While not as irascible as Burkett, Tebeau was a hard-nosed player who battled over every pitch and every ground ball. He was supposed to ignite the team, his natural state supposedly the dynamite stick.

Showing that nothing was sacred, Tebeau lifted Young from the starting rotation in August after he lost four straight starts. Instead, his demotion featured bullpen work. In those days, that was an insult. Of course, Tebeau had to show the rest of the Spiders that no one was immune from his perform-or-don't-play dictates. Young interpreted this move as punishment and felt that he was no longer wanted by the team. He kept quiet for some time, but when the equivalent of being benched stretched on for weeks, he spoke out, saying, "[I'm] being used to pitch out the fag end of losing games."[4]

This was not a page from "How To Make Friends And Influence Your Manager." Indeed, Young compounded his grumpy comment with the exact type of sentiment that endures today when such matters arise. He suggested he wasn't paid well enough for this type of duty, and he might be better off playing for another team. Perhaps even more of an indictment in Tebeau's mind was that when the team engaged in a serious brawl with Cincinnati, where punches were thrown and it was reported that bats were even swung (though presumably they did not connect with human flesh), Young was a viewer, not a participant. Tebeau loved players with feisty souls, in other words, like him. That was not part of Young's temperament.

Tebeau spent 13 years in the majors as a player and hit .279, most of them as a player-manager in Cleveland. He did turn around the Spiders, but every day seemed to be the hard way for the combative Tebeau. Much later, Sid Keener, a long-time St. Louis sports writer who died in 1981, wrote a story that was equal parts appreciation and character study of the man Keener met when he was a youngster and Tebeau got him entrance into a game for free.

The Tebeau Young was introduced to in 1891 was encapsulated in some of Keener's prose. He wrote of Tebeau, "[He] was a born leader and he was going to be the boss or he was not going to play." Tebeau brooked no insubordination, and Keener mentioned that Tebeau said, "If there's any one on this club [the Spiders] who wants to fight, just write it out and mail the challenge to me."[5]

Young was certainly not going to match fists with Tebeau. He was better with verbal snappiness if his ire was truly up. Young in a sense prevailed with his point of view by being Young. As the season was winding down in 1891, he again received opportunities to start games. And win them. Young shed his slump, returned to his normal form, and completed the season with a 27–22 record. Whether their truce was officially agreed to or not, Tebeau stopped bugging him about not throwing at hitters or throwing punches and learned to accept Young for what he was—a superb pitcher—and one who was about to break out as a superstar in the game.

In 1891, the most famous Americans were William F. "Buffalo Bill" Cody, who was touring the world with his Wild West exhibition, writer Mark Twain, President Benjamin Harrison, former President Grover Cleveland, who was gearing up to retake the Oval Office in 1892, and General Nelson Miles, who had outlived Generals William Sherman and

Philip Sheridan. In sports, the best-known athlete in the country was heavyweight champion John L. Sullivan, the "Boston Strong Boy."

Baseball players had not yet reached Sullivan's level of glory, but that was coming as the popularity of the game spread and more attention was paid to the sport by the nation's newspapers. Despite his flashy nickname of "Cyclone," Young was not necessarily suited for the role of celebrity. He was neither a jokester nor a boaster. He was the kind of man and player who let his work stand on its own. Some of his comrades at home in Gilmore even wondered if becoming a star player would swell Young's head. They asked his family members if Dent was coming home after the season, as if they expected the answer to be no because he had better things to do in bigger cities.

After 1891, his testy conflict with Tebeau aside, Young was now an established pitcher, one of the best in baseball. In spite of his slump and his time spent in the bullpen pretty much as a mop-up man, his 27 victories stood out. The winningest pitcher in the National League that year was Bill Hutchinson of the Chicago Colts with 44 triumphs (a year after winning 41 games). John Clarkson, shortly to be a Spider, won 33 games that year, as did Amos Rusie. The great "Kid" Nichols won 30 games. So Young's total was the fifth-highest in the NL.

It was obviously to Tebeau's advantage to settle things with Young, who was just 24. There was no way the Spiders management wanted to trade him elsewhere. After being happy with his $1,430 deal the year before, but griping about low pay late in the summer, Young was rewarded with a $2,000 contract for 1892.

This turned out to be a very wise deal for the Cleveland Spiders. Young was on the cusp of greatness, and he would make that supremely clear the next season. Even Tebeau conceded that he must let Young be Young.

As a matter of fact, it was time to let Cy be Cy. The sports writers who covered Cyclone's pitching feats shortened the name for convenience. Just as Denton had little choice in being labeled Cyclone a few years earlier, by the end of the 1891 season he was being referred to as Cy whether he appreciated it or not. It was amusing mostly because most fans eventually came to believe Cy Young was his real name. When they asked for autographs, Cy Young is what they expected to read on their pieces of paper.

5

Mowing Them Down

In 1890, Denton "Cyclone" Young was breaking boards in fences with his hard stuff. By 1892, Cy Young was breaking bats held in the hands of big-league hitters.

No longer anonymous, somewhat seasoned, considerably more educated about Major League ways, Young was now the best pitcher in the National League, a lucky get for the Cleveland Spiders initially, turned ace of the staff. This was the season that made Cy Young, that began cementing his reputation and boosted him to a new level of stardom around the league, the sport, and the country.

Whether Young was too good to be true, as in his middle name True, or just that his gift was larger than anyone else with a strong arm, he matured into peak athletic form with a bang. In the new season, Young was king of the hill. As Cleveland improved to 93–56, second in the league to the Boston Beaneaters. Young himself was second to none, compiling a league-best 36 wins (the most in a single season in his career), a league-best .750 winning percentage, a league-leading 1.93 earned run average, and a league-high nine shutouts.

Actually, the 36 wins were equaled by Chicago's Bill Hutchinson, who pitched 622 innings that season. Hutchinson led the league with 314 strikeouts while making 70 starts for the Colts and 75 total appearances.

The Spiders were very good, and Young was great. He also threw a career-high 453 innings, and quite possibly Young cornered his local market share of ice cubes for post-game soothing treatments. If he didn't, he should have. That type of innings burden ruined more than one good pitcher of the era, so Young was fortunate he did not demonstrate the weariness that others suffered. Hutchinson didn't have a winning season after he was 32.

The sheer volume of work Young was called upon for by manager Patsy Tebeau illustrated how much more trust the boss had in him than during the rougher season before, when the men were first getting to know one another. Cleveland definitely fielded better personnel during the 1892 season. While Young emerged as something special, he was ably supported in the rotation. John Clarkson became a Spider, and although management anticipated more production out of him, Clarkson did win 17 games.

From season's start at spring training in Hot Springs, Arkansas, optimism surrounded the Spiders. Sports writers surveyed Cleveland's lineup and suggested this was going to be Cleveland's best team in a while, maybe the best of all. When they talked to Young, he too said he was ready to go. His phrase was, "The old arm is as good as ever now."[1] Naturally, his arm was not old, but still quite young, and it should have been fine.

The new guy was a rookie hurler from Logansport, Indiana, named George Cuppy, who had the unfortunate nickname of "Nig." This nickname did indeed stem from Cuppy being of somewhat darker skin complexion. It was not taken as such a supreme racial insult at the time, unlike nowadays when it would not be tolerated for a moment. Cuppy was another of what would now be considered an undersized player at 5-foot-7 and 160 pounds. He was a right-hander, 22 years old, beginning a 10-season major-league career. Cuppy was a fresh, electric presence and the winner of 28 games.

While Young delivered his pitches with a somewhat standard form, Cuppy had a distinctive style on the mound. He went through contortions as he labored to get the ball to the plate. His fastball was useful, though not as marvelous as Young's. Cuppy's primary weapon was his curveball. That pitch sent batters into the same kind of contortions Cuppy engaged in while pitching.

When baseball first burst upon the American scene, players did not wear gloves. Then they began wearing thin leather gloves such as workmen may don today. Gradually, they adopted styles with more padding. During the 1880s and 1890s, more and players learned how to play the game wearing gloves. Cuppy was still pitching without a glove on his non-throwing hand when he joined the Spiders. For that matter, so was Young, until 1897.

One day when he was scheduled to pitch, Cuppy decided to make the change. Teammates, along with other patrons, were gathered at a drugstore that was a usual hangout before games. Cuppy announced that he had a surprise for viewers that would become apparent when he took the mound. The anticipation teased those sitting around, and gossip began about what this could all be. It turned out that Cuppy made his debut in a glove that day.[2]

Whether bare-handed or gloved, Cuppy was terrific for the Spiders that season. His earned average was 2.51, and his arrival represented a huge bonus to the pitching staff. He too was an innings eater, compiling 376 innings on the mound for Cleveland that season. Unexpectedly, Clarkson was not as good as he had been, but it didn't much matter.

Day in and day out over the long season, the Spiders' best hitter was Cupid Childs, who hit .317. Jesse Burkett, then 23, had not yet busted out. He hit .275. The three biggest run producers were shortstop Ed McKean with 93 runs batted in, first baseman Jake Virtue with 89, and George Davis with 82.

This was a peculiar season for the National League. For the first time, the circuit broke the campaign into two parts. Cleveland got off to a so-so start and was just fifth in wins at the end of the first half. Then the Spiders rallied and came in first during the second half. The winners of each half-season met in a championship series. This was not a direct forerunner of the modern World Series. That did not begin until 1903, but there was incentive for teams to keep playing hard and build up victories as the summer went on.

McKean, three years older than Young, grew up in Cleveland and was the captain of his hometown team after pro experiences in Youngstown, Ohio, Providence, Rhode Island, and Rochester, New York. He was a man after Tebeau's heart, fiery, with a big mouth, ready to taunt umpires and opposing players. He hustled full-time and treated the game as if every little thing mattered to victory. His spirit was infectious and added to his leadership qualities. A 13-year big-leaguer, McKean's lifetime average was .302.

As someone who had joined the Spiders before the team was any good, McKean was as happy as anyone to be part of the winning 1892 club. The players sensed they had something good going for them. Chief Zimmer, Young's catcher, was a key partner in the pitcher's quest to win 30 or more games, and when he hit the 30 mark in early September, Zimmer expected his friend would keep on rolling. "He'll win 35," Zimmer said.[3] The prediction came true, and Zimmer even underestimated the total by one.

The question on everyone's lips—teammates, fans, competing players—was what made Young so good. There was his fastball, of course. But others possessed fast fastballs. By his third season in the bigs, Young was much more knowledgeable than he had been as a rookie. While Young had limited formal education, leaving school so early, that did not mean he wasn't an intelligent man. He adapted quite well to his environment, and the more he pitched and the more first-rate hitters he faced, the more he assimilated through experience.

Several years later, when he was long established as a big-time big-leaguer, Cy Young's picture appeared on the cover of *Baseball Magazine*. The featured article was titled "How I Learned to Pitch." Whether this piece gave away trade secrets or not, telling folks how he did it would never translate completely to hitters so they could stand in and topple him on methodology alone.

One thing Young stressed in his first-person story—perhaps just to intimidate the amateur reader not already completely enthralled by his reputation—was that pitching is hard work, and it took a lot of practice and effort for him to succeed at it. "Idiosyncrasy is a long and dangerous-sounding word used by doctors to designate something that goes against the grain," the story begins. "I have a severe case then of idiosyncrasies each spring, such a severe one in fact that many times I have come very near throwing up my job as pitcher."[4]

That was gloomy enough talk coming from a pitcher 18 years along in the majors with unprecedented success on his resume. Don't say Cy didn't warn you if you took up this demoralizing role, he was saying. He did an even better job of painting spring training as drudgery, far removed from romantic notions that often color the images of that season's annual reintroduction of baseball to the fans. In Young's view, it was mentally daunting to force himself into training again, "irksome duty," and once begun led to "exquisite agony."[5] None of that sounded like much fun. Apparently, unlike the modern player who stays in shape year-round and doesn't need much from spring workouts except to regain timing, Young made it sound as if he let himself get flabby in the off-season. Or maybe from the vantage point of his late 30s and with a nearly two-decade-long career in the books, he did let himself go a little bit over the winter. "Again and again I have made up my mind to quit the game, all on account of my disinclination to train in the spring," Young said, "but after a struggle I conquer myself and get through with the early spring training some way or other."[6] This seemed overblown for a hard-working farmer who later had to be dragged from the sport with a hook like the vaudeville act stereotype.

For those looking for instruction, Young got started early in the article, almost as if he was feeling out the other team's batting order in the first inning. He was just venting, doing some whining to let everybody know he definitely felt mortal at the start of each season as he aged. By that time, of course, Young had earned the right to say anything he wanted about pitching. It was as if he had invented it. No question he had perfected it better than any of his contemporaries or anyone who had come before him.

Intriguingly, one of the lures of spring training, for whipping a team into shape, as well as fans taking vacations to venture south to watch the squads develop, has always been nicer weather than northern teams were likely to encounter in March when there was still every chance of a late-season snowstorm. However, whether it was Jacksonville or Arkansas, Young only periodically seemed to warm up to these getaways. He

cited how likely there would still be bad weather that could affect pitchers' development. If there were soothing hot springs or other activities to
enjoy with time off, Young did not mention being attracted to them.

Young did offer his viewpoint on what pitchers need to become winning pitchers once the mind is set to take the task on. In some ways, it was
a scouting report. "The would-be pitcher must be endowed physically for
the strain of pitching, must have a good arm and a good disposition, coupled with a capacity for work. Another big item is patience. There is never
a game a pitcher does not have it taxed. A person can learn to be patient,
just as one can learn to play a piano or learn stenography."[7]

But wait, there's more. Young trumpeted the trait of coolness under
fire as if he spoke of going to war and facing bullets at the front.

> Coolness is harder to acquire. A person who is temperamentally nervous works
> at a disadvantage when he strives to be cool under all conditions. Some men are
> born cool and for this they ought to be divinely thankful. But with all that, cool-
> ness is a trait that can be cultivated. One must force himself to think and after he
> has thought for a moment he can regain his wits, which is another way of saying
> he is finally cool and collected.[8]

This was all general background, of a type that could have been written as a Be Like Mike description for Michael Jordan in basketball decades
later if he was asked what made him great. For a young man with aspi-
rations, this was worth reading, even if it would not give him the talent
to make it to the big leagues. That indeed had to come first, because will
alone would not carry a player to a professional roster and allow him to
stick with one of the top teams.

After this broad-based introduction, Young did offer some more spe-
cific advice based on what he learned growing up, during his brief stay in
the minors, and then during his long career in the majors to that point in
1908.

> A beginner should work a long time on straight balls alone. This does not seem
> very exciting, but contains a big secret that many overlook. The beginner should
> keep throwing this straight ball until he can absolutely put the ball where the
> catcher wants it. Next, cultivate a slow ball and get control of that. It makes no
> difference how long it takes, get control of it before you go on with something
> else.
>   Now learn to mix up the balls, that is, to alternate them. The secret of success
> in pitching is learning to change the balls to keep the batter guessing. The chief
> reason that batting is so weak these days is that the pitchers have more to offer
> than in olden days.[9]

That surely was an ironic comment, although no doubt made sin-
cerely by Young. What was current then is the olden days to the modern
baseball fan, when many weapons the pitcher had at his disposal were

later banned. It was a notorious period for pitchers scuffing baseballs on belt buckles, throwing the spitter, and spitting tobacco juice on balls. Just about anything went, and it wasn't until 1920 that such practices were outlawed. While there was no particular attention on Young as a specialist in tossing such pitches, all of those variations were legal until after his career concluded. However, much later he did mention tobacco pitches.

Young followed up this discussion with a rather optimistic outlook for the beginning pitcher who followed his advice, as if his words were a magic formula that could make a pitcher out of just about anyone. "An average man, if he will follow these simple words, keep everlastingly at it, and exercise common horse sense will win out sooner or later in the pitching game," Young wrote.[10]

Young's own habits were exemplary and had been when he was growing up. His disdainful annoyance over the rigors of spring training notwithstanding, he maintained those positive habits, and for him they yielded notable results. As the years passed, it became more and more apparent that Cy Youngs were not grown on farms as plentifully as vegetables or bred like cattle, no matter what workout programs they followed.

It became ever clearer as the 1892 season advanced through the warm weather that the big fellow on the mound had learned to pitch and might be getting smarter by the day. When the split regular season ended in mid–October, the Spiders led the standings. They were now scheduled to face the Boston Beaneaters in a championship series.

The Beaneaters finished 102–48 with an eye-catching .680 winning percentage. Boston was one of the original teams when the National League was founded in 1876 and won the flag with an 87–51 mark in 1891. A post-season series was a newfangled idea as an outgrowth of the experimental split season.

Boston's pitching staff featured Kid Nichols, who went 35–16 with a 2.84 ERA. An eventual Hall of Famer, Nichols was a known quantity who won 362 games during his career. This was the second time he reached 30 wins in a season, something he accomplished a phenomenal seven times in his 15-year career.

Less well-remembered was Jack Stivetts, a right-hander from Ashland, Pennsylvania, whose 1892 record matched Nichols' at 35–16. While he had neither Nichols' longevity (11 years), nor total wins (203), Stivetts was coming off a 33–22 season for St. Louis of the American Association.

The biggest name in the Beaneaters' lineup was outfielder Hugh Duffy, who hit .301 that season. A lifetime .326 batter, Duffy won consecutive batting titles in 1893 and 1894. During the latter season, Duffy produced a .440 batting average, the highest Major League total ever. He was going to create problems at the plate for the Spiders. The native of Rhode

Island began his professional life as a textile worker. He took up baseball as a semi-pro sideline. Then he spent the rest of his life connected to the sport, including 17 years as a player for a variety of teams. Elected to the Hall of Fame in 1945, Duffy won 535 games as a manager and scouted for the Boston Red Sox up until the year before his death in 1954.

Game One of what was billed as the World's Championship Series was played on October 17, and even as of 2020, 128 years later, must be considered one of the greatest games ever pitched. Cy Young got the nod for the Spiders and Spivetts was the starter for Boston. What began as an afternoon game went on and on until darkness resulted in umpires halting the action. At that point, 16 innings had been played with both starters still on the mound and a score of 0–0. Young allowed just four hits. The game went into the books as a tie.

That was as close as the Spiders came to taking a game off the Beaneaters. Boston captured the Series 5–0-1 and were proclaimed world champs. Young was Cleveland's pitcher on the day Boston won the title. Going up against Nichols, Young was beaten, 8–3.

For winning 36 games and becoming Cleveland's No. 1 starter, Young was rewarded with a $2,300 contract for the 1893 season. A few years later, a Boston sports writer listed Young as one of a few pitchers who might be worth $10,000 per season. Young never saw such big dollars during his career.

6

Me, Her and the Ball

By the fall of 1892, the direction of Cy Young's life was set. He was 25 years old and knew what he wanted. Young was neither a thrill-seeker nor flamboyant. He did not dream of alternative sources of income or capitalizing on his growing fame. The pitcher's preferences were straightforward.

Young was really a man of the soil. He grew up on a family farm, and he never showed much interest in being anything more than a farmer. That is, when he wasn't playing professional baseball. The third constant in his life, from the time he was a boy, was his girlfriend, Robba Miller. Young was no playboy. He always had the girl back home, and upon the conclusion of each baseball season he returned to her. The Young family farm and the girl of his dreams were in the same place— Gilmore, Ohio.

After Young posted his best season and the Spiders enjoyed their best season, Young covered the short distance between Cleveland and Gilmore for the off-season. There was one difference. This time Young was coming home to marry Robba. The couple's wedding was held on November 8 in Peoli. He was marrying the girl next door, although by city or suburban standards that was only technically true, since she was brought up on the farm down the road.

While Young and Miller had known each other for practically forever and it always seemed foreordained that they would marry, the couple made their own choice on the timing. Young wanted to be financially secure when he became a husband, and to him that meant having $1,000 in the bank. Major League ball enabled him to save that sum. Men and women married younger at the time, but if it mattered to the newlyweds, Robba turned 21 that year as well. The purchasing power of $1,000 in 1893 was close to $28,000 in 2019. That is a fairly tidy savings account for young people starting out in marriage.

Since the bride and groom were from farm backgrounds, somehow it seemed appropriate their marriage vows were taken at 10 a.m. In the big city, that would have been the equivalent of holding it when the rooster was crowing.

After they were wed, Cy purchased the farm where Robba grew up from her father Robert. Instead of moseying down the road to Cleveland as a permanent abode, the couple became the next-door neighbors of Young's parents. Once farm youngsters, they were now farm proprietors. The pitcher's new address was in Peoli, not Gilmore, but if he spent time practicing with rocks anymore, he probably could have thrown one between the two properties.

When the baseball season began, Robba joined Young, traveling with him and the team and absorbing more baseball than she had ever seen before. The 1893 National League season began with a different format from the 1892 season. The split-season plan guaranteeing a post-season playoff was scrapped. There was no world's championship at stake for two half-season pennant winners. The league champ was the team that compiled the best record during the regular season. Having tasted a bit of success in 1892, the Spiders sought to build on it, but despite becoming a very good hitting team, they did not improve on their record, and like everyone else in the league found themselves chasing the Boston Beaneaters again. Cy Young was Cy Young, but overall the Cleveland pitching was not as reliable as it had been the year before. The Spiders had won over the Cleveland fans in 1892, and that was a battle both hard-won and of incalculable value. They had to hang on to them.

Young recorded his second straight season of more than 30 wins, but in the big picture he wasn't quite as dominant as in the preceding season. The sturdy right-hander collected 33 victories and lost just 16 games. He was once again a powerful machine, throwing 422⅔ innings. But Young was a bit more hittable. His earned run average jumped from 1.93 to 3.36, though that may have been attributable to a rules change from the mound being extended from 50 feet to 60 feet, 6 inches from the plate. John Clarkson, another notable of the era, saw a similar result—his earned run average ballooning from 2.55 to 4.55 during that season of change.

The Spiders finished 73–55, in third place, 12½ games behind Boston. Pittsburgh grabbed second place, 7½ games ahead of Cleveland. George Cuppy was still good, this time going 18–10, but not in the same class as he was the year before. His ERA was much higher. John Clarkson was still an important hurler in the rotation but was fading at the tail end of his career, and his record was 16–17. That hurt.

Clarkson was one of the all-time greats, but at 31 his earned run average skyrocketed to 4.45 and he was only one season shy of retirement. Spiders management had hoped Young and Clarkson would be an unbeatable twosome, but it was too late in Clarkson's career to perform the way he had at 23 when he won 53 games in a season. Clarkson had been so good it was reported that he was actually approaching the end of a three-year contract with the Spiders that paid him $8,300 per season.

Clarkson was no stranger to big dollars in baseball. After the 1887 season, his contract was purchased from the Chicago Colts for $10,000. That seems to be an almost unbelievable figure for the times, but Clarkson was a coveted figure when the 1880s came to an end, and the Players' League was hustling for players. He won 49 games for the Beaneaters in 1889, and with more teams came more jobs, so Clarkson was approached to jump teams. Clarkson said he was approached by Arthur Dixwell, the magnate of the Boston club in the Players' League. Dixwell was known as a "players owner" who gave gifts to his favorite guys, from cigars to diamond pins, recliner chairs, and apparently cash in the form of loans that were of the wink-wink variety in that repayment was not sought.

Dixwell wanted Clarkson, who already had a big name in Boston, as a drawing card for his new team. Clarkson reiterated their discussions. "I told him to make me an offer," Clarkson said. The retort was $6,000. "I told him it was not enough. Negotiations ceased right then and there."[1]

Clarkson said that when the Boston National League team, the Beaneaters, offered him even more to stick with them, he agreed. Clarkson remained with the Boston NL team into 1892, when he was sent off to the Spiders. At the time, his throwing seemed fine. Between the two teams that year, Clarkson won 25 games, but he never again was the same dominating pitcher.

This decision to stay with Boston rankled pro-union members of the Players' League, but Clarkson said he had not intended to be anything but above-board, and he went to the new league's meetings in California to hear the organizers' pitch. By sticking with his original Boston team rather than helping to legitimize the challenger league, Clarkson made some enemies.

"I expect the players who belong to the Brotherhood were sore against me because I joined the League after I became a Brotherhood man," Clarkson said.[2]

It was obvious that at the time, he faced a career choice that offered more security and paid him more money. Clarkson was looking out for No. 1, much as so many future ballplayers have done since free agency took hold. By the time Clarkson was a regular for the Spiders, though, his deal didn't matter much anymore. He could not deliver the goods with the same authority. However, one thing Clarkson the veteran did was mentor the younger Cy Young. Young's primary pitch was his fastball, but in the majors no one gets by as a one-trick hurler. Clarkson did some

behind-the-scenes coaching with Young to improve his curveball, something Young acknowledged with thanks later.

What powerhouse hitters the 1893 Spiders were. Catcher Chief Zimmer took a backseat as backstop to newcomer Jack O'Connor, who saw
action in 97 games, about one-third more than Zimmer, and batted .286.
In less action, however, Zimmer out-hit him by banging safeties at a .308
rate. Player-manager Patsy Tebeau hit .329. Cupid Childs hit .326 and Ed
McKean .310. Chippy McGarr was 30 and had been out of the majors for
three years, but filled in nicely at third base and hit .309.

Buck Ewing was a rent-a-player essentially. He was already 33 years
old and had led the NL in home runs 10 years before. But the future Hall
of Famer still could wield a stick and hit .344. Ewing's natural position
was catcher, but the Spiders were well-stocked at the position, and he
shifted around where needed. This was the highest full-season average
of Ewing's career, and the Spiders put so many men on base Ewing's 122
runs batted in was also a career best by far. Although Ewing played a second season in Cleveland the next year, he was a far less critical asset and
hit just .251.

Much like Cy Young's nickname, Ewing's attachment to the surname
Buck was lodged in cement even though his given name was William.
Ewing did not break any fences on the way to becoming Buck, but said he
was given the nickname at age two while playing marbles. He told people
he played the game with an older boy called Buck, and the duo was referred to as "Big Buck" and "Little Buck."[3]

Ewing was pretty much a one-year wonder for the Spiders in 1893,
but one of the most notable developments from within the roster was the
emergence of Jesse Burkett as a supreme hitter. The outfielder, who was 24
that season and in his fourth year in the majors, began showing the stroke
that made him famous. Burkett hit .348, his finest average to date, but not
by a long shot the best he ever compiled. Burkett had become a big-time
threat at the plate.

Ewing was renowned for his defense as well, and he was the first
player who was primarily a catcher to be inducted into the Baseball Hall of
Fame. Late in his career, after he stopped playing, Ewing managed Cincinnati and the New York Giants for seven seasons.

Burkett was not a home run hitter, though he did knock in 82 runs
that season, but when he adjusted to big-league pitching, his style was to
bash line drives. Burkett worked doggedly to make himself a superior hitter, and he succeeded at his mission after a so-so hitting start to his career.
He was a relentless practice man, and he did not slack off once his average
approached .350 either. His excellent eyesight helped Burkett connect as
often as he did, and his work ethic kept him out on the field as late as he

could stay around without park lights. That habit went back to his youth. "They couldn't get me in for supper," Burkett said. "I played till dark."[4]

Still, in old age he told a newspaper visitor, "There were better players than me."[5] However, the list is a short one. Like so many early big leaguers, his vote for the best he ever saw was Ty Cobb, the Detroit Tigers' 12-time American League batting champ. "Cobb could do anything around the plate—hit, bunt, drag the ball."[6]

Burkett had much in common with Cobb, some of it in the batter's box and some of it sharing a gruff demeanor. Burkett earned his nickname "Crab" because of his testy nature. Not that he apologized for it. "You got to be a battler," Burkett said. "If you don't, they'll walk all over you. After you lick three or four of them, they don't show up anymore looking for a fight."[7]

Burkett was definitely Tebeau's type of ballplayer. And given Burkett's, Ewing's, Childs' and the others' hitting prowess, the Spiders might have been expected to win more games. If the pitching of 1892 was combined with the hitting of 1893, Cleveland may have dethroned the Beaneaters.

Author Reed Browning, who examined Young's life in a 2000 biography, placed some store on why the Spiders didn't win on intangibles, those things not measured in the box score that provide empirical facts. Apparently, the Spiders clubhouse was not as friendly as your typical high school locker room. There seemed to be seething dislike between Childs and Burkett "and [they] wanted to duke it out." There was an undercurrent of resentment towards Clarkson for his tap dance with the Brotherhood.[8]

Cy Young was not aligned with any of the unhappy factions. Just give him the ball, and he would go for the win no matter who was backing him on the field or in the dugout. Young may not have been at his absolute best, but winning 33 games (one of which was his 100th career victory) was hardly a slump. Of course, it should be remembered that 1893 was the season when the distance from the pitching rubber to home plate was expanded to 60 feet, 6 inches. That well could have made Young more hittable. Some careers were destroyed by the change. Young adapted, though somewhat unhappily.

Young and two other greats, Kid Nichols and Amos Rusie, remained pitchers at the top of their games. Still, this was not a rules change Young welcomed. He worried he might become a victim of it, saying "base ball legislation is tending to put the game back to the old three-cat game, when old women and babies could play as well as men, and when 80 or 90 runs were made in a game."[9]

Did this change spell the demise of Clarkson, who relied more on his breaking ball than his fastball? Some hitting stars of the time suggested that the best of the best fastball pitchers like Young, Nichols and Rusie were good enough to roll with this punch, or perceived assault on their livelihood. Those who came to the majors like Young were living through a time of change. This era saw those who played the game bare-handed add rudimentary hand-wear to their equipment, the distance from the mound to the plate altered, the elimination of pitchers taking a step forward towards the hitter before throwing, and the shift towards the overhand throw, though some sidearmers still persisted.

Some 126 years later, the mound is still situated at the same distance from home that it was moved to in 1893. Since there have been no major attempts at revision since, it seems likely that baseball authorities made the right call. If anything, looking at the recent number of pitchers throwing faster than ever, it seems that just maybe Major League Baseball will one day push the mound back a few more feet. There is no chance the mound will move closer to the plate. It's too late to help Cyclone anyway.

There were definitely some unknowns at the start of the 1893 season, and certainly many pitchers had to be skittish about adjusting to the main change pushing their release point back so far compared to the past. This was apparently enough of a topic of conversation that Young was asked by sports writers how he might fare under the new regulations.

Humor in manner of tone does not always jump off the written page, so it is not possible to know how serious or playful Young was when asked if he was thinking of quitting baseball because of the change, though it is most likely he had a twinkle in his eye and at least a minor smile on his lips when he said he would "try and stand it if the rest did. I've got a little strength left yet."[10]

It wasn't so much a question of whether the big-league pitchers of the day would be able to reach the plate with their tosses as whether the added distance would take the edge off their fastballs to provide more advantage to the hitters and whether their control would be maintained. While Young may have been flip in his pre-season response, it is also quite possible that his allowance of more hits and earned runs than in the year before was due to the distance change. Before one early-season game, Young said he had "no speed, no curves, no control."[11]

On any given day, even top pitchers can be out of sorts. Sometimes those words can be interpreted as an indicator of a demoralized pitcher, or merely one speaking frankly about a particular outing. Yet the combination of all factors in that 1893 season still left Young among the league's best. No one who wins 30 games in a season can be overlooked. Fans who always seem to believe even a superstar can improve every year may have counted on Young exceeding his previous year's total.

If Cy Young seemed more vulnerable during the early stages of the season, he put the slower start behind him and won 25 of his last 32 starts.

If Young had been anywhere else but the top of the heap, he was back. No, he did not exceed his win total of 1892 (he never would again). But 33 wins is 33 wins, and even when the feat was more commonplace, any pitcher who never caught a whiff of such exalted air might be jealous.

Exhibiting the same traits often seen in the makeup of professional sports team owners not only in Major League baseball, but in professional football, hockey and basketball, Frank Robison was unhappy because Cleveland did not finish higher than third place. After all, he had invested in bringing in several top-notch players. Worse, from his vantage point, was that the Spiders' attendance was not better. So Robison was neither making money nor gaining glory. There were hints in the off-season that Robison was trying to sell his team. Before the end of the decade, ownership and management in Cleveland would affect Cy Young in a material way.

That still lay a few years in the future. Meanwhile, the No. 1 pitcher on the Cleveland team was recognized with that designation. For winning 33 games in 1893, Young was given a $100 salary raise to $2,400 for the next season.

7

The Sometimes
Gay Nineties

The way the 1890s, also called the Gay Nineties in the United States, is viewed through an historical lens, it may have also been described as the best of times and the worst of times, the words penned by Charles Dickens in his 1859 novel "A Tale of Two Cities." While that phrase has become somewhat trite from overuse over the last 150 years or so, it wasn't yet a cliché by the 1890s.

It could be applied to the Cleveland Spiders. Owners Stan and Frank Robison craved both a winner and a financial success with the ballclub. But in the early and mid-part of the decade, they were at their high point as the best of also-rans, always looking up at one team in the standings. The Robisons had assembled a good ballclub and kept at it, adding pieces to the roster until they felt they could not fail. The cornerstone of the pitching staff was Cy Young. The Cyclone continued to do his job at a high level during the 1894 and 1895 seasons. He remained a big winner, but not the biggest winner in the league.

The fortunes of the Spiders varied as well. Manager Patsy Tebeau continued to try and squeeze everything out of his men, but with mixed results. In 1894, Cleveland's record was 68–61, above .500, but good for only sixth place in a 12-team National League. There was a new power-house team, the Baltimore Orioles, circuit pennant winners with an 89–39 record. Cleveland's attendance was as up and down as the team's perfor-mance. In 1894, the Spiders attracted just 82,000 fans total to League Park over the span of the season. They may have been a civic institution, but the civic was not playing its expected supporting role. The Robisons couldn't figure out why baseball fans didn't come out to the park more often. Their philosophy should have been rewarded, they felt. "Baseball, after all," said Frank Robison, "is like the show business. Give the public a decent attrac-tion and they will turn out to see you."[1]

Young hung in there in 1894 with a 26–21 record, though his earned run average rose again, this time to 3.94. Young endured a career-high seven-game losing streak this summer, and a headline writer in another city took notice of one of his off-days, writing, "A Cyclone Struck Cy Young." Young's innings total was 408⅔, another demanding work load. During that era, never a thought was given to the future health of pitchers whose arms were likely to burn out from overuse. There were no athletic trainers or team doctors. Regardless, there were no surgical cures for damaged goods. Pitchers threw until their arms practically fell off and then went on to another profession. Young did hold out during the pre-season, however.

Under the impression that he was the highest-paid player on the team, Young was dismayed to discover that John Clarkson was making more dough. Young was peeved at management, and that included manager Patsy Tebeau, who took a stance aligned with the bosses. Young got a small raise, but the situation bugged him. Contrary to other figures about how much Clarkson was paid, this publicized salary said he was making $2,500 with Cleveland. There was no players union around to keep track of the truth.

The trend to more offense in the game had shown up in 1893 when the pitching distance rule change kicked in, and life was better still for hitters in 1894. As a team laden with good hitters, the Spiders benefited from that upsurge. Cleveland was slugging the ball all over the lot, though not beyond the fences. Six starters and regular backups hit higher than .300: Jesse Burkett, .358, Ed McKean, .357, Cupid Childs, .353, Jack O'Connor, .315, George Tebeau, .313, and Patsy Tebeau, .302. George was Patsy's older brother. His career at bat was uneven, but his two best seasons, in 1894 and 1895 with the Spiders, were his best performances.

Two consistent problems for the Spiders were poor fielding and injuries. Some of the players were great when available, but other times they were sidelined by failing bodies. "No team in the league has had as much bad luck to contend with as we have," Patsy Tebeau said.[2]

George Cuppy went 24–15 on the mound, but his earned run average continued to climb to 4.56. And this was the disappointing career finale for John Clarkson, ending his superb big-league run with an 8–10 record. This was not what Spiders ownership bargained for. They hungered for more. As did the country at large.

The time period, going back a bit, was more broadly described as "The Gilded Age." The phrase was coined by Mark Twain, who also gave the world Huck Finn and Tom Sawyer. Although Twain was no baseball reporter, he was the American philosopher of the age, whose creative thinking provided healthy bromides to digest.

There is no indication that Twain made a comment specifically about

Burkett's career, but one fit. "Continuous improvement is better than de-layed perfection," Twain said.[3] It might be said that Cy Young should have listened up when Twain made another comment: "Keep away from people who try to belittle your ambitions. Small people always do that, but the really great make you feel that you, too, can become great."[4] That might suggest that Young steer clear of batters who wished to do him hard by cracking hits and scoring runs and that he would be in the best company if he spent his free time with Kid Nichols and Amos Rusie. Twain may have had a reminder message for the Robisons, too. "The world owes you nothing. It was here first."[5]

The Nineties are sometimes viewed as a playful time in American history. The age of the Industrial Revolution was lightening the load of laborers, providing more recreational and family time and making it easier for farmers to make a profit without working completely from sunup to sundown. Yet the Panic of 1893 depression erased some of the surety of financial stability. Wages increased for many, magnates made millions and millions of dollars, immigrants poured into the country with the belief that it was the land of opportunity, but there were not enough jobs for all, and an overheated economy took down some of the rich.

There was gilding coating the roster of the Spiders upon reading the names, but it masked some distress beneath the surface. The Spiders re-corded impressive numbers, but they did not always come through in the clutch. A review of the lineup might make an observer ask, "Why didn't they win more games?" That was the same question the Robisons were pondering too.

While there was no doubt baseball was a man's world, the country at large was feeling the first stirrings of women protesting their station in life. The focus was on obtaining the right to vote. Wyoming, which did not even become a state until 1890, as a territory in 1869 granted women the chance to vote. The sparsely populated land even then was looking to qualify for statehood, and by giving women the vote Wyoming prompted thinking that its cause would be advanced by adding more citizens. Even-tually, because of this early suffrage action, Wyoming became known as the Equality State.

The great equalizer in baseball was then, as today, the confrontation between the pitcher's best stuff and the hitter's keen eyesight. Perhaps if the pitching rules had not changed when they did, Young would have won even more games. But then, his achievements might not be taken as se-riously, since that view of 19th century baseball's inferiority seems to be today's overriding viewpoint.

It was probably a good thing Young lived a long life to burnish his legacy, lest he be overlooked by future generations. Although this might not be accurate (though there is no video to disprove it), Young had a tangy retort to a young sports writer following his career. The writer asked what Young's strategy was for coping with the bases loaded. "Young man," Young said, "I do not ever recall having to pitch with the bases filled."[6] Next question.

When he was much younger and still pitching, Young explained to an off-season visitor to his and Robba's farm in Peoli, Ohio, that from the time he was new to the game, passing through the minors, and during all his years in the majors he had been very consistent in his approach to training. Young stuck to the tried and true rather than embrace or experiment with newfangled conditioning methods. "You've heard the story about the postage stamp sticking to one thing till it gets there," Young said. "That principle has been the making of me." The questioner wondered whether Young had ever tried massage on his arm. "Massage, did you say? Huh! I wouldn't let one of those fellows get hold of my arm. It doesn't get sore, so what's the use?"[7]

That was a notable comment. His arm never got sore. That pretty much made him a freak of nature then. A pitcher going on year after year, throwing more than 400 innings, or even 300, per season, typically suffered a breakdown and loss of livelihood due to early retirement. The list of pitchers forced into early retirement, not just from Young's era, but over the decades, is a long one. One day they wake up with a throbbing elbow and their careers are toast. A ligament pops, an ache creeps in. It's always something. Sports medicine has traveled more than an ultramarathon's worth of distance between Cy Young's retirement and the Tommy John medical procedure.

Neither in the 1890s, when he was first making his way, nor in the early years of the 20th century, was Young benched because of a serious injury that would hamper him during a single season, or push him to exit the game.

During the off-season, Young was pretty much a workaholic of a physical nature. He and Robba had their own farm, and farm work does not get accomplished through wishing and hoping. Just doing the chores helped keep Young in shape, never mind calisthenics or throwing the baseball. Farm work was Young's personal style of cross-training.

"I was up at four o'clock yesterday," Young said on a winter day. "We eat breakfast by lamplight. There's always the feeding of the stock to do. This winter I am also helping clear some timber land. You ought to see me swing an axe. I have never worried about condition. I try not to worry about anything. I never have a ball in my hands during the winter and never use my arm to throw."[8]

The old days of tossing the rocks or apples at the barn were over. Young had learned something about overall physical fitness and applied it. Besides, he also believed that pitchers won as much with their heads as their arms.

> Say, if a pitcher hasn't got nerve, he had better pack up his grip and get back home. You can't get along without it. Why, sometimes when I am in a hole I have to say to myself, "See here, Cy Young, you can win out and you've got to do it." And it works. I'll tell you something else. I believe most pitchers are born, not made. But I want to tell you there are more good pitchers hid away in the hills than on the diamond.[9]

He was one of them. Young did endorse the concept of running for pitchers. One ballplaying cliché is that the legs go first. Young had a powerful torso and strong legs and stressed how important those good legs were to him. Speaking at another time, it seemed by the time Young got done analyzing his 1890s pitching, all of his success could be narrowed

down to his relationship with squirrels. "I always had a good pair of legs." Young said. "Got them chasing squirrels back on the farm. I guess the squirrels gave me a good arm, too. I hunted them with rocks. Got so I could hit one at 60 feet right between the eyes. One day I killed a squirrel 300 feet away."[10] The older Young got, the folksier his tales got, and the more they were enjoyed by younger generations.

What Young did not do was diminish his accomplishments on the mound during the 1890s and the early 1900s. Yes, it was a different game back then, without much happening on the home run front. But as he reminded

The great Larry Lajoie, whose .426 batting average in 1901 is the highest of the modern era starting in 1901, admired Young and convinced him to play for his American League club in 1909 and 1910.

people, there were other great pitchers who targeted him, always relishing their matchups, several of them also members of the Baseball Hall of Fame.

> And don't think it was easier to win games in those days than now. Whenever I got into a city, I'd find they saved their ace for me, so that record of mine was piled up against fellows like Walter Johnson in Washington, Bill Donovan in Detroit, Kid Nichols in Boston, Addie Joss in Cleveland, Rude Waddell in Philadelphia and Bill Hutchinson in Chicago. I once pitched a 20-inning game and allowed no passes, but lost to Waddell because of two errors behind me.[11]

Although the Spiders had not lived up to advance notices in 1894 when they contended with what seemed the bright lights of Broadway, that did not prevent manager Patsy Tebeau from issuing rosy predictions for 1895 before that campaign began. "I'm mighty sweet on Cleveland's chances this year," he said.[12]

There occasionally had been fan or writer comments, low-key, but nevertheless present, some watchers of the national game wondering whether Young would again ever match his 36-win season. Well, he wouldn't, but in 1895 he won 35 games. That was a mouth-closer. Young's season mark was 35–10, a .778 winning percentage. He logged a 3.26 ERA, all in fewer innings (369⅔) with fewer starts (40).

This was a gay season indeed for the Spiders. With a record of 84–46, they placed second in the National League. Pleasing numbers, yet Cleveland could still not capture the flag. The Baltimore Orioles were still three games better. This was the year Jesse Burkett truly blossomed. He had improved by the season, but he reached a rarefied zone in 1894 when hit .405. This was the first of three batting titles claimed by Burkett. He cracked out 225 hits that season.

Burkett was at last reaching his peak, and he was a darling of the fans, although it did not last. Some players are indifferent to booing and engage hecklers with retorts to their supposed funny comments, while others ignore repartee altogether. When Burkett was going this good, there was nothing to razz him about. However, sooner or later even the best players have an off-day in the clutch and leave the potential winning run on base, strike out looking, or go oh-for-four. On those days, Burkett did not merely brush off either the downturn or fan criticism. None of this let-it-roll-off-your-back stuff for Burkett. That's how he eventually got tabbed with the "Crab" nickname. No one said he didn't deserve it.

Near the tail end of Burkett's playing days, when he was still trying to make a buck from the game in his 40s and playing minor league ball, his personality and responses to insults were the same. One day, after being chastised for not being in the best of shape, he was irked and said what was on his mind. "Hell's bells," Burkett said, "there's men my age up there in the stands yelling about me showing up who couldn't run half a block to catch a streetcar."[13]

Burkett also recorded an extraordinary .482 on-base percentage in 1895. The Spiders were again a first-rate hitting team with pop throughout the order. Chief Zimmer may have been 34, getting up there for a catcher, but he batted .340 with 56 runs batted in and 14 stolen bases. One thing about Patsy Tebeau as player-manager, he always held up his end at the plate, this time batting .318. Ed McKean hit the finish line at .341, and George Tebeau, in his second and last big year for the Spiders, hit .326. Cupid Childs saw a drop-off but hit a still-respectable .288.

On the mound, George Cuppy, still saddled with the unfortunate nickname of "Nig," won 26 games behind Young. But there was no really solid third starter. Clarkson was retired. The next-best pitcher went 12–14, and although Bobby Wallace eventually made the Baseball Hall of Fame, his big seasons were to come when he switched away from the mound. Few people today even know of Wallace fulfilling that role. Except for a single appearance in 1902, Wallace was done with mound duties after 1896. Wallace played in the majors for 25 seasons, with the vast majority of his efforts in the infield. While he had some good years as a hitter, Wallace was primarily an asset as a glove man.

One of Young's highlights during the 1895 season was blanking the Orioles on four hits to win, 1–0. The Orioles had replaced the Beaneaters as the team with swagger. The Orioles were managed by Ned Hanlon and featured several prominent ballplayers whose names are still revered. Starters included Wilbert Robinson, later known for managing the Brooklyn Dodgers, John J. McGraw, the famed future manager of the New York Giants, "Wee" Willie Keeler, one of the best hitters of all time, Hughie Jennings, and Joe Kelley. Jennings' .386 average actually topped Keeler (.377), McGraw (.369), and Kelley (.365) that year. The Orioles' top hurler, Bill Hoffer, went 31–6. That was Hoffer's best year, and he burned out quickly.

Hanlon, Robinson, McGraw, Keeler, Jennings, and Kelley were all inducted into the Baseball Hall of Fame. Now that's depth in greatness. This was a scrappy, hard-nosed bunch, and their aggression helped McGraw form his aggressive managing style that he applied for three decades with the Giants. The best of them all on the field, though, had to be Keeler.

Right-fielder Keeler was born in Brooklyn, New York, in 1872. His nickname, whether he liked it or not, made sense because Keeler's height was 5-foot-4, and he weighed just 140 pounds. In those days, players wielded bats so large they were often compared to clubs, but somehow Keeler managed to handle his stick. He batted .341 lifetime and stroked 2,932 hits at a time when there was little or no attention placed on reaching the milestone of 3,000. Too bad for him. Keeler won two batting titles, and in 1897 he hit .424 with 239 hits in 129 games. One of Keeler's secrets, a testament to his sharp eyes, was that he hardly ever struck out. Keeler fanned just once for every 63 at-bats.

The Orioles had arrived fully formed in the National League by transferring from the American Association. Their terrific showing, taking the pennant in 1894, gained them entry into the first Temple Cup series. William Chase Temple, a rich businessman with varied interests who was a part-owner of the Pittsburgh Pirates, put up $800 to buy the cup. It was intended as a rotating trophy going to the winner of the showdown between the National League's first- and second-place teams.

The Temple Cup was the award succeeding the Dauvray Cup, which was named for actress Helen Dauvray and presented to the league champ between 1887 and 1893. The folding of the American Association brought the Orioles to the National League starting with the 1892 season. In 1895, the Orioles were in the middle of a three-season run as the best regular-season team.

A sizzling finish, going 27–3 down the stretch, enabled the Orioles to pass the New York Giants for the 1894 pennant. Keeler actually swatted the hit that clinched the pennant off Cy Young as Baltimore topped the Spiders in Cleveland. Baltimore fans reacted with delirium. Businesses—except for taverns and saloons—closed immediately to let the party begin.

The Orioles still had games to play to complete the schedule, but when the team returned to Baltimore, the town went crazy. Their train was escorted by fans for the last 40 miles into Baltimore, and some 10,000 supporters joined a parade to fete the players. The parade route was five miles long, and an estimated 200,000 cheering spectators came out.

Mayor Ferdinand Latrobe was a gushing host, exclaiming, "We have always had the most beautiful women and the finest oysters in the world, and now we have the best baseball club."[14]

That year, Kelley batted .393 and Keeler hit .371. While not nearly as well-remembered as Keeler, whose reputation was burnished by the catchy "Hit-'em-where-the-ain't" philosophy he espoused and has forever stuck to him, it was clear that Kelley was a special player. "Joe had no prominent weakness," McGraw said of his teammate. "He was fast on the bases, he could hit the ball hard and was as graceful an outfielder as one would care to see."[15]

With the Temple Cup less prized than the World Series would become, the Orioles must have used up all of their energy celebrating their pennant because the Giants came at them full force and swept the best-four-out-of-seven series in four straight games.

The Orioles were just as dominant during the regular season in 1895, and that qualified them for another Temple Cup championship series, this time against the Spiders. During Cy Young's time with Cleveland, the club had not won anything, no trophies, no particular recognition. This second-place finish with such a fine record was an achievement, but the Spiders and their owners wanted to cement the season with victory. Of some note, too, some additional cash would come into the coffers.

Baltimore's players did not seem to have much zest for this series. Their primary aim when the season began in the spring of 1895 was to win the pennant. They did so, playing superb baseball over the summer months. They were kings of the long season and did not seem terribly excited by having to prove themselves once more as kings of a short series.

Although he was shakier than sharp, Young was on the mound for the first game, won at League Park by Cleveland. One must wonder what got into the local fans, who behaved abominably towards the Orioles, throwing garbage on the field and shouting insults. There was not such an intense rivalry between the clubs, except for that year's closing stretch of pennant race, but it was inexcusable activity nonetheless.

It is difficult to imagine that bunch of Orioles players being intimidated, but this collection of great players mounted little offense. Cuppy won the second game, and Young came back out to put the Spiders up 3–0. When the season shifted to Baltimore, Orioles fans retaliated by throwing items at the Spiders—outside the ballpark—and also defeating Cleveland. However, Young was tabbed as the starter for the fifth contest and conquered the Orioles again, going 3–0 in the win-loss column as the Spiders became champs, winning 5–2, hoisting the Temple Cup in celebration. It was a great moment for Cleveland, but the series did not conclude with a gracious, sportsmanlike send-off. Baltimore's fans were so menacing, seeming bent on attacking the players while pelting them with fruit and rocks, that the Spiders had to be safely escorted away from the premises by the local police.

Some 1,500 fans greeted the Spiders when they returned to Cleveland, and they were honored at a banquet attended by about 300 people. Then, as today, after the World Series, players on teams in the championship series are awarded extra pay from gate receipts. Compared to the old days, when even small amounts of extra cash were helpful to the budgets of players who did not make much money, there are full shares, half-shares, and the like divvied up by the team members.

Choosing to be generous, the Spiders gave everyone on the team, whether he played or not, an equal share of $528. Those who did not get their whacks in against the Orioles were grateful. "I tell you this is a club of good fellowship," said backup catcher Jack O'Connor, who did not play against Baltimore.[16]

Champagne flowed like rivers and was appreciated by the champs. Maybe the Spiders turned rowdy and maybe they did not, but one account of the revelry suggests that late in the proceedings some players actually kicked the Temple Cup around as if they were playing soccer.[17] It is an amusing story but seems a little far-fetched. The 30-inch trophy was a heavy metal object. No matter what type of kick form may have been used, it seems it would have taken a larger toll on a toe than a foot might have made upon impact with the emblem of the championship.

Regardless of the accuracy of Temple Cup abuse, it sounded like quite the shindig for the happy Cleveland Spiders.

8

1896

Coming off the farm after a winter of wood chopping and cattle feeding, Cy Young was in an optimistic mood as he headed to spring training with the Spiders in Hot Springs, Arkansas again. Cleveland had reached new levels of achievement in 1895, and the glow of the Temple Cup victory over the Baltimore Orioles still shone bright. Almost always after winning a championship, a victorious team will think highly of its chances to repeat at the start of the next season.

That is the attitude Young brought to camp to kick off the 1896 season. There was a much smaller body of evidence in the late-19th century showing how difficult it is for sports teams to repeat their golden moments than there is now. Many managers and coaches have said the most challenging thing to do in sports is to repeat winning a title. If that outlook was even in place at the time, no one passed the message down to Cy Young. More likely, the prevailing thinking mirrored his own: We did it once, so we can do it again. "I am in fine shape," Young said, "and if the other Spiders are in as good shape as I am, no team in the league will be in it with Cleveland this season."[1]

The Spiders were riding a high after polishing off the Orioles in the post-season. Why wouldn't they think they were hot stuff? For the most part, Young was right. The Spiders played at a scorching .625 winning pace during the regular season, finishing at 80–48. The only problem was that once again the Orioles were a little bit better, actually 9½ games better in the standings, with a 90–39 mark.

Like many of his teammates, Young had been taking the field without a baseball glove, barehanded, for the first several years of his career. Gradually, other players began wearing first those thin work gloves that more resembled bicycle racers' gloves of the 20th century, and then gloves that were actually professionally made for the sport. It seems incomprehensible to envision professional ballplayers on the diamond not wearing gloves. Not only are gloves fundamental to the sport, they prevent hand injury and provide players with face protection against line drives. Interestingly, in some vintage photographs of Young, it is not entirely clear whether he is wearing a glove, with one hand out of sight of the camera's lens.

Even more intriguing is that a modern-day fan can purchase a Cy Young-model baseball glove online. A shopper can google "Cy Young baseball glove" and come up with an opportunity to buy a used Cy Young glove. It is called "1930s Hutch Cy Young Baseball Glove," with a price tag of $275 attached. This is not a spanking new mitt. The selling description reads in part: "Cy Young Split Finger Glove. Made by Hutch. Stamped famous Cy Young Model. Believe this is his only store model glove ever sold." The glove is very much faded leather, the string connecting the thumb and forefinger not completely tied, with some fraying areas on the bottom and back. This is not a glove that Young wore, though perhaps he owned one like it during the latter years of his career.

In 1896, once again the Spiders fielded a lineup loaded with excellent hitters. Jesse Burkett had topped .400 the year before, and in 1896 he became that rare ballplayer to hit higher than that twice during his career. Burkett was super again, batting .410 and leading the National League in hitting for a second time in a row. He stroked 240 hits and scored 160 runs. With numbers like those next to his name on the lists, Burkett could crab all he wanted.

There was some drop-off in Spiders hitting, but Burkett's was not the only big gun. Cupid Childs came through with a .355 average, and Ed McKean hit .338. Patsy Tebeau did fall off to .268, and George Tebeau was gone. Jack O'Connor hit .297 off the bench in a more limited, but still active role.

No matter how good Young might be in any season, it had been proven that the Spiders needed more than one arm to get anywhere. George Cuppy kept hurling at a high level as Young's sidekick. This season, Cy Young finished 28–15 and Cuppy went 25–14. Cleveland introduced a new face to the pitching staff. Zeke Wilson was the third man, going 17–9, and before he quit pitching, Bobby Wallace compiled a 10–7 record. For a fourth man, that was collecting his share of wins. Wilson was a right-hander from Alabama who spent just five years in the majors. That 1896 season was his best.

Young led the NL in strikeouts that season with 140, a rarity for him. He led his league in Ks in only one other season during his long career. His earned run average was 3.24, but one indicator that prevented him from winning 30 games again was permitting a league-leading 477 hits. Young was about as busy as ever, throwing 414⅓ innings.

As well as Cleveland played overall, the Spiders had taken on the aggressive, somewhat cantankerous personality of manager Tebeau (and perhaps coincidentally the approach and attitude of the Orioles). Their own field play was not gentlemanly. It was intended to be intimidating. At one point in a game against Louisville, the events deteriorated into a brawl, not something the Spiders would shy away from (although Young was never pugnacious). Not terribly surprising (and perhaps even correctly), Louisville baseball officials felt like the aggrieved parties and initiated procedures to have the entire Cleveland team arrested before a Saturday game.

Cleveland players were hauled into court (in full uniforms, a vision not often seen on the police beat), and Tebeau, O'Connor, McKean, and Jimmy McAleer were fined $100 each. Worse, the Spiders wore the label of the black hats all around the league after that. In a sense, they were like the Detroit Pistons' "Bad Boys" of NBA basketball of the 1980s, already viewed with suspicion and dislike when they showed up at the stadium before any action took place.

Watching with concern the mounting hostility, which did nothing to quell Spiders behavior either, the National League announced a $200 fine for Tebeau. Bosses of other teams announced they would add more police protection at their home games versus the Spiders. In hindsight, it is difficult to know whether there was genuine worry about what might break out in those games, or the owners were using Cleveland's reputation for publicity purposes and hoped to take the Spiders out of their usual style through intimidation.

Owner Frank Robison, who may well have reveled in his club's image, but would have enjoyed it even more if fans backed the team in larger numbers (Cleveland was 11th out of 12 teams in attendance that season), acted outraged about this animosity directed at his squad. He challenged the league in court to withdraw the Tebeau fine and ordered his men not to pay any fines. It was unfair to pick on the Spiders, he said. "It is war, and I like nothing better," Robison said.[2]

Young liked baseball and nothing better. He was a non-combatant in the midst of the whirlwind, a conscientious objector of sorts. Young wanted to pitch and defeat the opposition with his guile and speed. He had no interest in throwing punches or having games disrupted by brawls, snarls and nastiness. His tune was Play ball!

In mid-season of 1896, Young pitched one of his favorite games and, until that point, his best. Although the Cyclone threw three no-hitters in the big leagues, he had not thrown one yet. On July 23, it was Young versus the Philadelphia Phillies in Cleveland. As Young said after his eye-opening performance, he was ready that day, felt so good he was positive he was going to dominate the Phillies.

The Phillies were not especially good that season, finishing with a 62–68 record, but their lineup featured some of the most dangerous batsmen in the world. Future Hall of Fame outfielder Sam "Big Sam" Thompson, was large for his day at 6-foot-2 and 207 pounds. He had a lifetime average of .331 and hit 20 homers in 1889, an unusual accomplishment for the era, and 126 in all. Thompson, whose handlebar mustache was in a style seen only in exaggerated cartoon depictures today, once drove in 166 runs in a season and 61 in a single month. He was nearly at the end of his career by 1896.

So was Dan Brouthers, another superior hitter of the 19th century, whose physical dimensions were listed as the same as Thompson's. Brouthers, another future Hall of Famer, hit .342 lifetime and cracked 106 homers. The third high-profile hitter in Philadelphia's lineup was Ed Delahanty. That season the outfielder batted .397, which was actually a slight drop-off since he batted over .400 the two preceding seasons and did so a third time later.

Delahanty's story is one of the strangest in baseball history. He was born in 1867, the same year as Young, and his .346 lifetime batting average is one of the highest ever. Like Thompson and Brouthers, Delahanty was later elected to the Hall of Fame. Born in Cleveland, he was from a ball-playing family. Four brothers played in the majors, though he was the best amongst the siblings. Called "Big Ed," Delahanty was on his way to driving in 126 runs in 1896.

Big Ed spent 16 successful years in the majors, winning batting titles in both the National League and the newer American League. The mystery about Delahanty surrounds the night of his death at 35 on July 2, 1903. Part of the evidence of what occurred in the last hours of his life is clear, and some of is murky. Traveling on a train at Niagara Falls, Delahanty was said to be so drunk as to be unmanageable, scaring the other passengers with his unruliness and even perhaps brandishing a straight razor as he threatened them.

A bold porter gained control of Delahanty and ejected him from the train at the famous Falls, and the train moved on without him. Delahanty began to walk across the International Railway Bridge. He soon disappeared, leading to speculation that he committed suicide by jumping, lost his footing due to clumsiness brought on by alcoholic imbibing, or was even pushed and murdered as part of a robbery by a stranger.

While mostly forgotten in the 21st century except by keen students of baseball, Delahanty was not only a contemporary and competitor of Cy Young and Willie Keeler, he was better known by the public at the time. His nickname was the "King of Swat" because of his high averages and hold on the sport as a dashing (456 stolen bases' worth) and excellent player.

Naturally, Young and Delahanty crossed paths in games, with each man winning the confrontation some of the time. In one incident described by one author, Delahanty refused to accept an intentional walk. The catcher, probably Chief Zimmer, was said to signal for the intentional base on balls because the potential winning runs were on base in the ninth inning. The walk was intended to neutralize Delahanty's threat. The story goes that when Young threw the ball far outside to Delahanty, he stepped across home plate and swung with his might, knocking the ball out of the park and capturing the game for Philadelphia. "I told you to let him walk," the catcher told Young after the game. Young said he was aware of that. "Oh, I know you did," he said. "But I had to pitch the ball somewhere, and I thought I had a wild pitch until I saw it going over the fence."[3]

Despite Philadelphia's loaded batting order for the July 23, 1896, game, Young was not fazed by any wielder of big sticks. He whizzed through the lineup with the prospect of the first no-hitter of his career looming in front of him as the teams entered the late innings. Cleveland led, 2–0, and Young had allowed just one batter on base through a walk. Delahanty stepped into the batter's box and hefted his wooden weapon.

Slash. There it went. Delahanty drove the ball to the outfield and broke up the no-hitter. Young quickly ended the threat and walked off the mound with a dazzling one-hitter, in complete command of the game except for one pitch. Young said he knew pre-game, "I would pitch good ball. I played to shut the Phillies out without a hit. I don't think any team would have hit me the way I was working Thursday."[4]

Not every day on the mound was as satisfying as that Thursday. Overall, Young still shined with his 28 wins, but at times—like every professional athlete—he was vulnerable. So were the Spiders. By finishing second in the standings with their strong record, Cleveland earned the right to play for the championship again, renewing their rivalry with Baltimore in the Temple Cup series. The Orioles had dominated regular-season play, but whether through indifference, failure to focus completely, or weariness, they had not won the Cup. This time the Orioles seemed to feel that was an oversight on the team resume.

Hughie Jennings batted .401 that season and Keeler .386. Four other regulars and two part-timers also hit more than .300. Bill Hoffer led the staff with a 25–7 record, and four other starting pitchers turned in double-figure victories. The reason the Orioles finished nearly 10 games ahead of Cleveland in the standings was that they had more of everything.

That was proven in the Temple Cup challenge. Baltimore swept the Spiders in four straight games. Young pitched the opener against Hoffer but was beaten, 7–2. Young took a line drive off his wrist clouted by John McGraw that left him with painful swelling—he was lucky it wasn't broken. He remained on the sidelines for the next three losses. The series was never close.

Young especially respected Keeler's bat-handling skills. He recognized Keeler as an extraordinary hitter. "The talk that it is impossible for a batsman to send the ball where he pleases is utter rubbish," Young said. "It can be done. Willie Keeler does it almost every day of his baseball life."[5]

At the party celebrating their decisive triumph, the Orioles, and others in attendance, including William Temple, drank champagne in abundance from the Cup. A handful of the players then went on a European tour, sailing across the Atlantic Ocean. As Keeler said, surprisingly to the players and to those who had warned them, few experienced any seasickness. He visited the home of his ancestors on one of the stops that included England, France, Belgium, Holland, and Ireland. "You can't imagine how beautiful it looks," Keeler wrote of seeing land once more that was as green as ballpark grass, "until you are on the sea for 10 or 11 days. We are close to the shores of Ireland, the home of our parents."[6]

Although the Robisons were vocal about their lack of crowd support in Cleveland for the Spiders, the fans who did avidly follow the club always had a soft spot for Cy Young. During the 1896 season, the fans showed their affection for Young by presenting him with a cane carved out of a baseball bat. While a Young in his 20s may not have known what to do with such a present, he brought it back to his Peoli farm and kept it.

When Young was much older—he lived to be 88—and he needed some help getting around, he pulled out the cane and used it as a "walking stick," as he put it. Young's last year of life was 1955, and he made a visit to the Baseball Hall of Fame in Cooperstown, New York, that year and donated his keepsake cane to the museum. "This is my last baseball souvenir," he said.[7]

That may not have been completely accurate, unless there was a transfer of another item at the same time. The Hall of Fame has a big, fat, tightly wrapped, heavily protected Cy Young scrapbook in its archives. The contents are mostly old, yellowing newspaper clippings saved from Young's playing career. During that era of baseball coverage by the city's newspapers, with no other mass media around, the writers' main job was to report the game doings. They did not often venture onto the field or the dugouts to interview players after the contests. Only periodically did the writers approach players for more in-depth talks. So most of the time, the players' thoughts remained hidden. Young was a big name long enough that his thinking was probed on occasion, even if it wasn't always right after a game took place.

He also lived for a long time after he retired and was often approached for interviews about the old days. Young was cordial enough, chatty enough, and welcoming enough, and his memory seemed pretty solid, so there are more remarks on the record from different sources than there might be of some of the other stars of the 1890s.

Neither team owners nor managers evidenced too much concern that they were wrecking their pitchers' futures by sending them to the mound day after day and accumulating 400 or more innings each year. Only a small number of top-rate pitchers could withstand it. If that were not so, then there may have been more challengers to Young as the all-time winningest pitcher. Several pitchers won more games than Young in a single season, but they could not keep up with him in the long run.

Pud Galvin, winner of 365 games, once threw 656⅔ innings in one season. Although he stayed around the majors for 15 years, the last five years of his career saw a diminishing workload. John Clarkson won his 328 games, but was retired by age 32 after his effectiveness began waning. Kid Nichols won 362 games over 15 years of play, hung in longer than most, but started showing signs of decline by his 30th birthday.

Charles "Old Hoss" Radbourn won 310 games, including the all-time single-season record of 60 in 1884, but was out of the sport after 11 seasons. Tim Keefe won 342 games in 14 seasons, but only once as many as 19 over his last six years.

Cy Young was more durable than any of them. He pitched for 22 years, and he had those seasons when he was asked to be the go-to guy for much of the campaign, backed up by just two other starters. Five times during the early years of Young's career in Cleveland, he was called upon to toss more than 400 innings in a season, a total that would be regarded as insane in 2020. Young averaged 334 innings during his career. There was not much medical research to tell teams and players they were jeopardizing careers when they undertook these assignments, but the suspicion began to grow among the pitchers. Young was smart enough to realize those massive innings totals could ruin a pitcher.

> Every year the strain on the pitchers becomes greater. The explanation lies in the fact that a present-day twirler must have a large assortment of curves, and then, what is more, be able to deliver them at high speed. Formerly pitchers [in the 1890s] would work every day, but few of the present men [in the early 1900s] could equal the record made by Charles Radbourn when he, for the Providence Grays, landed a pennant single-handed.
>
> A pitcher that has to go into the box oftener than every four days complains of overwork. Several clubs carry as many as seven pitchers, and it often happens that for one reason and another all of them are unable to work.[8]

In part, Young seemed to acknowledge that pitching was more difficult towards the end of his career than at the beginning, but while recognizing that not all of that hard work was good for the arm, he also seemed to take pride in the heroic warrior model that the pitchers of the 1890s represented.

Still, by 1897, there were some signs that Young should pay attention to the number of innings he threw.

9

1897

As Cy Young stood atop the familiar mound at League Park in Cleveland on the afternoon of September 18, 1897, he was on the cusp of one pitching achievement that had eluded him to that point in his star-spangled career with the Spiders.

There were two outs in the top of the ninth on the balmy day with a temperature of about 70 degrees, although winds blew in to somewhat cool off the atmospheric conditions. Actually, though, Young had more or less taken control of those atmospheric conditions with his sizzling pitching. There were about 2,500 fans in the park waiting to see how Young handled the Cincinnati Reds' next batter.

The man walking to the plate was an unusual player, most assuredly someone who could handle a bat, but different from most ballplayers. The Reds outfielder, a native of Ohio, was born William Ellsworth Hoy, who was deaf. In those more insensitive times, when players could get away with nicknaming Spiders pitcher George Cuppy "Nig" because of his relatively dark skin, it was not deemed inappropriate to Hoy to be nicknamed "Dummy" because he could neither hear nor speak clearly. He communicated with his teammates by writing them notes. Hoy never displayed resentment over his nickname and seemed to embrace it to a point, as if that and not William was his birth name.

Hoy was a tremendous fielding center fielder who set several early records, and he could hit well, compiling a .288 average over 14 seasons in the majors. He also accumulated 2,048 hits. Young knew enough about Hoy to understand he had to pitch him carefully. This was true under all circumstances, but most importantly in this situation.

Hoy contracted meningitis as a three-year-old, and that left him with his affliction. Of course he faced some disadvantages during games. The commonplace situation in the outfield when a fly ball is hit is for the closest fielder to shout, "I've got it!" in order to alert one of his partners. Hoy could not easily form the necessary words, but managed to make an approximate noise. "Whenever I take a fly ball, I always yell 'I'll take it,' the same as I have been doing for many seasons," Hoy reported, "and, of course the other fielders let me take it. Whenever you don't hear me yell, it is understood I am not after the ball and they govern themselves accordingly."[1]

If Young could get Hoy out, the righty would fulfill an ambition of throwing a no-hitter. The score was 6–0, Spiders. Almost from the game's start, manager Patsy Tebeau liked what he saw from Young and offered positive feedback. Tebeau was not one to keep quiet when he had anything on his mind. "You've got them off-balance," Tebeau told Young early in the game.[2] After that Tebeau said nothing more, though the crowd, if only 2,500 strong, kept up a buzz.

Cleveland glove men had made three errors. Not even future Hall of Famer Bobby Wallace was immune that day, committing two of them at third base, one on a throw and one on a muffed ground ball. Still, the Young no-hitter was in reach.

The first Reds batter in the ninth was pinch-hitter Claude Ritchey, an infielder in his rookie year. Ritchey stood in for pitcher Billy Rhines and got a piece of a Young offering, but when he made contact the ball flew to Young for the out. Moving to the top of the order, up came right fielder Bug Holliday. He got wood on the ball, too, but it was a grounder to Wallace at third.

It was a good thing Wallace made that play. Fans would have ridden him hard after the two errors. He might not have been such a close pal of Young's either at the end of the day. As it was, there was a lot of talk about whether or not the official scorers were fair on Wallace's two failures. Some thought the plays should have been marked as hits, but Wallace lobbied against his own cause and in favor of Young's, and the shots stayed as errors. Wallace said it was inexplicable that the ground ball should beat him, but things happen. "The ball came straight at me," Wallace said. "But in some way got through me."[3]

Wallace's clean play in the ninth made for two outs.

Here came Hoy to the plate. Young was ready and still strong. He whiffed Hoy to complete his masterpiece. In many other games, Young struck out more men. Polishing off Hoy was only his third K of the game. It was a grand moment for the Cyclone. There had not been a National League no-hitter in four years. As often happened during those early days of baseball, the game was swiftly played. Young disposed of the Reds in an hour and 35 minutes.

Recognizing that Wallace had come to bat for him with words taking the blame for the botched ball-handling, Young expressed his appreciation. "I have never forgotten the little fellow for that," Young said.[4]

The world of baseball was young at that time and no-hitters scarce.

Young's feat was celebrated by a delightful headline in the *Cleveland Plain-Dealer*: "Young's Record—It May Be Tied, But It Can Never Be Beaten."[5] No one could picture fewer than zero hits.

A bigger deal in Ohio and Cleveland earlier that year was the swearing in of William McKinley of Canton as President of the United States. The citizens of Ohio were excited about that occurrence in March, and there seemed to be no reason why they shouldn't be excited by the Spiders starting in April. But that was not to be. The Cleveland turnout was anemic, just 115,000 strong in 1897, making them last in the 12-team league in attendance.

Young was pleased to record the no-hitter. In some ways it was a consolation prize for his season, which had not followed according to plan if a 20-victory season can be termed disturbing. Neither Young nor the Spiders truly clicked that year. Young's record was 21–19 and his earned run average 3.74. Not bad, still tops on the staff, but not vintage Young. Zeke Wilson, 16–11, Jack Powell, 15–10, and Cuppy, reduced to 10–6 with an innings plunge to 138, followed him in the rotation.

While the Baltimore Orioles maintained their outstanding winning pace during the 1897 National League season, finishing with a record of 90–40 and a winning percentage of .692, that was not good enough to capture the pennant flag. And it was not the previous runner-up Spiders who gave them difficulties. The regular-season winners that year were the resurgent Boston Beaneaters, who surged ahead of the Orioles with a 93–39 record and a .705 winning percentage, as impressive as it gets over a long season. The Spiders fell to fifth place with a 69–62 record. They were not in the hunt for post-season play that year.

This was the fourth year of the Temple Cup's existence, but it would also be the last. An excellent idea on the surface—and with thanks to William Temple for his generosity—the NL ceased matching the top two teams for the right to gain possession of the silver trophy after 1897. There were good intentions, but the series did not produce the type of frenzied support the organizers expected. As good as Boston was in the regular season, the underdog Orioles handled the Beaneaters easily in the series, winning four games to one.

But that was the end of the year, not the beginning. If no one was making outright predictions of greatness coming off of the 1896 victory campaign, there was still every reason to think the Spiders would still be in the mix at the top of the standings. Although Burkett did not bat .400 again that season, he was in the neighborhood with a .383 average. The man had become a hitting machine. Likewise, Cupid Childs swung away to the tune of .338. Outfielder Ollie Pickering hit .352 in 197 plate appearances. Good old Chief Zimmer, then 36, showed more luster with the bat than at almost any other time in his long career, hitting .316. Although Wallace was just 5-foot-8, he was the biggest power source for the club, clouting four home runs, driving in 112 runs and batting .335 with 14 stolen bases. That was an MVP-caliber, all-around year.

There was also a key newcomer who burst on the scene. Outfielder Louis Sockalexis hit .338. The Cleveland team was still known as the Spiders, but would later become the Indians, accepting the nickname they still display today. Sockalexis was later termed "the original Cleveland Indian" because he was an Indian, or Native American.

Sockalexis was born in 1871 in Indian Island, Maine. Sockalexis had been a logger there before turning to baseball, and he was 25 when he joined Cleveland. He played in 66 games for the Spiders in 1897, and many thought a legend was born. His life did not turn out that way, however. He was a shooting star, barely in the public eye longer than Halley's Comet. Never mind fans, Sockalexis took racist abuse even from some teammates, who found Sockalexis' presence something new to crab about. A half-century later, with the Brooklyn Dodgers, when Jackie Robinson broke the color line for African Americans in the 20th century, he faced the same type of ridicule and harassment, again sometimes from teammates, until general manager Branch Rickey harangued them for their behavior and traded some elsewhere.

The nation had not really come to terms with its feelings about Native Americans in 1897. The country had been built on the backs of those who had been there before the settlers and the cavalry troops swooped across the plains, herding Indians onto reservations, slaughtering the bison, and making the West safe for settlement. Just as white Americans treated black Americans with disdain and contempt even after the Civil War was over, lingering hatred, racism, and in some cases, just a disrespectful indifference, were deeply felt.

The Plains Indians Wars, from the late 1860s to about 1890, reshaped the country. The government and the growing population were greedy for more and more land and desperate to acquire valuable minerals wherever they were found. Gen. George Armstrong Custer became the martyr of the wars when he and his troops were massacred at the Battle of the Little Bighorn in 1876 Montana. Famed Sioux chief Sitting Bull, architect of the Natives' victory, was chased and hounded until he gave himself up to reside on a reservation.

In a memorable essay in 1890, Frederick Jackson Turner declared that the American frontier was closed. The Indian tribes had been rounded up, the many millions of bison had been reduced to a relative handful. Americans from the East could go forth and multiply and grow corn and wheat in newly opened territory. William F. "Buffalo Bill" Cody, the most accomplished scout for American cavalry officers in the West, and winner of the Congressional Medal of Honor for his performance in the field, over the ensuing decades became the best friend Native Americans had. Cody stumbled into show business, first on the stage and then with his riveting Wild West exhibition that kept alive the myths and truths of the West. Through his connections with highly placed generals in Washington, D.C., from his fighting days, Cody received permission to hire Native Americans for his shows. Some even joined him in travels to England, France, Russia, and other European nations.

Cody had pretty much transformed his outlook. From a hired scout who fought for his government, he became the leading employer of Native Americans in the country. One of his best friends and top assistants (while also being a highly paid employee) was Iron Tail. For one six-month period in 1885, Buffalo Bill even secured Sitting Bull's release from reservation confinement to join his show. As part of his pledge to Sitting Bull, Cody said the chief would not have to take part in any skits. His only job, Cody told Sitting Bull, was to be himself. Sitting Bull bought in. Those who attended the show just wanted to see Sitting Bull, although he also distributed autographed pictures.

Although Sitting Bull was long gone (dead three years, murdered by his own people), by 1893 when the World's Columbian Exposition, known as the World's Fair for short, opened in Chicago, Cody and his performers were denied the opportunity to be part of the event. Instead, Cody set up his own exhibition right outside the gate and drew more than one million people. Not so far away, the Chicago Colts and the not-quite-as-famous Adrian "Cap" Anson were playing baseball. Buffalo Bill was trying to educate people about the past. Baseball was the sport of the future.

In 1897, again not far from where baseball was being played in New York, Cody's Wild West was selling out an early version of Madison Square Garden.

Sockalexis was not as popular as Sitting Bull, and he went through some rough times. If he had a significant go-between to help him relate to the Spiders the way Cody stood up for Sitting Bull, perhaps Sockalexis would have become more than a famous footnote in Cleveland in the long run.

More than merely a lumberjack, Sockalexis had attended college at Holy Cross in Worcester, Massachusetts, and played baseball there. That was Sockalexis's connection to the Spiders. Jesse Burkett, who coached and lived in that town, brought him to the attention of the Cleveland owners with an endorsement. "He is a wonder," Burkett wrote in his telegram scouting report, "but I can't spell his name. Just send on a blank contract and I will try to sign him."[6]

The Spiders offered Sockalexis $2,000 to play the 1897 season in Cleveland. However, he made a stopover in South Bend, Indiana, home of Notre Dame, to enroll there instead. He didn't last long at Notre Dame. After someone insulted his heritage and Sockalexis punched him out, he was expelled from school.

It was generally conceded that Cleveland was pretty much a racist town, but Sockalexis came highly recommended by Burkett as a worthy outfielder who was fleet afoot and possessed a rocket arm, and the local papers ate it up, heralding his arrival. Surprisingly, sports writers began urging management to ditch the Spiders name and adopt Indians to replace it. That was not officially done in the 1890s. One substitute nickname for Spiders was the Cleveland Lake Shores. The team went through some other name changes over the next 15 or so years, but has been the Indians since 1915.

Tebeau was quite accepting of having a Native player on the team. He only cared if Sockalexis could play, and he showed he could. There was little warmth towards Sockalexis among the players, though. He was often on his own on train trips and the like. Owner Frank Robison was approached by a sports writer in spring training and asked for an evaluation of Sockalexis. "He's a fine young man, a fine ballplayer," the boss said.[7]

Sockalexis earned a spot in the lineup. He was 5-foot-11 and 185 pounds, but he could take care of himself physically. He had also played football at Holy Cross and showed his toughness. He was happy to fight if challenged, but with a Jesuit background he did prefer to turn the other cheek. There was an incredible amount of pressure on him. He was expected to perform on the field, but he was not viewed as an equal citizen outside of the ballpark, on the team's travels, and between games. During games, too, he was the object of fan verbal abuse and taunts from opposing players. There were no other Native-American players in the league to bond with—not yet. Sockalexis was a lonely pioneer. "No matter where we play, I go through the same ordeal," Sockalexis said, "and at the present time I am so used to it that at times I forget to smile at my tormentors." He also termed this abuse "part of the game."[8]

Sockalexis' main coping mechanism was anesthetizing himself through drink. He became a well-known figure in Cleveland bars. He also swiftly became known as a player around the country, the so-called first of his kind in the majors drumming up much-needed attention for the Spiders. Some of the welcoming sports writers also trafficked in clichés, interchanging Spiders for Warriors because of Sockalexis' presence. Using even less taste, when Cleveland won a game it was sometimes said that the team "scalped" their opponents.[9]

The Robisons didn't care what kind of coverage the Spiders received as long as it was favorable enough to lure fans to the park. Behind the scenes, Frank Robison was exploring the possibility of moving the team out of Cleveland. At the least, he wanted to see the prohibition on Sunday baseball lifted, so that workers with the day off and families with children could come to games.

The Spiders had been a financial loser for several years, even when good records were recorded. He definitely thought the grass had to be greener somewhere else, although he wasn't sure where. The East was the stronghold of baseball, but all of the major cities had teams, and in recent years some had more than one when leagues were pitted against one another. There was no indication that moving into staked-out territory as a second club would be beneficial. And the West was a vast open area with no large cities prepared to go Major League because the distances were too great to cover on long train rides. Heck, Buffalo Bill was still proving just about every day that most of the country still believed in a Wild West.

If Sockalexis' face in the lineup was controversial among some and he suffered in his own way from a surfeit of negative attention, there is little evidence on record of what Cy Young felt about his young teammate of a completely different background and race. Young was an easy-going guy, accepting of all his teammates in general. He may have been surrounded by several grumpy players and may have heard the taunts of others towards Sockalexis, but it is unlikely that he would have been a player who gave the young man any trouble. On the other hand, there are no tales of Young reaching out to Sockalexis with a hand of acceptance or comfort. He was reserved, usually keeping to himself, not uttering controversial statements. Experience and performance may have given Young's voice authority in the dugout, but there are few, if any, reports of him raising it for political reasons within the team. Was it in his nature to stand up for someone?

As it so happened, Sockalexis was a likeable man, and after some tense moments in the early going, his teammates supported him. And Frank Robison raved about him a few weeks into the season. "Today I consider Sockalexis the greatest find of the year. His work has been 100 percent better than I thought he would ever play."[10]

Sockalexis hit well, fielded divinely, threw to the plate from right field with stunning speed, was good-looking enough to attract considerable female attention, and was hailed by local papers wherever the Spiders traveled. He was a phenom, a sensation, the Mark Fidrych or Fernando Valenzuela of his time. It was a temporary condition, but Sockalexis was having more fun than he did at the start of the season, even if prejudice seemed to be always waiting around the next corner. Sometimes when Sockalexis was the object of narrow-minded fan scorn, he tipped his hat to the crowd. When he went out on the town in Cleveland night spots, Sockalexis, smoking Cuban cigars and upgrading his wardrobe, was a popular fellow. He drank too much and entertained women of ill repute. The drinking, more than the lovemaking, became something to worry about within the Spiders' management.

Then it happened. Sockalexis spent one too many reckless nights on the town. He suffered a broken foot while carousing on July 4. The combination of the injury and Sockalexis' failure to tone down his drinking cost him playing time. He could no longer perform the way he had early in the season. Then things got worse. Again under the influence, Sockalexis jumped out the window of a brothel, aggravating his broken foot. He developed blood poisoning and was hospitalized. Years later, Spider infielder Ed McKean said of Sockalexis, "He was a wild bird. He couldn't lose his taste for firewater. His periodic departures became such a habit, he finally slipped out of the majors. He had more natural ability than any player I have ever seen, past or present."[11]

The Spiders went into a tailspin and fell farther behind in the pennant race as Sockalexis tried to recover in time to play again before season's end. Somehow, Sockalexis reappeared for a game on September 11. He was limping on the field but made two hits. A week later, when Cy Young pitched his no-hitter against Cincinnati, Sockalexis was not in the lineup. The recently acquired Pickering, who contributed one hit to the win, was on the field instead of him.

The first half of the 1897 season was the final high point for the Cleveland Spiders in their city. They slumped decidedly in the second half as the sensational Sockalexis was grounded. Even Cy Young went home to the farm that season wondering not only went wrong with his club, but what went wrong with his pitching. Cy was not used to 21–19 records. He wanted to avoid becoming a flameout like so many other star hurlers of the 1890s.

10

Cleveland's Last Gasp

The 1898 season began for the Cleveland Spiders with significant undercurrents. Was Cy Young's 1897 season to be dismissed as somewhat of a fluke, or did it represent the beginning of the end of a brilliant pitching career? Could Louis Sockalexis' shaky end to the 1897 season be reversed and his true potential on the diamond realized? Were the owners of the Spiders at the end of their patience over the lukewarm fan interest in their team, and were they poised to move the club to a more welcoming environment?

And, and almost as an aside, oh yeah, what were the Spiders' prospects on the field?

Young was in the middle of it all, but he could only influence part of the developing situation, always by what he did best. If he rebounded to pitch better than he had in 1897, that would be personally satisfying. And if he pitched better in 1898, the team would likely have a better record.

While strikeouts often came in the course of games since foes could not often keep up with Young's fast ones, he did not seek strikeouts. There was no such thing as pitch counts, or anyone keeping track of them, in the 1890s. Innings counts, yes, and Young was definitely aware of the toll throwing so many innings could take on a pitcher's arm. He may not have experienced any troublesome soreness, but he was observant and knew other top pitchers in the league did suffer ailments that cut down on their effectiveness and often ended careers. With that as a background, going for strikeouts meant throwing more pitches.

During his career, Young did amass 2,803 strikeouts, but that was due to his longevity, a total compiled over 22 seasons. Only twice did Young collect as many as 200 strikeouts in a season, 200 exactly in 1904 and 210 in 1905. However, he also led his league in strikeouts twice with lesser totals. That stands to reason since during the Deadball Era, there were few power hitters swinging away and the best batsmen hit to make contact.

"I've got seven men behind me," Young said of his philosophy of relying on his infielders and outfielders to make putouts.[1]

Despite being aware of the catastrophes suffered by other pitchers, one of Young's most notable characteristics was never burning out, always taking his turn on the mound, pitching more complete games than most men pitched. The fragileness of pitchers, especially in the modern game, is legendary. The starters have five days between starts, not every-other-day recovery periods the way Young did. Complete games are an endangered species, rarely even permitted by managers from their hardiest starters whether they hunger to go the distance or not. Team management has so much money invested in bullpen throwers that it would be a waste to pay them and not use them. Young had previously mused on how some teams, in his experience during the latter stages of his career, even carried seven pitchers on a roster! That number two decades into the 21st century is usually a dozen. Young would barely comprehend the strategy behind the constant shuffle of pitchers in and out of games, often to face one batter at a time.

A wonderful quote attributed to Young when he was well into retirement stemmed from an encounter with a young sports writer. Either the young man was too ignorant for his job or the story is apocryphal. Young was asked, "Did you ever pitch in the major leagues, Mr. Young?" He answered, "Son, I won more games than you'll ever see."[2] That sounds like a snappier reply than was common to Young, but it was witty.

It was also true for many of those who approached Young. One thing Young repeated several times in his life was that he never spent much time warming up his arm before games. Whether he believed that would save wear and tear or not, it mathematically cut into the number of throws he made in his career. Those modern relievers inserted late in games often throw more pitches in the bullpen than they do on the field. Recently, announcers have taken to regularly commenting on the amount of time relievers have spent warming up in recent games as a disqualifier for their use in following games. Young would have split his side laughing about that. In his world, you saved your stuff for the real thing, not pretend moments. "I needed only a dozen pitches to get ready," Young said.[3]

The Robison brothers' feud with local authorities over Sunday baseball intensified with Frank becoming bolder and bolder in his pronouncements and challenges. This was a marriage seemingly on the way to divorce, if not during the 1898 season, then after it. Robison wanted his team to be appreciated by local fathers as well as fans. He did not skimp on trying to bring in winning players. He was proud of what the Spiders accomplished when they won the Temple Cup. He definitely wanted to win, but he was just as keen to make money on his business. "I am not in

the baseball business for fun, nor for patriotism for my own city," Frank
Robison said, "and I do not propose to have a few people in Cleveland run
my team to my disadvantage when I can see good money in it elsewhere."[4]

Things were getting tense and ugly between Robison and the cler-
gymen of Cleveland, who wanted to maintain Sunday as a holy day, and
just as firmly did not want baseball entertainment competing with church
attendance and their sermons. Robison had been trying to get Sunday blue
laws changed for several years and was getting nowhere. The rupture between the Robisons and Cleveland was now happening.

To demonstrate both the seriousness of the situation and how ticked
off the Robisons were, in July, with much of the season remaining, the Spiders committed to play the remainder of their home games beyond the city
line, elsewhere in the county, or elsewhere period, not in League Park. The
Robisons were past caring about good relations with Cleveland's religious
and governmental figures. It may seem preposterous, but the Spiders went
on the road to play "home" games. Such locations included Cincinnati,
Rochester, New York, and Weehawken, New Jersey. They were destined
to be mere curiosities in those communities, with no chance of building a
following any more rabid than the Spiders already had in Cleveland.

Naturally, this raised the question of whether there was a major-league
future for Cleveland. Frank Robison was beyond caring about that, and he
and his brother Stanley began investigating other possible landing places
for their franchise.

As in most controversies, Cy Young sought to stay at somewhat of a
remove. Certainly, Cleveland was the most convenient city for him to play
big-league ball in, but decisions were being made well above his pay-grade
and level of responsibility. Being a star player and having played his entire big-league career for the Cleveland National League entry, Young
was asked for his thoughts about whether the Spiders would be around
in 1899. Most assuredly, Young preferred to play in Cleveland versus any
other city. His home was a short train ride away, and he was basically a
homebody. Sure, he wanted to stay in Cleveland, but it was not his place
to issue opinions that ran contrary to ownership. He had no say in the
matter of the Spiders' future, but Young was probably at least speaking
from the heart, if not from any basis of knowledge, when he spoke up for
the local ties. "I expect to see the Cleveland team in the forest city," he
said, invoking a Cleveland nickname. "I have no proofs for this. It is only
my opinion."[5]

With no true home field and little backing because of the complex is-
sues surrounding the team, the Spiders were semi-homeless. This was not
good for team morale, nor did it provide any kind of on-field advantage
when the Spiders entertained visiting teams. Given the disarray and the

awkwardness of off-field adventures dominating headlines, the Spiders did not play badly in 1898.

The Boston Beaneaters were again overpowering, finishing 102–47, with the Baltimore Orioles again chasing and finishing 96–53. The usual suspects were at the top of the National League standings. The Cincinnati Reds and the Chicago Orphans also placed ahead of the Spiders. Cleveland came home in fifth place with an 81–68 record. It should be noted that the 12th and last-place team was the St. Louis Browns, with a 39–111 mark. This was particularly noteworthy because it was said owner Chris von der Ahe wanted to sell out, and the Robisons thought St. Louis was fertile baseball territory and fans would react positively to a winning team.

Always a marvelous hitting club, as a group the Spiders slumped in 1898. Jesse Burkett was high man in average at .341, although it marked a drop in performance from his two previous seasons when he topped .400. You couldn't much fault a man for hitting "only" .341. But the rest of his teammates who normally hit at better than a .300 clip had off-years. No other regular hit higher than Cupid Childs' .288. Not Ed McKean (.285), Bobby Wallace (.270), or Patsy Tebeau (.259). Were they all getting old together?

More problematic was Louis Sockalexis. After his exhilarating start, his closely watched fizzle in 1897 became a sad tale. No one wanted him to rebound more than the Robisons, Tebeau, and other Spiders. Between his broken foot and his constant battle with alcohol, it did not happen for Sockalexis during the 1898 campaign. It would have been a beloved story of redemption. Sockalexis, who was only 26, was used in just 21 games, drove in 10 runs and batted .224. It was a depressing scenario for him and for those who saw him at his best at the start of the 1897 season.

When Sockalexis departed Cleveland at the end of his rookie season, he was chastened but hopeful. He promised Tebeau that he would give up drinking, then retreated to the Penobscot Indian Island Reservation in Maine for the off-season. The Spiders, or Indians, depending upon who was doing the writing, gathered for spring training for the 1898 season once more in Hot Springs, Arkansas. The team met in Cleveland and the players had dinner together, Sockalexis included. However, when the players congregated for the train ride south on March 6, Sockalexis was a no-show. Everyone else got the word and was on time. Tebeau sent word back to the team offices, asking those present to watch for Sockalexis and send him on a subsequent train, hopefully one a few hours later the same day. That didn't work out either. The newspapers took an interest in Sockalexis' whereabouts, too, and actually received reports of sightings on the local nightlife scene. He did not seem in earnest to be poised to make his way to a team reunion.

Finally, a couple of days after the Spiders began taking mineral baths in Hot Springs, Sockalexis appeared in Arkansas. Tebeau and Frank Robison were just about ready to give up on him, so showing up, albeit later than teammates, was at least a starting point to making the team again. Sockalexis had some explaining to do, especially to Tebeau, who was in his corner and just praying that the player he saw at the start of the 1897 season could emulate his actions all over again a year later. First they needed a reconciliation, though, and it apparently took place on the practice field where at least one sports writer overheard the exchange.

The player might have given any type of excuse for his tardiness, but as someone used to priests, confession seemed to be his preferred method of mea culpa to his manager. Yes, he told Tebeau, being drunk got him again back in Cleveland. "I did it again, Cap," Sockalexis said of his carousing upon returning from Maine to the city that so embraced him with friendship and reverence. "A crowd got hold of me and before I knew it they had loaded me. I had not taken a drop in so long that I did not know my capacity, and before I knew it, they had me. I am through for good now. My friends in Cleveland are my worst enemies, I fear, even though they do not want to be. After this I will defy anybody to get me started."[6]

This was the kind of speech Tebeau wanted to believe, even though he had been burned sufficiently the year before that he did not know whether he should trust it or not. Sockalexis at his best, though, was a welcome addition to the roster. He had shown tremendous athleticism for half a season, and it was fervently hoped he could do it all over again.

Also contributing to the late-season collapse of 1897 was the departure of veteran outfielder Jimmy McAleer, who did not want to play anymore and abandoned the team after only 24 performances. McAleer was not the best player on the team, but he filled a role. He was a solid center fielder and he hit fairly decently, compiling a lifetime .253 average. Even with the late pickup of Ollie Pickering, losing McAleer and Sockalexis were costly one-two blows.

Tebeau decided he wanted the 6-foot, 175-pound McAleer back, and he made an off-season visit to Youngstown, Ohio, to convince him life would not go on properly for him without playing baseball. As he was departing for his lobbying visit, someone asked Tebeau if he believed he could sway McAleer. Yes, he did. "Oh, I'll land him all right," Tebeau said. "He can't get away from me. First, I will open up a Saratoga full of inducements and spread them out before him. If he remains obdurate, I will try hypnotism, and I am becoming quite a smooth article in that line. We have got to have him, so that settles it."[7]

Apparently, Tebeau was a good salesman because McAleer rejoined the team, competed in 106 games while hitting .238, and then retired again. Still, he did make a few cameos in games in 1901, 1902, and 1907. Despite Tebeau's expression of need, McAleer was no game-changer for Cleveland in 1898.

While McAleer and Sockalexis were welcomed back into the Spiders fraternity, the United States was in more turmoil than the ballclub. The country was at war. The Spanish-American War began in April of 1898, right about the time as the baseball season. It also had a spring training of sorts as prelude. Cuba was clamoring for independence from Spain, and this idea was of great appeal to many Americans, including newspaper publishers who agitated for invasion to help the Cubans after the U.S.S. *Maine* was sunk in Havana Harbor in February.

Even though it did not involve the West, this was one of those Manifest Destiny wars that the United States felt it had a divine right to stir up and enter. The rallying cry, in large headlines, especially in New York newspapers and those administered by Joseph Pulitzer, was "Remember The Maine."

Although previous to the war breaking out, Theodore Roosevelt was on a political track, the reputation he gained from his fighting in Cuba made him a household name and boosted him first to the vice presidency and then the presidency. Roosevelt was assistant secretary of the Navy, but resigned to form the First U.S. Volunteer Cavalry, which became known as the "Rough Riders." The irregulars had their exploits well-documented during the short, satisfying American victory.

When the smoke stopped curling in the air from pistols and cannon fire, Cuba had its independence from Spain. The United States gained possession of the Philippines, Puerto Rico, and Guam for $20 million. The whole war was over in less than four months, actually shorter than the baseball season lasted.

While the nation's main focus was on the war, the Spiders were not winning nearly as many of their battles as Roosevelt and his men. McAleer was fairly mediocre, most of the regulars' batting averages cratered, and Sockalexis' flirtation with a comeback misfired. In early spring training showings, Sockalexis was criticized for lackadaisical fielding. He had excelled in the outfield in 1897. As often occurred when the nation's attention turned to war (this occurred during World War I and World War II also), able-bodied athletes were questioned about whether they were going to volunteer to join the service.

Sockalexis' response was lively. In saying that the only way he would join up was if he was given a company of Penobscot Indians to command and pay equal to his baseball salary, he added, he "would be slow putting on the war paint."[8] Native Americans had certainly had enough of war in the 19th century and were not necessarily keen on suiting up for the same Army that had treated them so rottenly.

During World War I, the baseball season ended early in 1918 because of conscription and the need for full military staffing. During World War II, many players could not enlist quickly enough, Cleveland hurler Bob Feller being one of those to enter service immediately. The Spanish-American War was over so swiftly this never became an issue.

In 1897, the Spiders had been one of the most ill-behaved and verbally assaulted teams. Where they traveled, fights broke out. The National League was tired of such shenanigans, and in a pre-season league meeting adopted stronger guidelines for behavior, including a prohibition against swearing at the umpires. To this day, a player or manager cursing at an umpire will almost automatically result in game ejection.

The NL demanded adherence to this policy and made every player on every team sign a contract agreeing to the terms. The players of 1898 were even less likely to be choirboys than those of 2020. The Spiders' first reaction was to make fun of the phrasing. Sockalexis was asked for his reaction and told a sports writer, "I'll cuss the umpire in Penobscot." Burkett actually took swearing lessons from Sockalexis in his native tongue so he could also make vulgar points with umps without the arbiters being aware of what they were being called.[9]

Choosing a cleverer path, catcher Jack O'Connor showed what his approach would be in protesting an umpire's call. "Pardon the intrusion, my dear Mr. Umpire," O'Connor said, "but do you not agree with me that your decision is a slight injustice? I have no desire to question your ability or fairness, but merely suggest under some misapprehension you have inadvertently wronged us in a slight degree."[10]

Likely any umpire, then or now, would give the heave-ho to a player for such a Shakespearean performance on the grounds that he was being ridiculed.

Sockalexis seemed to be his usual self (non-drinking variety) in interactions with teammates, but he was playing lousy ball. That wouldn't do at all, and Tebeau was worried. Realizing his spot on the team was in jeopardy, Sockalexis pulled himself together and began to show his genuine talents again. He got the picture of his status. "As to my falling by the wayside," Sockalexis said in a renewed pledge to steer clear of alcohol as the Spiders headed to Cleveland, "there is no chance of it. I made a big fool of myself and know it. Mr. Robison [Frank] and Mr. Tebeau stuck to me longer than I deserved and I mean to repay them. When I get to Cleveland I intend to get a place near the ball grounds to live in and then I will not go downtown all the season. My mind is made up and it is no joke. I have a good future as a ball player and only have to take care of myself to keep in the game."[11]

This was an essay of note, the team bosses wanting to believe the words flowing from Sockalexis. The only problem was that Harry Blake, previously an unheralded member of the team, outplayed Sockalexis in spring training and was awarded a starting outfielder's spot. Although Blake was just 24, he had never shown the kind of promise Sockalexis had. Still, he played in 136 games that season while batting .245. Sockalexis was soon an afterthought on the bench.

Most of these developments—outfield competition, Robison battling with Cleveland officials, the imposition of the umpire-abuse contract—did not directly distract Cy Young much. He was concerned about his 1897 performance and was determined to rejuvenate the short decline of his aura as a mound magician.

Young came through. He finished the 1898 season with a 25–13 record and a much-improved 2.53 earned run average in 377⅔ innings. "I threw as few pitches as possible," Young said of the philosophy he came to embrace. "I aimed to make the batter hit the ball."[12]

The 1898 season was only the second one where Young wore a glove in the field. This aspect of his early play has often been overlooked, but he gradually got used to the extra appendage and came to appreciate how it helped moundsmen make plays they were not able to accomplish before. Also, its addition altered some throwing habits. "The glove changed fielding a lot," Young said. "We used to cup both hands and close them over the ball like a clam shell. When the glove came in players began to depend on the gloved hand to stop the ball and the right hand to hold it. Naturally, their reach and range improved."[13]

The 1898 National League season concluded with a Cy Young content about his performance, Louis Sockalexis' baseball future hanging by a thread, and the Spiders' future relationship with Cleveland torn asunder. Frank and Stan Robison were happier, though. They hatched a creative scheme that might yet make them money from the sport and might provide a better atmosphere for winning.

11

St. Louis

The culmination of the Robisons' and the Spiders' divisive relationship with the leaders of the community in Cleveland created major ripples not only in the life of Cy Young and his wife Robba, but throughout the National League. There was no ignoring the developments and hoping they would just go away so the Youngs could resume life as usual.

St. Louis was the home of the St. Louis Browns, the worst team in major league baseball in 1898. The Browns were last in the 12-team league, and team owner Chris von der Ahe declared bankruptcy. Sensing opportunity, as well as the solution to the ongoing feud with Cleveland, the Robisons bought him out.

That left the brothers owning two baseball clubs in the same league, creating a situation ripe for a conflict of interest. While such a development would not be countenanced in professional sports in the 2000s, this circumstance was allowed to ride for a while, though with disastrous results.

Cy Young had no desire to play for a team based in St. Louis. He wanted to remain in Cleveland. Briefly, he thought he might be able to since the Robisons retained ownership of the Spiders. The Browns had previously been a successful and popular team, but in recent years, as the amount of cash in von der Ahe's bank account dwindled, the caliber of players declined.

One of the first things the Robisons did was change the name of the team from Browns to Perfectos. That certainly was wishful thinking if the reasoning was that the team had a chance to be perfect. It soon became clear that the Robisons were going to favor one team over the other, not attempt to make the Cleveland squad and St. Louis squad equals on the field.

The Robisons essentially stripped the Spiders of their most important assets, transferring all of the best players to the Perfectos roster. This included Young. He frowned on the move to St. Louis because he was well aware the summer heat and humidity in the Missouri city could be brutal and sap the energy of a pitcher. Young was not likely thinking in this manner also, but that oven-like climate would help keep pounds off him.

Weight gain had begun to be an issue of concern for Young. In the past, his off-season farm chores kept him fit and trim. Whether he had eased up on them during the off-season between 1898 and 1899 or not, his appearance at spring training in Hot Springs in early 1899 was cause for comment. His belt was definitely a notch looser due to midriff bulge encroaching. "Training is not a picnic for a man of my build," Young said, reminding sports writers of his 6-foot-2, 210-pound frame. "No one knows what I went through last spring to get in condition."[1]

The new St. Louis entry did cause excitement with its new look. The Perfectos played well, even if they were not pennant contenders. They finished 84–67, in fifth place, far behind the Brooklyn Superbas, who posted the best record of 101–47. There were no rules against Sunday baseball in St. Louis, which left Frank Robison gleeful. The combination of fresh blood ownership, a winning team, and more exciting players brought in fans. The Perfectos' attendance for the season was 373,909, second-highest in the league. In 1898, the Spiders drew 70,496 fans, lowest among the 12 teams. The total was so low, devoted fans who showed up regularly must have been able to claim their own rows of seats.

In 1899, the fans recognized that they had been stiffed and refused to support the remnant Spiders at all. Baseball Reference cites an amazingly low total of 6,088 paid attendance—for the entire season. With the best players shifted to St. Louis, the Spiders became the equivalent of a AAA minor-league team, crushed on a regular basis by the league's other 11 teams. His feelings about Cleveland versus St. Louis notwithstanding, Cy Young would not have been happy being left behind.

Frank Robison assigned brother Stanley to take care of the Cleveland property, but gave him no tools to work with. His good riddance comment to Cleveland was dismissing the 1899 Spiders as "a side show" to real baseball action.

His career in shambles after being unable to quell his thirst, outfielder Louis Sockalexis, then 27, was left behind, too. It was an indicator that neither Patsy Tebeau nor Frank Robison had any patience or faith left in the once-prominent player. Sockalexis played only a small part in the catastrophe that was the 1899 Spiders season. He appeared in just seven games, batting .273 in 23 plate appearances—and never played in the majors again.

Although abandoned by his real team, Sockalexis pronounced himself fit to play for the Spiders. They were once again bold words, and all the people who liked him wanted them to come true. "I will be in right field when the bell rings Friday," Sockalexis said as the season was about to begin, "and if I feel as I do today, I will knock the ball over Lexington Avenue."[2] Since he clouted no home runs at all that season, apparently Sockalexis never again felt the way he had "today."

Cleveland released Sockalexis on May 17. He had drunk himself out of the majors. Sockalexis hooked on with a couple of minor-league clubs after that, but his drinking finished off his pro career altogether. Sockalexis died at 42 in 1913, back in his home state of Maine, his life so full of potential, but ending as a tragedy.

The Cleveland Spiders, almost if preordained by Frank and Stan Robison, were on a similar downward trajectory. Their 1899 season was a travesty, a full-speed journey on a highway to hell. Although less well-remembered in detail compared to some truly horrible ballclubs such as the 1962 expansion New York Mets, the 1899 Spiders have been labeled the worst team in baseball history by many.

Cy Young was not particularly psyched up to move to St. Louis for the season. He talked it over with wife Robba, but the only alternative was retirement, staying on the farm year-round. "I don't like it, Robba," he said. She replied with a fact that Cy already knew. "It's hot there in St. Louis," she said. He also noted one other point, that St. Louis was much farther away from Peoli than Cleveland. "It's a long way from home," Young said. "It's a long trip."[3]

Boy, did the transplant Spiders, now the Perfectos, have it good compared to life in Cleveland. Opening Day of the season ironically put both of the Robisons' teams together in one location—St. Louis. As a clear demonstration of how grateful they were to possibly be seeing good baseball again, about 15,000 loud, cheering fans showed up. The Perfectos, with Cy Young on the mound, on a quest of his own, won 10–1. The score illustrated the general fortunes of both teams during the 1899 season.

It was a good omen for Young, too. He was back in the groove, more like the Cy of 1898 than of 1897. Young went 26–16 for the Perfectos with a 2.58 earned run average. He also pitched 40 complete games. The way the game is played in the 2000s, probably no pitcher will finish with 40 complete games in their career ever again. Ever busy, Young tossed 369⅓ innings. Even if the big right-hander was not enamored of St. Louis, it was a good year for him, if not perfect for the Perfectos, who slumped late in the season.

Almost comically, given the league rules about being politer to umpires, or at least not verbally abusing them, a restraint difficult for Young's teammates to abide by, an encounter between Young and umpire Hank O'Day was reported. It almost appeared to be a parody on the order of

Jack O'Connor's joking around when he heard the proposal about shutting up.

Young waited until after a game to approach O'Day and file a complaint. "Mr. O'Day, I think that was a strike," Young said. O'Day had not changed his mind about the call. "All right, Mr. O'Day, but in my opinion it was undoubtedly a strike."[4]

Was Young really that much of a Boy Scout (though there were no Boy Scouts yet)? In the hands of other Perfectos, with their tempers and grudges taken into account, the challenge to the call would not have waited until the end of the at-bat, and someone might well have kicked dirt on the umpire's shoes.

The Cy Young of 1899 brought comparisons to the Cy Young of earlier in the decade. He may have been 32 that season, but he seemed as sharp as he had at 22. He was obviously still one of the best pitchers in the game. "You will notice that Cy seldom uses a slow ball," manager Tebeau said that season, "but depends on control and the knack of his quick-breaking shoot. He is constantly whizzing them over at top bursts of speed."[5]

Although being a winner in St. Louis beat being a big-time loser in Cleveland, Young's advance fears about the summer weather were confirmed. Neither he nor his wife liked the steamy conditions. At least once, he complained about it. Young said the air was stifling, "hot, humid and malarial," although he avoided being afflicted by malaria in Missouri. "I attribute many of our defeats in the home grounds to the change of climate."[6] There was no obvious direct correlation between the Perfectos' wins and losses at home and the daily temperature. That part was all in Young's head, but it was definitely a thought brought on by his general distaste for what he felt were tropical conditions.

Climate had little to do with the Cleveland Spiders' defeats in 1899. The ranking of the Spiders as one of the worst teams ever, if not the absolutely worst, presumably gets short shrift if only because the season was recorded in the 19th century, prior to the so-called modern era of baseball. The ways in which the Spiders were terrible can be measured by amazing numbers that leave a baseball fan slack-jawed. For starters, Cleveland finished the season with a 20–134 record. That translates to a puny .130 winning percentage. Cleveland finished 84 games out of first place. The pitching staff's earned run average was an abominable 6.37. Two men shared the manager's job. Lave Cross was 8–30, and Joe Quinn was 12–104. Cross was 33. Quinn was also in his 30s, having managed the Browns for part of the 1895 season to an 11–28 record. Neither ever managed in the big leagues again.

Only subs who did not play very often batted over .300. Catcher Ossee Schrecongost was at the start of a productive career and hit .313 in

43 games. Harry Colliflower, who also tried pitching, hit .303 in 23 games in his only major league season. Chief Zimmer, who was 38 and was not invited to join his old teammates in St. Louis, batted .342 in 20 games. Despite his close relationship and long-enduring partnership with Young, the phasing out of Zimmer as No. 1 catcher had begun the year before. Zimmer was only a part-timer then as the team and Tebeau forged a new alliance between Young and fresh backstop Lou Criger.

As Zimmer was aging towards retirement, he found himself caught up in the Robisons' gamesmanship, stuck in Cleveland with the retreads and wannabes. If he wanted to play ball in 1899, that's where it had to be. If baseball was the game being played by the Spiders that season, that is. The Spiders were so bad they tortured onlookers.

Never mind the mediocre hitting, Cleveland's pitching was stained by some of the worst records in history. It had to be an awful experience to be a hurler for the Spiders in 1899. In place of Cy Young, there was Jim Hughey, whose record was 4–30 with a 5.41 earned run average. No pitcher has lost 30 games in a season since. In place of George Cuppy was Charlie Knepper, with a 4–22 record and a 5.78 earned average. Frank Bates finished 1–18, 7.24. Crazy Schmit went 2–17, 5.86. It is not clear if Schmit, whose given name was Frederick, was called Crazy before playing that season, or playing that season drove him crazy.

Historians compare the 1899 Cleveland Spiders to all other contenders for the worst-ever crown. Casey Stengel's 1962 Mets are always in the conversation. In their first season, the Mets finished 40–120. Stengel, who was a Hall of Fame leader, used to lament, "Can't anybody here play this game?" Famed New York newspaper columnist Jimmy Breslin wrote a book about the foibles of the team using that title. But the Mets won 25 percent of the time. They were 20 wins better than the Spiders.

Between 1936 and 1945, the Philadelphia Phillies lost at least 100 games seven times, with a worst record of 43–111 in 1941, and three other times lost at least 90 games. That is an eye-opener for sustained futility. Not to be overlooked, the Phillies of 1916 finished 36–117. The Pittsburgh Pirates of the early 1950s were terrible, too, with a low point of 42–112 in 1952. However, the long-forgotten Pirates of 1890 finished 23–113. There have been some other bottom-of-the-barrel teams over the years, including the Detroit Tigers of 2003, chasing the Mets to the wire with a 43–119 mark while hoping to avoid permanent negative attention.

The Spiders of 1899 were worse than all of them, though, and during the 2003 season, when the Tigers were pursuing ignominy, Cleveland sports columnists pulled out their 20–20 rearview vision glasses to remind fans of the ghastly days of yesteryear. "No question, Spiders are the worst ever," one headline read.[7] Another summed up the Spiders of

1899 as "the worst team in baseball history."[8] No waffling comparisons made.

The bonafides are established and sound exaggerated, although they are not. One latter-day Cleveland area sports columnist shared his findings with Cleveland baseball fans in 2003, numbers that are almost gruesome body punches. The Spiders had a 24-game losing streak. They also had losing streaks of 15, 14, and 13 games. They committed 395 errors, including nine in one game. They were not pristine fielders at other times either. Author Jim Ingraham summarized it all by saying, "Losing? These guys invented it."[9] That's something you want on your tombstone, all right.

Although he had seen time with the club in 1896 (only two games) and in 1897, the Spiders/Perfectos' transition at catcher really began in 1898, with Lou Criger appearing in 84 games and batting .279. In 1899, in St. Louis, with Zimmer stranded in Cleveland, Criger appeared in 77 games. Jack O'Connor was still around, and Schrecongost was rescued from Cleveland to play more in St. Louis, hitting .278.

With Zimmer and Young separated fully for the first time in Young's career, he had a new main catcher in Criger. They became famous battery mates and worked very smoothly together. Criger was born in 1872 in Elkhart, Indiana. He stood 5-foot-10 and weighed 165 pounds. He was an accomplished fielder but not much of a hitter, batting .221 lifetime in 16 seasons. That .279 performance in Cleveland was the highest Criger ever hit. He was a smart player and communicated well with Young on pitches, and the ace trusted him.

He also brought attitude to his game, according to one of his managers, Louie Heilbroner. "Many players tackled Criger because he looked like a weakling," Heilbroner said. "But Criger would fight any six men on earth in those days and if someone didn't pull them apart, Lou would lick all six by sheer perseverance."[10]

That was a testimony to Criger's toughness. Young was no fighter, but he seemed to appreciate it in a man he liked. "As a backstop, a thrower, for quick, intelligent action, he ranks with the best who have ever handled a ball," Young said of Criger.[11]

Criger became so identified as Cy Young's catcher that one newspaper put that fact in its headline when Criger died at 62 in 1934. Young and Criger played together on the Spiders, Perfectos, and the new Boston American League team until the end of the 1908 season, when Criger was swapped by the Boston Red Sox to the St. Louis Browns. Young was very sour about the deal, knowing how much he would miss Criger. Not even when long-time teammate Jack O'Connor asked him for a reaction, did Young wish to engage the topic in conversation.

"When Young told me last fall that he thought Criger would be traded to the Browns, I asked him what he was going to do for a catcher," O'Connor said. "The old fellow thought I was kidding him and walked away without giving an answer. I felt hurt and followed him. 'What's got you,' I said to him, 'that you can't give a fair answer to a fair question from a friend?'" O'Connor said Young replied, "'That's a sore subject with me, Rowdy, and I had an idea you were trying to get me started, so I ducked.'" Before the men split, O'Connor said Young told him how much he thought of Criger as a player and a man, and O'Connor added, "Old Cy will be lonesome next season."[12]

When it did come to pass that Criger was traded, ending Young's working relationship with the catcher after a decade, Young offered a very gracious parting message, confirming O'Connor's opinion and their conversation.

> In Criger, St. Louis will get one of the greatest catchers that ever donned a glove. I've pitched to him so long that he seems a part of me, and I am positive no one will suffer from the departure more than I. Lou is a great student of the game and knows the weaknesses of every batter in the league. So confident am I of his judgment that I never shake my head. It means that I have to learn a great deal about the batters, features to which I had heretofore paid no attention.[13]

That is pretty much admitting later that he learned a lot from Criger's observational powers. It is to be recalled that in 1899, there was no videotape, film, or any slow-motion apparatus that would allow Cy Young to study opposing hitters between games, advantages that exist now. At best, Young would have picked up clues as he threw, analyzing a fresh batter after he saw him in person for the first time, not knowing things pre-game.

All those glowing words came later, but in St. Louis, Young and Criger probably bonded more (Chief Zimmer was no longer competition) and realized how well they really clicked as a tandem. Was it Batman and Robin? Certainly, Young was the bigger name. But Criger made Young better, and Young's connection made Criger better known.

Young was inclined by his growing-up lessons not to be a trouble-maker or a late-night party guy, or become involved with any substance that would make him high, or drunk, and his farmer's lifestyle played into the good-habits advice he offered to other budding pitchers. The way he was raised in the Young family, and the way he lived with Robba, just reinforced his notions that living clean was the road to success. Early in his career, Young even had a clause in his contracts that he would not be forced to pitch on Sundays because of his religious beliefs. That was easy enough to observe during the Cleveland days when Frank Robison was sparring with local authorities over even being allowed to stage Sunday games. Whatever Young's precise convictions, he did eventually yield and volunteer to pitch on Sundays when needed.

Young saw more sunrises than midnight hours during his lifetime and recommended such living for ballplayers.

> In the first place it is advisable to keep good hours. This sounds like a triviality no doubt to many of you, but in the end you will find it a big item. A queer thing about my trade is that I have found that many of the so-called little things are the big ones after all. Go to bed early and get your sleep. A ballplayer must be one 24 hours around.
> Cultivate good habits. Let liquor severely alone, fight shy of cigarettes, and be moderate in indulgences of tobacco, coffee and tea. Small things you say? A player should try to get along without any stimulants at all. Water, pure cool water, is good enough for any man.[14]

This debut season in St. Louis had several highs. Young won his 26 games with Jack Powell right over his shoulder with 23 wins. Lave Cross, who had been stuck managing the helpless Spiders at the start of the season, escaped as a player for St. Louis and hit .303 the rest of the year. It was probably common for people to tease him about which role he had more fun in.

Jesse Burkett nearly hit .400 again, reaching .396. For some years, many believed he did top .400 for a third time, but later re-evaluation of the statistics dropped him just below that barrier. The Perfectos started out strong, but either began showing signs of age, fatigue in the heat, as Young worried about, or lost some key players. Rookie Mike Donlin, who would bat .333 in an 11-year, major league career, was just 21. He appeared in 66 games and batted .323. If Donlin could have stayed under control all season, he may have made a difference.

In 1898, as the United States was polishing off the Spanish-American War, helped along by Admiral George Dewey's victory in the Philippines, Donlin, then in the minors, painted his bat red, white, and blue and named it "Dewey." He craved fame, once approaching a well-known sports cartoonist, handing him a picture of himself, and asking the cartoonist to put him in the paper. Donlin was a 17-year-old minor leaguer at the time. "Now, here's one of my pictures, pal," Donlin said. "You can print this, but be sure to get my name under it. That's important, too."[15]

When Donlin was first invited to join the big-league club in 1899, he was in jail for public drunkenness in Santa Cruz, California. It would not be the last time. He went to prison for six months in 1902 for "accosting" chorus girls while drunk. Donlin probably never read Young's suggestions for clean living. If he did, he did not digest them. Donlin, from Peoria, Illinois, was the anti–Young in lifestyle, a reckless, fun-loving, imbibing party animal who somehow did not let the games get in the way of a good time and only rarely let his carousing interfere with his baseball. He was a tremendous hitter, married a vaudeville star, and was in 66 Hollywood movies. Nicknamed "Turkey Mike" because of the way he strutted, Donlin probably knew every bar that Young had never visited.

In 1900, the St. Louis Perfectos became the St. Louis Cardinals, the team that represents the city to this day. The nickname changed to Cardinals because of the splash of red on the uniforms. But unlike the 1899 Perfectos, the team roster went through significant change. As a slugger, Jesse Burkett still stood out with a .363 average and a .429 on-base percentage. Much of the old guard was gone, though, into retirement or on to other teams. Criger was established at catcher. Bobby Wallace still held down shortstop. The old nemesis, the fiery John McGraw, came over from the Baltimore Orioles and batted .344.

Patsy Tebeau and Jack O'Connor barely appeared in uniform. Although he lived on the edge, Donlin was there, at 22 still trying to win a regular spot. When Donlin played, he excelled, hitting .326 in 78 games. There were some new faces and even some good hitters added to the mix. But overall the team was not very good and finished 65–75. Yet the fans, proving St. Louis was a good baseball town, kept coming. The Cardinals drew 270,000, and that ranked them second in attendance.

Although Cy Young did reach the 20-win plateau, it was not one of his finest seasons. His record was 20–18, with a 3.00 earned run average in 321⅓ innings. But he had no help on the mound. St. Louis used mainly five starters, and Cyclone was the only one with a winning record. Jack Powell was 17–17. Brought along from his nightmare in Cleveland, Jim Hughey got some chances to pitch for the Cards. He was just 5–7, but that was a fabulous improvement over 4–30.

Young may have been frequently hot and sweaty in St. Louis, but he was only lukewarm about pitching there. There was no free agency, and it was clear that there was no going back to Cleveland for the Robison brothers. Young was a little bit uneasy about his ongoing tenure in Missouri, but he did not have a breadth of choices. Highlights of Young's 1900 season were 3–0 and 1–0 victories over Rube Waddell, the initial stages of their mound rivalry.

The nation was excited about the birth of a new century. Young had turned 33 years old, but neither felt old, nor believed his skills were diminished. He, too, was looking ahead. However, he was taken aback by a surprise turn in the off-season. A fresh opportunity was floated his way, and when he grabbed it, Young began a strong second act to his career.

12

The American League

Rarely, if ever, did even the best players in baseball have contracts that lasted for more than one year. From the time Cy Young became property of the Cleveland Spiders in 1890, then the St. Louis Perfectos, either at the end of the season or later in the winter, he was offered a deal for the next year by management.

Players had no bargaining power after the American Association and the Players' League folded. There was no one to compete for their services, so they were usually in a take-it-or-leave-it position. If the player did not wish to accept the terms offered, what was he supposed to do? He could retire and go into another profession, or perhaps make an arrangement with some minor-league outfit. The owners in the National League held all of the cards.

Then, abruptly, things changed. Starting with the 1901 season, the NL had competition from a fledgling rival league. Cy Young was not particularly paying attention to the sport's politics of the moment when he was home in Peoli with his wife during the off-season. One February day, he received a surprising piece of mail.

This letter was sent by a man named Ban Johnson, an individual who would change the course of baseball history The contents called for Young, already on his way to recording more victories than ever, and one of the most recognizable drawing cards in the National League, to accept an offer to join the Boston team in the new American League. The arrangement called for Young to be paid $3,500 to pitch in the "hub of the universe" for the 1901 season.

Young's 1900 salary was $3,000, the second year in a row Frank and Stan Robison paid him that much. He was about to turn 34, which to him was just a number since he did not believe age was slowing him down. But when he had an off-day or a slow stretch, others always seemed prepared to talk about it, raising the issue of how much more mileage he had in his right arm and whether he would be able to maintain the high standard he had set when more youthful.

The pitcher had given no thought to moving to another team. Yet he was definitely not as attached to St. Louis as a home base as he had been to Cleveland. The steamy summer stretches of high temperatures and humidity just about as high, were not much removed from the front of his thoughts. Yet especially being the kind of man he was, Young felt loyalty to the Robisons.

The story goes that Young had been out in the barn, feeding hay to horses or handling some other chore, when he returned to the warmth of the house and was shown the letter by Robba. The look on his face when he unsealed it and read the contents got her attention. "What is it?" she said.[1] Young handed her the envelope from Ban Johnson and said, "What do you think of it?"[2] Mrs. Young read over the materials about the American League and the Boston franchise, as well as the dollar figure mentioned. Her first-blush reaction was: "Wonderful."[3] So much for marital discord as any result of a team and city shift. Certainly, Boston, the Youngs knew, had the more variable New England weather going for it and was unlikely to get bogged down in weeks-long heat waves.

An account of this session in the Young household does indicate Young did take into consideration his long relationship with the Robisons. He felt he had been treated fairly over the years. But maybe it was time to try something new, to take a gamble in a new place, and for more money as well. Any modern-day baseball free agent affiliated with a team and a city that has supported him probably goes through the same mental gymnastics. Most often those players who have their heartstrings tugged upon by nostalgic feelings are also debating whether or not they will be receiving five- or six-year contracts, and the difference in the offers may be measured in the millions of dollars. Young likely had similar thoughts about his past, but his contract differential was merely $500. To him and his wife that was substantial, however. The comparative purchasing power of $500 more today is nearly $15,000.

One thing that may have also influenced Young was the parting shot of Frank Robison at the conclusion of the 1900 season. Robison had warned that the salaries he paid were going to drop for the next year. Also, taking a second crack at it, the players were using the off-season to try and start another union. Young was actually one of the Perfectos' representatives in talks.

The Perfectos, with roster membership tracking some of the old Spiders' list, were known as rambunctious. Frank Robison highlighted extreme behavior off the field as a reason to cut salaries. He exempted just four players from this rant that came as a notification by mail to returning players. Young, who was likely the most decently behaved gentleman in the crew, a man who did not drink, keep late hours, or get into trouble away from the ballpark, was not included on the short list of players whose salary would be preserved.

As a star and a significant figure on the team, Young was caught off-guard, not only by Robison's action, but by the reaction of teammates, some of whom turned to him for advice or beseeched him to stand up to management. "Just as if I was in the position to help them out of their troubles," said Young, who did not see himself as having the kind of power the other players must have thought resided in his veteran status.[4]

Robison may have been a benevolent owner—to a point—but he was still a dictator. Although he backtracked from his stern stance, the mere act itself angered players. He must not have given much thought to the possibility that those same players whose contracts he held in his hands and wished to devalue compared to the previous season, might well contemplate taking the risk of joining the new league.

Was all of that part of Young's thought process? There is no sure way of knowing, but it was all on his mind. A good-sized raise, the paper mailed to him, not merely promised in conversation, but in black and white, had to aid his decision. Young signed the contract and became a member of the new Boston American League baseball team for the 1901 season. For that matter, he became part of the new American League, the upstart rival to the long-established National League where Young had played all but a couple of months of his professional career. "I'm in the game for Cy's wife and babies," Young declared a bit defiantly, especially since he had no babies, "and will go where the money is most obtainable."[5] The comment about babies, of course, was metaphorical. The Youngs never did have children.

Byron Bancroft Johnson, born in 1864, was president of the Western League, a minor league that began play in 1885. He watched from afar, with great ambition in his breast, as the National League established a monopoly on Major League Baseball. Even though the NL had a claim on 12 populous cities, Johnson believed some of the teams were vulnerable to competition because their attendance was low and the clubs were not winners. He may well have been thinking of the Spiders, who sank to the lowest of the low in on-field record and attendance.

Something else bothered Johnson. Teams misbehaved, featuring players who away from the diamond were not role models, but suspects in police lineups, or in danger of becoming so. He saw a league that fostered a ready environment for drinkers, whoremongers, gamblers, drug takers, or name-that-vice. His vision for a new league was that it would encourage "clean" play and behavior and generally be more wholesome.

Johnson also knew that to be credible, the new American League would also seek to woo away established stars from their old teams, pay them the money worth taking on the challenge, and then promote them with savvy marketing. He knew the paying customer for the new teams must be able to see their guys as the real deal. Cy Young was the perfect example of the type of player Johnson wanted to cross over to the AL. He was a long-glittering star. He was a big winner on the mound year after year, and he was of sterling character. No skeletons in Young's closet that would prove embarrassing to a club. So Young was exhibit A for the new operation.

There were many doubters who did not believe Johnson could pull off such a daring enterprise. A glance at recent history indicated as much. The National League could be seen as the last man standing in a donnybrook, the survivors of other magnates with deep pockets and stars in their eyes who wanted in to the baseball ownership fraternity. Most of the would-be directors of clubs underestimated the financial risk, and even if they did not, they might be dragged down by their partnership with other owners.

Johnson was a determined man who had done his research. He had studied law and been the sports editor of a newspaper. He wore horn-rim spectacles and parted his dark hair in the middle. He was invariably photographed wearing suits, a main of distinction. He played the part to fit his office during what became a long tenure as president of the American League. He served in the job for 30 years and helped revolutionize and grow the sport.

Will Harridge, who was the AL's second president, talked admiringly of Johnson, who did have his share of enemies, many rooted in the National League, but beyond as well. Harridge credited Johnson as the one who made baseball into the true National Pastime and gave it the structure it has forevermore been defined by. "He was the most brilliant man the game has ever known," Harridge said. "He was more responsible for making baseball the national game [than anyone] in the history of the sport."[6]

Johnson had faith in the proposition of a new league rising up, and he was shrewd enough to make it happen. He allied with Charles Comiskey (like Johnson another future Hall of Famer), who played in St. Louis and became a kingpin owner in Chicago, Charles Somers, who backed the Boston team, and Jimmy McAleer, a former Young teammate, as recruiters of talent. These men, and others, knew the players of the National League, knew who was disgruntled with their present situation and might be ripe for the plucking for the right amount of money. Johnson had to be an optimist, as all dreamers are.

A key element was an ill-timed salary cap of $2,400 applied to players by the NL. That gave the new AL considerable room to maneuver without going bankrupt from over-spending. Johnson was abetted by owners of high-level minor league teams moving operations into big cities when the

NL shrank. That provided a foundation, but the bigger money was waved at defecting players.

Not only in the 19th century was going all-in on a new sports league equal parts whimsy, dedication, and bankroll. But throughout major sports history in the United States going forward, any first-of-its-kind league had to fend off all comers to thrive. The more successful the league, the more likely pretenders would convince themselves there was room on the landscape for competition, and they were the ones who could strike gold. Rarely has the challenger prevailed. Whether the National League owners were too smug, too arrogant, foolish, or simply didn't take the upstarts seriously, Johnson seized every opening to place a new team in a big city. Just how extraordinary Ban Johnson's success was can be seen by perusing a long list of failures, not only in baseball (some still to come), but in three other major sports—football, basketball and hockey—that form the cornerstone of professional team sport in the United States. In a few cases, the new people did provide enough of a challenge to force a merger with the old-timers, or at the least to convince the original league to absorb some of its teams.

Although the National League and the American League play on today under the umbrella of Major League Baseball, it was less than a decade and a half after the American League's inception that a new set of entrepreneurs took them on. The long-gone and often-forgotten Federal League came into existence in 1913 and took a shot at the NL and AL during the 1914 and 1915 seasons before going down the drain financially.

The Federal League was founded with the belief that there was room for three leagues and disintegrated when proven wrong. However, during its short existence, the Federal League stirred things up. The longest-lasting legacy of the Federal League is Wrigley Field. The venerable park was constructed and opened in 1914, making it the second-oldest ballpark still in use to Fenway Park in Boston, which opened in 1912.

Wrigley was originally Weeghman Park, named for Charles Weeghman, owner of the Federal League's Chicago Whales. After the league died, the Cubs, under the guidance of the Wrigley chewing gum family, assumed tenancy of the ballpark. It was called Cubs Park from 1916 to 1926 before the name was changed to Wrigley.

The Federal League employed some of the same tactics that the American League did in 1901, waving bigger-bucks contracts in the faces of established stars. The circuit was somewhat successful in this effort when players like Joe Tinker, Eddie Plank, Chief Bender, Mordecai "Three-Finger" Brown, and Claude Hendrix suited up for Federal League teams. Perhaps the most amazing aspect of the Federal League's short-lived existence was that Major League Baseball ultimately accepted the statistics of the players as ones to be counted in their lifetime records.

It was much later in the century when there were a few other aborted efforts to start another major league, but the Federal League was the most serious competition presented. In other sports, the National Football League has fended off many fresh leagues, as far back as the 1920s, when superstar Red Grange and his agent, "Cash and Carry Pyle," founded the first American Football League. Immediately after World War II, the All-America Football Conference caused great concern to the NFL. The older league eventually absorbed several AAFC teams, including the Cleveland Browns and San Francisco 49ers.

In 1960, the American Football League, buoyed by the growing hold on the American public of the sport, and most importantly a real audience for more televised football, took its shot. The AFL forced the NFL to negotiate and settle. A step-by-step merger culminated with a complete union, leading to the NFL as it exists today. Along with the American League, as fostered by Ban Johnson, this was the most dramatic instance of a brand-new league gaining acceptance.

The World Hockey Association took on the National Hockey League in the 1970s. Star players—no one bigger than Wayne Gretzky—and rich owners, forced the WHA on the older league over time. As the WHA began hemorrhaging money and teams began folding, a ceasefire was called, and eventually four WHA teams were accepted into the NHL.

The NBA faced a similar situation when the American Basketball Association came into existence in 1967 with guns (or at least three-point shots) ablazing. The ABA went under in 1976, but once again fabulous players found homes in the NBA. Among them were Julius Erving, George McGinnis, George Gervin, Moses Malone, Mel Daniels, Artis Gilmore, and Rick Barry. They were clearly better than many players in the NBA, and their talents were factors in the merger as four whole teams were accepted into the fraternity—the Indiana Pacers, San Antonio Spurs, Brooklyn Nets, and Denver Nuggets.

Over the decades, the equivalent of billions of dollars were torched in the pursuit of the professional ownership dream, with only a small number of winners hitting the lottery. If Ban Johnson understood the odds against him, one must wonder if he would have doggedly worked to create the American League and nurture it to equal stature with the National League.

When the 1901 baseball season began, the National League had eight teams, not 12, as it had recently fielded. The squads were the Pittsburgh Pirates, Philadelphia Phillies, Brooklyn Superbas, St. Louis Cardinals, Boston Beaneaters, Chicago Orphans, New York Giants, and Cincinnati

Reds. The American League teams were the Chicago White Stockings, Boston Americans, Detroit Tigers, Philadelphia Athletics, Baltimore Orioles, Washington Senators, Cleveland Bluebirds, and Milwaukee Brewers.

The Brewers are not to be confused with the Milwaukee Brewers of today. These original Brewers became the St. Louis Browns in 1902, which became the Baltimore Orioles reincarnated in 1954. That was a throwback, since the 1901 Orioles became the New York Highlanders in 1903 and later switched their nickname to the Yankees. After the horrible 1899 season, the Robisons disbanded the Cleveland Spiders. Johnson stepped in with this new club, the Bluebirds. They were also called the Blues because the players wore blue uniforms. Their 54–82 record could have had them singing the blues, too.

That year, the Pirates won the National League pennant with a 90–49 record. The White Stockings took the flag in the AL with an 83–53 mark. Dummy Hoy, at 39, was a member of that White Stockings team. The most important individual associated with the club was pitcher Clark Griffith, who went 24–7 and was also manager. Attendance was a robust 354,350, first in the league. Milwaukee was the worst team, although Hugh Duffy was lured from the NL and hit .302 for the Brewers.

These Baltimore Orioles were not as good as the National League version, although they had Wilbert Robinson and John McGraw. Mike Donlin batted .340 in 121 games. "Iron Man" Joe McGinnity, another future Hall of Famer, won 26 games. Candy LaChance, a one-year teammate of Cy Young's in Cleveland, batted .303 back in Cleveland. Ollie Pickering, also back in Cleveland, hit .309. The new Detroit Tigers, with Roscoe Miller winning 23 games, did OK, capturing 74 games. The Washington Senators did not fare as well. Joe Quinn, who suffered through two-thirds of the Spiders' worst-ever season, hit .252 in 66 games.

The new Philadelphia team, managed by Connie Mack, who was on his way to 66 years in baseball, went 74–62. Eddie Plank won 17 games, but the hero of the club was Napoleon Lajoie, one of the greatest players of all time. Lajoie batted .426 that season. That was the best average of the modern era, from 1900 to the present, represented the first of five batting titles Lajoie won, and helped him compile a .338 lifetime average. Lajoie's .426 average was 50 points higher than anyone else's in the majors.

That was Jesse Burkett's .376. Burkett led the National League in average, hits (226), runs (142), on-base percentage (.440), games played, plate appearances, and at-bats for the Cardinals. Burkett's greatness was well-established by then.

Boston placed second in the American League with a 79–57 record. The Americans (one of the plainest of nicknames) drew well, with crowds totaling 289,448. That was the second-highest attendance mark in the new league. Boston was a pretty good club given that it was assembled essentially out of thin air.

Ossee Schrecongost, once exiled to the terrible Spiders, was becoming a very reliable player. He batted .304 as the No. 1 catcher, appearing in 86 games. Player-manager Jimmy Collins, a third-base star elected to the Hall of Fame, hit .332 that season. Buck Freeman had been emerging as a top player in the National League despite a late start. Freeman hit 25 home runs in 1899 for the Beaneaters, fairly astonishing at the time. He was 29 in 1901, but hit a career-high .339 with 12 home runs and 114 runs batted in. He stole 17 bases, too. Freeman was on his way to becoming the first player ever to lead both the National League and the American League in home runs.

Freeman was a noted slugger for his time. Many years later, just when Babe Ruth was bursting into Americans' consciousness, but before he established new heights for a power hitter, Freeman was asked what he thought of the greatest demolisher of pitchers who had ever come along. "I was convinced several weeks ago Babe Ruth would at least equal, if he did not surpass, my home-run record," Freeman said in 1919.[7] At the time, Freeman was working as an umpire in the minors. Ruth set a new homer mark that season with 29. A year later, he bashed 54, stunning the baseball universe, and in 1927 he clouted 60 home runs. The Deadball Era was over.

"I never could hit like Ruth," said the 5-foot-9, 169-pound Freeman. "I couldn't take a swing like the big fellow because I didn't have the physique. When I was sent to Boston I thought it would be easy for me to make a better record for home-run hitters because of the short right-field fence on the Boston grounds, but I was mistaken."[8]

Cy Young never had to contend with Babe Ruth at the plate (their careers barely missed overlapping), and Ruth never had to contend with Young on the mound.

It was all a renewal, a revival of reputation-building, for Young in Boston in 1901. Comfortable in his new environment, he was superb, winning 33 games, his first 30-victory season since 1895. Young's friend and favorite catcher Lou Criger joined him in Boston. Although Schrecongost was considered the first-stringer, Criger played in 76 games (some at first base) and hit unusually well at .270. Teaming with Young helped both of them make the adjustment to a new team, new city, and new league.

Once the American League was created, grew, and endured, other executives offered praise for Johnson's life work. "[His] contribution to the game is not closely equaled by any other single person or group of persons," said Hall of Fame executive Branch Rickey.[9]

Lee Allen, a sports writer and long-time historian for the Baseball

Hall of Fame, echoed Rickey about Johnson's importance. "Ban Johnson succeeded in establishing his American League as an equal rival of the National," Allen said. "That crowning success elevated baseball to a high level of public acceptance and forced the birth of the modern game. For a half century there would not be a single change of franchises. Baseball would grow up."[10]

In 1901, Young was at least as good as he ever was during a single baseball season. It may well have been his finest overall season.

13

A Star in Boston

Cy Young's new adventure would have rated five stars as he immediately became the freshest Boston celebrity. The big right-hander came
across as 24, not 34, when throwing the ball, as if he had been re-energizing
by drinking more milk in the off-season on the farm.

Young recorded some spectacular seasons, but his first, with the
Boston Americans in 1901, was up there among the best of his long and
storied career. For the fourth time in his career, Cyclone won more than
30 games. His 33 victories led the new American League, and his earned
run average of 1.62 did also. Only once in his 22 years of Major League
pitching did Young post a lower ERA. He was complementing his fastball
and curve with a heavily practiced change-up that gave him more in his
arsenal.

Many of the players in the new league had gone up against Young in
the old league. But many of the players in the just-born circuit had never
seen him throw before. Many of them had to be cowering in the batter's
box as Young worked magic and set them down. Although not a particularly high proportion of the outs Young accumulated with his arm in
Boston, his 158 strikeouts also was first in the league that season, while
he tossed 371⅓ innings. Just like old times—old good times—with the
Spiders.

Cy Young first became acquainted with his new team in spring training of 1901. The club gathered in Charlottesville, Virginia, home of the
University of Virginia, and where President Thomas Jefferson presided
over his manor. Of all the familiar faces on hand, one of those who could
have been a difference maker if his arm was still as reliable as Young's, was
George "Nig" Cuppy. But Cuppy, whose lifetime record was an excellent
163–98, and was once Young's back-up ace so to speak, didn't have much
juice remaining in his right arm. Although Cuppy made the cut, at 31 he
was really finished. This was his last season, and his record was just 4–6.

While Young was iron-armed, by 1901 his physique had undergone some transformation. Far removed from the days of his youth when he reported to camp at a spindly 170 pounds, there were hints his widening waist-line had expanded sufficiently that he would weigh in at 230 pounds. If accurate, that was too much, even Young would say. He did take some pains to shave off some pounds, but for the rest of his career, that seemed to be an ongoing battle, the same fight waged by so many middle-aged men. Like those optimists on a perpetual diet whose weight shifts with the wind, Young could have weighed anywhere between 210 pounds and perhaps 230 at various points during the season.

Yet although being fit and trim would seem to be of much greater value to a professional athlete, somehow in 1901, whatever Young's weight really was did not seem to matter at all. His portly figure was cause for comment at times, however, with one newspaper referring to him insultingly as "the fat fossil from the Ohio Valley."[1] It was hardly a flattering observation, but presumably that critic shut up when Young surpassed 20, and then 30, wins over the summer.

While Young may have increased his consumption in the off-season, he was still at heart an outdoorsman, living off what the farm produced, cultivating crops and livestock like chicken and sheep, hunting in the woods when he got the chance, and, it was reported, even sometimes jogging, for the health of it. Young would have been ahead of the American jogging, running and marathon craze by several decades. Anyone watching him running without a finish line would be liable to ask, "Where are you going, Cy?" The answer of "Nowhere" would have perplexed them. Young was no fitness trainer, but he did realize he had best keep his body somewhat in shape if he was going to throw nine innings in the hot sun every few days.

In modern parlance, Cy Young always gave 101 percent. Not merely during games, but during all outings. Going all out, doing his best, was imbedded in his sinew. Although a tumultuous, black cloud was approaching for baseball when gamblers bribed players to affect game outcomes, especially the 1919 World Series between the Chicago White Sox and the Cincinnati Reds that became known as "The Black Sox Scandal," Young maintained the highest standards of integrity. He bristled when anyone suggested he ever took a batter or pitch off to gain a break from the hot sun, or for any other reason. Not him. Not me, he replied. "When you see me let any club make runs off my pitching on purpose, come around and I'll give you a brand-new $100 bill," Young said.[2]

It was not in Young to be anything less than honest in all of his dealings and even in his interviews. He may well have prevaricated when recognizing there was no good to be gained if he spoke out strongly against some issue, team owner or the like. Just as he behaved with that umpire he only questioned quietly and after the game about a strike call, Young did not wish to embarrass others or to draw attention to himself in a disagreement. He was no tycoon, but he saved and invested his money wisely, and when he cut a deal with someone he honored it. "My word is just as good as my signature to paper," Young said.[3]

It was as if Young adopted the old code of the West, his word being his bond, business to be conducted on a handshake. That was by no means his policy in dealing with baseball team owners, however. He knew better than that, understood that not everyone in the world was as scrupulous as he was. Since the common practice in the business of his profession was a player selling his services to an organization and signing a contract on paper, Young very much kept his eye on that process.

Many times Young expressed his philosophy in a brief summary. What it took to get along comfortably in daily life and in sports, to deal with society and its demands, he said, could be summed up in one simple bromide. "Common sense is all a man needs," Young said.[4]

It worked for Cy Young, even if it would not work for everyone.

Many pitchers younger than Young had lost their stuff and faded out of the picture. As a joke and gesture of camaraderie, Young's new teammates started calling him "Uncle Cy."[5] Except for Frank Foreman, who pitched in a single game at 38, Young was the oldest player on the roster. Even manager Jimmy Collins was only 31.

In 1901, the city of Boston had recently had its census confirmed at a population of 560,892. That size represented quite a metropolis at the time. Boston was the largest city in New England and a thriving, active

Cy Young as a young man in his twenties, while pitching for the old Cleveland Spiders of the National League. Young broke into big league ball in 1890 with the Spiders, the club based less than two hours north of his original Gilmore, Ohio, home.

community that had a history as old as the country. The first non-native Americans sailed via a ship called the Mayflower from England and disembarked at Plymouth Rock in 1620, long before the baseball cap was invented. Those who first settled the area of Plymouth Colony were called Pilgrims. They sought religious freedom, not the chance to adapt cricket into a new sport.

Over the following century and a half, more and more settlers flooded America. There were 13 original colonies, and although the British Empire still ruled from afar, rebellion was brewing. When the Revolutionary War concluded, the Americans had their independence, and the United States adopted a constitution and elected a president, George Washington.

The heartbeat of the revolution thumped in Boston. Paul Revere made his famous horseback ride alerting the populace that the British were coming. Boston was an old and staid city, not quite as liberal in politics as it is in 2020. As it was from the start, Boston was a city of immigrants. What began as an energetic port city expanded into an industrial city, as well, by 1880. A tremendous influx of newcomers came from Ireland, and Boston became known as the most desirable place for Irish immigrants to settle.

Like so many other Americans, Boston residents were fascinated by the new game of baseball as it grew to professional stature. The Beaneaters, one of the Spiders' major rivals in the National League, were formed in 1871. The Boston baked bean is a famous cuisine in the city, so fielding a team with that nickname made some sense. That was not the team's original name, though. At its inception, five years before the NL formed in 1876, the Boston club was called the Red Stockings. Then it was named the Red Caps.

The Beaneaters won eight pennants and were led by an incredible array of talent that showed off future Hall of Famers Mike "King" Kelly, "Hoss" Radbourn, John Clarkson, Kid Nichols, Hugh Duffy, Jimmy Collins, Billy Hamilton, and manager Frank Selee.

In 1907, the Boston National League team was called the Doves. In 1911, observers called it the Rustlers. In 1912, the new team nickname of Braves was adopted through incarnations and stuck in Boston, Milwaukee, and now Atlanta.

Fans in Boston knew baseball and appreciated good baseball before the Boston Americans were created. To compete with the Beaneaters, the American League team had to put on a good show. Those spectators knew Cy Young from his finest moments in the National League, so having him as a hometown player was a great marketing tool. They wanted to see him pitch, and better yet, he was pitching for them.

The oddest thing about the first season of the Boston team was that it didn't have a nickname. Americans was certainly all-inclusive for the fan base. Over the following years, the club and sports writers experimented with various names. At one time or another, the Boston Americans became the Boston Pilgrims, Puritans or Somersets, stemming from owner Charles Somers' name. It was not until 1907 that they became the Boston Red Sox, and there has not been a hint it might be changed ever since.

While it might seem logical that Cy Young would be the starting pitcher in Boston's first American League game, that was not the case. Young took ill and was not capable of going that day. Instead, the man chosen to make history on April 26, 1901, had what perhaps manager Jimmy Collins perceived as a lucky first name. The 5-foot-10 lefty from Ontario, Canada, was called Win Kellum. However, the Bostons lost the opener, 10–6, to the Baltimore Orioles. Kellum, whose lifetime mark was 20–16, but just 2–3 that season, pretty much disappeared as a key figure for those Red Sox predecessors. The game was on the road, so Collins was perhaps thinking ahead to using Young in the home opener for the locals' pleasure.

The *Boston Globe* reported that the Americans fell behind early and stayed behind. "The Baltimore boys jumped away with a lead at the first move and were never in serious trouble after that as Kellum, the Boston left-hand pitcher, was a poor match for the foxy [Iron Man Joe] McGinnity. Doubles and triples were thick and nearly every long hit counted for runs."[6]

Attendance was listed at 10,000 fans, and beforehand a parade in the downtown area enlivened the festivities. The Orioles had way more fun than the Americans, who lost their first three games of the season. On April 30, in Philadelphia against the Athletics, Boston finally won its first game, 8–6, in 10 innings. Young was the winning pitcher. As Young went that season, so did the Americans. He only lost 10 games compared to his 33 wins.

It wasn't until May 8 that the Americans finally played a home game at the Huntington Avenue Grounds and picked off the victory, 12–4, topping the Athletics. In a rousing good indication, the Americans attracted 11,000 spectators for the game. That was more people than the park could hold without standees. Across town, the Beaneaters were also playing, and their attendance was just 2,000.

Weight aside, Young was as crisp a thrower as ever. He never let down, anyway, but there was little doubt he was also motivated by a new feud with Frank and Stanley Robison. Young had vacillated over the offer from the Americans, in part because he was loyal to the men who gave him his first opportunity in the big leagues. As was clear from watching everyday Cy, he was a man who cared about his public image, never sullied it, and lived the way his parents taught him. So he did not depart St. Louis and the Robisons' employ lightly. But he was outraged when they lashed out at him, essentially saying good riddance as he walked out the door. Their verbal assaults irked him, especially when Stanley Robison said, "Young is through. In the new bush league he may have lasted a year, but we couldn't have used him."[7]

That was a rash misjudgment in more ways than can easily be counted. Not only did the comment fuel Young, a person who needed no extra motivation, but it was quickly proven to be foolish. Not only could the Cardinals have found a spot for Young in their rotation, Young could have played for any team in the world. He was so good that season that he would have won his own Cy Young Award if it had existed at the time— and not for the first time. Young wasn't to be merely a trophy, he was basically a human traveling trophy.

While Young represented a special hire for the Americans, one other figure was at least as important. Jimmy Collins, the player-manager, defected from the Beaneaters. His show of confidence in the new enterprise signaled to other Beaneaters players, and indeed to other National Leaguers, that the American League might be for real.

Collins, who was elected to the Hall of Fame in 1945, was born in 1870 in Buffalo, New York, and made his big-league debut with Cincinnati in 1895. He was 5-foot-9, and his playing weight was 178. Collins' lifetime average was .294, but if anything his fielding contributions were bigger. He practically invented modern baseball play at the third sack. His innovations included fielding a ball bare-handed in the gloved era and throwing in one motion, and he was one of the first to make underhanded tosses to other infielders. He was a cat pouncing on bunts in an era when the bunt was a more popular hitting weapon than the home run.

When the Americans convinced Collins to shift across town in Boston, an offer of $5,500 for his dual role did the talking. It should be noted that when Young jumped, he felt he was also obtaining security because that first contract sent to Peoli was for three years, the first time in his career he had a multi-year deal.

Collins was a slick enough fielder that he limited the damage players like John J. McGraw and "Wee" Willie Keeler could do with their usual bunt-and-run tactics. He played both of those smart competitors on the infield grass to steal away their jump on the ball. "They say I was the greatest third baseman," Collins said, "and I would like to believe it. But I don't know. There were many great third basemen in my day. I gave baseball everything I had and when I quit I was like the guy who died with his boots on. My arches had broken down. My legs ached. I had Charley horses."[8]

Young made up for being sidelined for the season opener later in the year. At one point, he won 12 straight decisions. The Americans, too, heated up for a stretch, briefly claiming first place, although they could not hold it. The team liked playing at home and over one stretch captured 23 of 26 games at Huntington Avenue Grounds. Making good money, making new fans, reveling in the reception for his new team, and winning games at a pace he had not kept since 1895, Young was a happy man in Boston in 1901. "I guess there is a little pitch[ing] left in me yet," he said.[9]

Not only did Young add a change-up to his repertoire, as always he was thinking on the mound. For such a conservative man in daily life, Young said he did not mind taking a risk once in a while by trying an unconventional strategy. Sometimes it worked, he admitted, but sometimes it didn't. But it was worth trying, and he didn't like it if a manager imposed a hard and fast rule against a pitch choice. "With the count two balls and no strikes, generally it's better to waste the next pitch," Young said. "But do you know when I'd occasionally groove the 0-2 throw? To a strong hitter! He's the one who'd be thinking, 'The pitcher wouldn't dare make the next one good against me because I could wallop it.' In any case, it's wrong to impose an automatic fine and rob the pitcher of a rare, but useful weapon."[10]

When the season ended, a good one, if not a pennant-winning one, the Americans actually played a short barnstorming tour throughout New England, buttressing the franchise's hold on the region. That pattern was established way back when, but is still very much in evidence today. In the era before commercial air travel, when trains did not run as frequently to rural areas, having Cy Young visit your small hometown was a major deal. It was something to be remembered, something to be savored. It would not have been difficult to imagine Young chatting away with some of those states' farmers, comparing crop and weather outlooks. After all, he may have been the best pitcher in the nation, but he also had much in common with them.

The air was probably fairly cool when the Americans traipsed around New Hampshire and Vermont, much to Young's liking. It is to be recalled that Cy and wife Robba disliked St. Louis' heat and humidity. At one time during the season, Robba proclaimed, "I just love Boston."[11] What was not to like?

Young hoped the Robisons were paying attention—as they likely were—though it was more significant, once he switched teams, that the Boston fans were following his every throw and liking what they saw.

14

Feeling at Home

It took practically no time for Cy Young to become the face of the Boston Americans. Swiftly, he became admired by the fans, who realized that the chance to watch him pitch was an experience to be relished. Young was not the type of man who was going to make friends with the public through force of personality, but in 1901, in a new city, he became an adopted son through the force of his fastball.

That 33–10 record and minuscule 1.62 earned run average was all the introduction needed to his new team and city. Young shed the description of stranger very quickly. Winning 33 games makes comrades fast. Talk about becoming "our guy" as someone to root for, and with Young as an individual barely known.

Then, in 1902, after the American League made a good first impression in its debut season, Young did it all over again. Cyclone was 35 years old in 1902, and he displayed the live arm of a high school player being scouted for the first time. This season, Young's pitching mark was 32–11, the fifth time he won more than 30 games in a season. Young's earned run average was 2.15.

Proving his stamina wasn't waning and defying any hint of creeping athletic old age, Young threw 384⅔ innings, the most in the AL. He also ranked first in games pitched with 45, first in games started with 43, and first in complete games with 41. Although he struck out 160 batters, two more than the previous season, Young did not lead the league in that category in 1902.

Following the pattern of the early years of professional baseball, when Young started a game, he believed he was in for the duration, all nine innings. Manager Jimmy Collins probably didn't know how to define the word "bullpen" without looking it up in the dictionary, because it was pretty much outside his frame of reference. During the 1902 season, Young won one game by going 15 innings and another game by going all 12. When a manager gave Young the ball, he was lucky if he could get it back if he wanted it.

In an intriguing departure from his usual off-season routine, Cy Young and Robba actually spent part of the 1901–1902 big-league break in Boston. He was hired as a pitching coach for the Harvard baseball team. Willie Keeler was the hitting coach. Let it not be said that the Crimson skimped on personnel to make Harvard's diamond nine as good as it could possibly be. So Young spent some time hanging out in Cambridge, Massachusetts, and then joined teammates for the rest of spring training in Georgia. Young was an optimist about his season, the Americans' second year together. He predicted they would do damage in the pennant race. The team, he said, should be "in the running from the very start."[1] Which was basically true, but running along the route was different from being ahead at the finish line.

What Young could not do, and had failed to do the year before, despite his phenomenal pitching, was carry the Americans to a pennant. Boston was a good team with a 77–60 record, but in 1902 that was only good enough for third place. Young was pretty much a one-man band on the mound. A shortage of pitching did in the Americans. However, Bill Dinneen, a 26-year-old right-hander seemed on the cusp of big things. Dinneen's record was 21–21, and his ERA was a solid 2.93. He was no weakling on the mound, either, tossing 371⅓ innings.

Jimmy Collins was one of his own best hitters, his stick producing a .322 average, ahead of Buck Freeman's .309, just behind Chick Stahl's .323, but in arrears of Patsy Dougherty's .342. Dougherty was a 25-year-old rookie outfielder from Andover, New York, who also stole 20 bases in 108 games that year. Freeman did it all, smashing 11 home runs and driving in 121 runs.

Cy Young dropped out of elementary school, but after he became a star pitcher and was traded to the Boston Americans (the future Red Sox), he was invited to coach Harvard University pitchers before spring training.

This was a very popular team. The Americans drew 348,567 fans and ranked second in the American League in attendance. The most ardent of these spectators formed a demonstrative fan club that sat in a special section in the Huntington Avenue Grounds, sometimes traveled on road trips, serenaded the team with a theme song called "Tessie," and acquired the name of the Royal Rooters. The word fan is short for fanatic, but these guys were more fanatical than most.

Since the Beaneaters predated the Americans, it was not outrageous that a local saloon was later referred to as the United States' first sports bar, minus the television sets. In 1894, a gentleman named Michael McGreevy opened a drinking establishment called "The 3rd Base Saloon." Early on, McGreevy, who became better known by the nickname "Nuf Ced," befriended baseball players, and his place became their hangout, along with politicians and other baseball supporters, including gamblers. McGreevy even became a sports memorabilia collector, acquiring gifts from the ballplayers which he used to decorate the walls in his bar. This was the place to be and be seen in Boston. The arrival of a second big-league team in the city only gave the 3rd Base more cachet.

Since he was the owner and the boss, McGreevy was also arbiter of debates over who were the best players and whether the Americans or the Beaneaters were the best team. If he didn't like the tone the disagreement was taking, he would bellow "Nuf Ced" and bang his hand on the bar. It is surprising no-one gifted him a gavel. McGreevy was the law of the landscape inside the 3rd Base Saloon.

Ordinarily, the reserved, non-drinking Cy Young would not spend his evenings in an establishment of this ilk, but Young and McGreevy did become pals, even if it was not over multiple beers. This is the exact sort of place, where ballplayers were celebrated, that would have done in Louis Sockalexis.

Once the Americans opened for business, the 3rd Base increased in popularity. Overhead, light fixtures were made out of game-used Americans bats. McGreevy went all the way for his business, but the sport was also his passion. The Royal Rooters gathered and drank before home games and then marched down the street to the ballpark. "Tessie" became their team song. Not only was it sung on the route to the games, it was broken out at strategic times with the opposition batting in order to get on the nerves of hitters.

At one point, the Royal Rooters' chairman was John F. Fitzgerald, who was the mayor of the city and grandfather of President John F. Kennedy.

"Tessie" was not an original composition of the fans. It was part of a Broadway show from 1902 called "The Silver Slipper" and was swiftly appropriated by the fan club. Actually, the real, expanded title of the song is "Tessie (You Are The Only, Only, Only)," and it was written by Will R. Anderson.

In part, the lyrics go:

Tessie, you make me feel so badly.
Why don't you turn around?
Tessie, you know I love you madly.
Babe, my heart weighs about a pound.
Don't blame me if I ever doubt you,
You know I wouldn't live without you.
Tessie, you are the only, only, only.

Maybe it bothered hitters and maybe it didn't, but certainly fans through the years have shouted more vile things at visiting team members. In later years, the Boston fans reshaped lyrics to personalize them for individual players.

The song was identified with the Americans, and then the Red Sox, through 1918. In recent years, starting with a new version sung in 2004 by the popular Boston band the Dropkick Murphys, "Tessie" has had a revival. The Americans/Red Sox did not win the World Series for an 86-year period between 1918 and 2004, when they won it all again. Note the years of life without "Tessie." The superstitious might say that was no coincidence.

Cy Young may or may not have known the words to "Tessie," though it could have been unavoidable. But he did know the right words to say to catcher Lou Criger, who was still his main backstop when he called for fastballs, curves, and change-ups. It was one of those seasons when just about everything worked for Young. He liked his paycheck, too, since he was making $5,000 the season.

The American League, as well, had just about everything going its way in its turf war with the National League. Some top players who were cautious about making the jump to the AL in 1901 watched closely as the "junior circuit"—as the American League was called for a long time—played out a very successful season, its players content with their increased paydays and with the look of stability surrounding the challenger. That meant more stars could be persuaded to come on over, including Ed Delahanty, Jesse Burkett, Bobby Wallace, and Joe Kelley.

The Royal Rooters stood out as the most rabid of rooters around the league. They were veritable noise machines at the Huntington Avenue Grounds, doing their best to provide a home-field advantage. This ballpark was built to hold 11,500 fans at the most, but the demand for tickets sometimes exceeded the capacity. The field itself was spacious, but the seating area was not as commodious. In the early days of baseball, owners welcomed standing-room-only—in the outfield. Patrons were held back from interfering with play by ropes stretched across the lawn.

Of course there was plenty of room to stand around in this park constructed for a mere $35,000. One reason those dead balls did not carry very far when bats stroked them was that the distance to straightaway center field was 530 feet. It took a cannon to shoot a ball over the distant fence. Astoundingly, in 1908 the center field wall was extended to 635 feet. That provided a whole bunch of room to fill with fans, but nobody was going to hit the ball that far. It was 440 feet to left-center. Although strictly down the foul lines, it was shorter, Huntington Grounds seemed to have as much open space as Cy Young's farm. Some might say it was a pitcher's ballpark.

The Americans' home record was 43–27, far from the best in the league. The pennant-winning Philadelphia Athletics went 56–17 at home, and the second-place St. Louis Browns were 49–21.

Having the Huntington Grounds, with its quirky, extra-large dimensions as a home park, didn't do Young's earned run average any harm. Young found his added change-up to be a bully pitch that helped him win so many games. He said that when he weaved it into his arsenal, it did cause confusion to batters, not only because of him flashing a different speed, but because his motion disguised it. "Most pitchers change their grip on the ball for a change-up pitch, but not me," Young said. "I let the fastball leave from the fingertips, but when I wanted a slower throw, I'd straighten out my fingers so that the ball left from the inside of my finger joints."[2]

On another occasion, Young talked curveballs. He sounded like a man who did not completely trust them, as if their use could be both a plus and a long-term detriment. There was little science available during Young's era about how the torque of throwing curves or screwballs might take a toll on a pitching arm. Watching other top-rate pitchers pressed into early retirement because their arms gave out, Young formed his own thoughts about overuse.

> Too many curves may get a pitcher down. This sounds kind of funny, but in a curve the arm is under a severe strain. Constant use of a curve will tear down an arm. It is said that the unsparing use of a spitball will put a pitcher out of commission. But as there is no hard and fast rule in baseball, some pitchers use it steadily, seemingly without the slightest inconvenience to themselves. Each individual case must stand by itself.[3]

Much later in life, Young was in a conversation with a sports writer and showed off a little, something he was unlikely to do in his prime. He was trying to prove a point and demonstrated one additional advantage he may have had when active—very strong hands and fingers. The funny part was how this tracked Young's career in a metaphorical sense. Young pitched such a high percentage of complete games that his manager couldn't take the ball out of his hands. And here was an elderly Young telling a comparative stranger he would not be able to pull the ball out of Young's hand with physical strength.

"Here, try to wrench it out of my hand," Young instructed a younger man. The ball could not be budged from Young's hold even though he was 78 years old. It is unknown how much that physical gift aided Young, but he seemed to think it was considerable. There was definitely magic in Young's fingertips. If he was wise, he shouldn't have wasted any of it by even snapping his fingers.[4]

Once in a while, Young helped himself with his bat. Not very often, though, and as he aged his average plummeted. In his 22 seasons, Young's batting average was .210. He also hit 18 home runs. Young's highest averages were .321 in 1903 and .289 in 1896 with Cleveland. That year with the Spiders, he hit three home runs with 28 runs batted in. Young's best in those categories.

However, during the 1902 season, Young, who was never an Olympic-caliber sprinter, posted one achievement with his bat. On June 5 against Cleveland, Young hit an inside-the-park home run. This was the stuff of a Willie Keeler, not a comparatively lumbering Cy Young. He got good wood on the ball, and his bash soared over the head of Cleveland outfielder Charlie "Piano Legs" Hickman, who committed the crime of misjudging the swat. When the ball landed, it rolled to the outfield wall and became stuck there. Hickman had a trying time retrieving the ball, and Young chugged around the bases. If he did not do so artfully, he had plenty of time. Witnessing what was going on in the distant pasture, Young cost himself time as he strode. "I almost laughed myself out of a home run," he said.[5]

This was an amusing aside, but being on his way to a fifth 30-win season is what gained Young the most attention from scribes. At 35, he was just about winning his age, the way it is said the occasional golfer shoots his age when he is in his 60s or 70s.

"The veteran Young is like wine," *Sporting Life* asserted. "He grows better with age."[6] This phrase has become a cliché, but if it was not brand-new in 1902, it was not overused by then.

Cy Young did more than his share to make the American League a success, but there were other stars on other teams contributing in 1902. Socks Seybold led the league with 16 home runs for the Philadelphia A's, and Young's Boston teammate, Buck Freeman, was tops in RBI with 121.

Another important figure was Larry "Napoleon" Lajoie. He did not match his spectacular .426 average of 1901, but the 6-foot-1, 200-pound Lajoie, who was of French heritage, won his second straight batting title with a .378 average. His services were also the object of a battle between the leagues. The National League, as a method of fighting back against players jumping to AL teams, brought a lawsuit seeking to enforce the reserve clause binding players to their teams even after their contracts for an individual season ran out. Preservation of the reserve clause was overturned in a Common Pleas court in Pennsylvania. Upon appeal, however the Pennsylvania Supreme Court upheld the clause.

At first it seemed the NL victory might be a massive blow, if not the destruction, of the American League. The Philadelphia Phillies said Lajoie's rights belonged to them, and they won an injunction stating Lajoie could not play for any other team. More legal eagle work showed that the injunction could not be enforced outside of Pennsylvania. This remained a problem since Lajoie was on the roster of the Athletics. At that point, he had played just one game for that American League team in 1902. Once this loophole was discovered, Connie Mack and the A's willingly traded Lajoie to the Cleveland Bronchos, and so he won his second batting title for that club. Whenever Cleveland visited the Athletics, Lajoie did not travel with them, thereby sidestepping the state's injunction.

While the A's made a sacrifice for the good of the league—they would have preferred to keep Lajoie than dispense with him—the second baseman became a hero in Cleveland, the greatest player in the history of the franchise. Young often pitched against Lajoie and recognized the regular challenge.

> Lajoie was one of the most rugged hitters I ever faced. He'd take your leg off with a line drive, turn the third baseman around like a swinging door and powder the hand of the left fielder.
>
> You know, they tell a story. I can't vouch for it, but I wouldn't be surprised if it were true. Lajoie endorsed a certain kind of chewin' tobacco, as all ballplayers did in those days, just like they endorse cigarettes and clothes these days. And do you know what happened? The day after the advertisement was in the papers, half the kids in the country were sick from chewing. Yeah, they followed him around just like they hung after Ruth. He had what you call color. He was great, old Nap.[7]

Young with his right arm and Lajoie with his right-handed swinging— and his willingness to stick with the AL after his court struggle—were the two most important players in making the American League viable.

After two seasons of going head-to-head, it was obvious the American League wasn't going anywhere. The owners of the two leagues called a truce, and in a throwback move to the days of the "World's Championship Series" and the Temple Cup, agreed that in 1903 the pennant winners in each circuit would meet in a World Series.

That decision effectively presaged the same type of settlement that occurred at the end of the 1960s, when the National Football League and its challenger, the American Football League, cut the deal that led to the creation of the Super Bowl. More immediately, the agreement introduced to baseball fans the World Series that is still enjoyed today.

15

A Championship Club

By all definitions, the 1903 baseball season was a glorious one for Cy Young and his Boston Americans. It was also an historic year for major-league ball, enough so that many people recognized it at the time and did not need to train binoculars on the past to figure it out.

Cyclone led the AL in several pitching categories, the Americans won the American League pennant, and the first modern-day World Series was played. Perhaps even Young would have been so bold as to toast the season by hoisting a beer, though that is wild speculation.

The fact that in negotiations, American League president Ban Johnson was able to attain an agreement with National League owners to announce that there would be a championship series between the leagues once the pennants were decided, was a coup for the new league. After exchanges of nasty words, roster raiding, and skyrocketing salaries in the competition for big-name players, this was a key element in formulating a truce. The creation of a world championship series was a de facto declaration that the leagues were on equal footing. Compared to other embryonic leagues challenging other professional sports leagues in the coming years, this was a minor tug-of-war rather than a hardcore war.

Leagues such as the 1960s American Football League, the World Hockey Association, and the American Basketball Association were badly bloodied after the National Football League, the National Hockey League, and the National Basketball Association sniped and blitzed and bombed them with dollars stacked high. Even the survivors limped with wounds while making their circuits viable.

Even though the National League had fended off the American Association and the Players' League in the 19th century, this time the NL authorities did not seem to dig in as deeply. The American League, mostly in the persona of a highly focused and highly motivated Johnson, drove the process. A mere two years into its existence, the American League had legislated parity with the 26-year-old National League. In the immediate big picture, this approach was not that great for the players. Once teams in the different leagues ceased pursuing players that were protected by the reserve clause, the athletes' salaries were sure to decline.

To preside over administration of the sport, the owners organized a National Commission that included Ban Johnson, Harry Pulliam, the new National League president, and Garry Herrmann, owner of the Cincinnati Reds. It was not until 1920 that baseball went to the one-man, strong-man commitment with the hiring of its first commissioner. While it seemed Johnson may have been out-numbered two-to-one on the governing body, he had a stronger force of personality than the others and saw Herrmann as a reasonable bargainer and compromiser. Johnson's top priority had been accomplished, that the American League be seen as co-equal to the National League

The legacy of the settlement unified big-league play, formed a new post-season world championship, and made one significant playing rules change for pitchers. The National League employed a rule that called the first two foul balls struck by a batter strikes. The American League did not count foul balls as strikes. When the two leagues essentially merged, they went with the National League rule. It made sense that Cy Young, a man who pitched many innings and was conscious of the potential strain on his arm, would support the National League approach because it would give him an advantage over hitters and make them easier to strike out.

Strangely, Young came down on the other side of the issue despite admitting, "the foul-strike rule is certainly a good thing for the pitcher."[1] As an individual, Young stood to gain from the change. The reasons he gave for opposing it seemed odd. He said the games would be shortened, and the offensive production would decline. Both of those things seemed likely because batters' time spent in the box would diminish as shorter counts were tabulated. If Young had been an independent sportswriting critic bringing up those points, they would have been valid. But since he made his living as a pitcher, and an aging one to boot, it seemed a certainty the rule change and those side effects would all be to his benefit. It could have been that Young was simply being candid when asked and that he was thinking of the overall good for the game. In any case, it seems peculiar that he would stake out this political position.

On the salary front, the worries of the players and the anticipatory satisfaction of the owners were sure to follow, if not instantly, then gradually. Young was a separate case. He made $6,000 for the 1903 season. He had certainly delivered the goods his first two seasons in Boston and proved worth it.

It was not clear at first how much the players cared about a World Series. Yes, it would provide bragging rights and some extra income, but they had been conditioned for several years to think that winning the flag was the ultimate on-field accomplishment a team could aspire to—witness the lukewarm reception to the Temple Cup. The players had to be convinced to elevate the importance of the new World Series in their minds.

First, two teams had to get there, though.

This was Boston's year. Management felt the Americans were among the best teams in the league over the first two seasons, but there was a difference between being among the best and being the best. Boston wanted to close that gap. No more could be asked of Cy Young. In 1901, the team notched 79 wins and Young was the winner in 33 of them. In 1902, the team collected 77 wins and 32 of them went on Young's resume. This was a good offensive team, so it was apparent that what was needed was help for Young on the mound. As often as he pitched and as many innings as he piled up, Young could not pitch every day.

Photographs of the young men on the Americans that season reveal that most players parted their hair in the middle, as was the fashion of the day (Cy was one of them), and the rest seemed to be blessed with particularly thick, wavy hair. The players, of course, given the time period, were universally white-skinned. Almost none of them were smiling. Whatever happened to "Say cheese" before the poof?

The big man did not win 30 games again in 1903, but that was just about the only thing Young missed on the stat sheet. Young finished 28–9 with a 2.08 earned run average. It was the third consecutive season Young recorded the most wins in American League play. He also led the league in winning percentage at .757, complete games with 34, shutouts with seven, and innings pitched with 341⅔. Young was 36 years old, and the friendly teasing called him "Uncle Cy" (down to a nickname for a nickname for a nickname), but the anonymous behind-the-scenes thinking (until the season actually began) was that he was too old to maintain his level of performance. Wrong. Even more absurd was Young's hitting that season, for which there is no good explanation. Making 146 plate appearances, Young batted .321. He was no power man, but he even scored 21 runs that season.

Cy Young was still the head honcho on the mound, not only for Boston, but in the American League. He remained the best of the best. For a change, however, Young had some solid assistance from his pitching staff. He was backed by a group that could—and did—win, yet from the vantage point of more than a century later, the totality of the team's pitching staff cannot be looked at as anything less than freakish.

No. 1, there was Young, carrying the big weight on his shoulders, as he had done for years. Bill Dinneen, who had his act halfway together in 1902, was at the top of his game with a 21–13 mark and a 2.26 earned run average in 299 innings. While Dinneen was clearly a No. 2 starter, all of a sudden Boston had five capable hurlers to throw at opponents. That season, those five men were the entire pitching staff with the exception of the legendary Nick Altrock, who was basically passing through. Altrock's record was 0–1 in 1903 and represented the only decision not recorded by the five others. Tom Hughes went 20–7, Norwood Gibson 13–9, and George Winter 9–8.

Not even the most avid Boston baseball fan knows much about those pitchers, if their names are known to them at all. Yet they were key difference-makers for the Americans when the team that evolved into the Red Sox won its first pennant.

Hughes, born in 1878 in Chicago, was 24 during the 1903 season. He was a rookie who spent 13 years in the majors, a journeyman with a lifetime 132–174 record. The right-hander was property of the Baltimore Orioles when the Americans bought his contract. That 20–7 mark was easily the best of Hughes' career, so Boston's move was timely.

Gibson, another righty, was also from Illinois, in his case Peoria. A rookie that season, Gibson was 26. He was starting a short, four-year career, and only once, in 1904, did he throw better than he did in 1903. More good timing by the Americans.

Winter also threw righty. He had been with the club since its first year, 1901, when he compiled a 16–12 record. Winter spent eight years in the majors with a record of 83–102, though his earned run average was a very solid 2.87. He lasted with Boston into the 1908 season, when he lost his stuff and was sent to Detroit to wrap up his career.

Altrock, whose lifetime record was 83–75 with a 2.67 earned run average, finished his season with the Chicago White Sox (4–3) and matured into a successful pitcher for a few seasons before an arm injury killed his career. There is little doubt that if Altrock had stuck around all season, the Americans would have had more fun than simply winning provided. Altrock was far more famous for his other contributions to baseball that did not stem from mound appearances. A long-time coach following his playing days, Altrock was best-known as a baseball clown, co-conspiring with partner Al Schacht to entertain fans and players for years.

At 27, Dinneen was in the middle of a three-season stretch when he won 20 games each time. Dinneen had another 20-win season earlier and won 170 games in a 12-year career that ended in 1909. He may have been the most important piece of the Boston puzzle, even as his throwing achievements were overshadowed by Young's. To say that Dinneen knew the strike zone is an understatement. Almost immediately after retiring, Dinneen became a big-league umpire and spent nearly 30 years in that job until stepping away in 1937. Whether players became a scout, coach, manager, or front office executive, it is far more common for them to stay in the game following one or more of those paths rather than switching to umpiring.

Dinneen was actually more renowned as an umpire than as a pitcher, selected to officiate in eight World Series and the first All-Star Game in 1933. One of the great umpiring stories of all time involves Dinneen. The tale was told at a testimonial dinner for Dinneen in his hometown of Syracuse, New York, when he was retiring from the sport. It goes: A drunk fan tumbled out of his box seat onto the field of play one day near ump Dinneen, and the man in the mask approached the disheveled man with kind words, saying, "You'll be all right tomorrow." The fan retorted, "Yes, I'll be OK, but you'll be blind forever."[2]

Whether throwing from the mound or standing over the catcher's shoulder, Dinneen knew where the strike zone was better than his tormentor believed.

Although the Americans were on their way to a 91–47 record, good enough to appease the Royal Rooters, as a team this group did not particularly hit well in 1903. One player, whose prime was all too short, however, had a monster year. Playing left field, Patsy Dougherty lit it up all year long. Dougherty was a left-handed swinger and righty thrower in his second big-league season at 26. In 1902, he broke in with a .342 average in 108 games. In 1903, when he was needed the most in his 10-year career, Dougherty batted .331, tops on the team. Even better, Dougherty led the American League in hits with 195 and runs with 107, and he came to the plate more than any batter in the league. As part of his all-around campaign, Dougherty hit 12 home runs, bashed 19 triples, and stole 35 bases. It was a "Where did that come from?" season.

Buck Freeman was still hanging in there, too, with another reliable season, featuring a batting line of 13 home runs, 104 RBI, and a .287 average, complemented by 20 triples. Manager Jimmy Collins helped himself with a .296 average while holding down third base. Chick Stahl, who had introduced himself to the Americans with a .303 season in 1901 after jumping from the Beaneaters, had a comparatively off year at .274 in 77 games. Somehow, Lou Criger was employed in 96 games even though he hit just .192 that year. Shortstop Freddy Parent made an impact. He was 27, eased into the lineup two years earlier, but hit a worthy .304 during the pennant-winning year. Parent spent the heart of his 12-year career in the middle of Boston's infield.

Parent, who was 97 when he died in Maine, also his birth place, outlived all of his teammates on the 1903 Boston Americans. When talking about the sport late in life, Parent stuck up for the old-timers over the newcomers for talent and gave examples of how the sport was rougher way back when. In 1970, Parent expressed some disdain for the quality of play in the majors then.

"Most of the clubs today are stocked with Class A players," Parent said. "There are only about three or four major league players on each team. Well, that's the way I see it. I may be an old-timer, but I'll tell you one thing. I know a ballplayer when I see one."[3]

He recalled wilder scenes from the game of the early 1900s, too, referring to a fight between Americans Hobe Ferris (second baseman on the 1903 team) and a back-up outfielder named Jack Hayden, who had a short stay—82 games—with the team. This one was a doozy. The way Parent told it: "I remember one time in a game with the Yankees [then Highlanders], our second baseman and our right fielder, let a fly drop between them. After the inning, Hayden was sitting in the dugout and Ferris got up, grabbed the top of the dugout, swung in like an ape and kicked Hayden right in the mouth."[4]

Ferris blamed Hayden for being lazy and indicated it was his fault the ball was not caught. An extraordinary incident to be sure, with Parent exhibiting a good memory. Police had to be summoned, and this was the first time in baseball history two teammates were thrown out of a game for fighting with one another. Hayden didn't play another game in the majors for two seasons. When it came to the team favoring one or the other, Ferris won that showdown. He had a much more expansive track record with the franchise as a Boston infielder for seven years.

Parent must have had a bit of a thick skin himself. The atmosphere was rougher at the ballpark in general way back when, too. "People get real excited when someone throws a paper cup or something at a player," Parent said. "They didn't throw those kinds of things in my day. They threw beer bottles—and they aimed at your head."[5]

Much later in life, Parent was a fan of Boston's Hall of Fame outfielder Carl Yastrzemski, but he said the best player he saw in his life was Larry Lajoie. That was hardly a controversial selection because there was no disputing that Lajoie was the best hitter of his era, helped put the American League on the map, and has been characterized as baseball's first superstar.

Lajoie and Cy Young had parallel, but overlapping careers, although Lajoie was about six years younger. The men had great respect for one another. Young and Lajoie each started in the National League, turned to the American League at the same time, and were crowd-pleasers who helped establish the league. Lajoie was a premier hitter who hardly ever struck out, and Young was a premier pitcher who hardly ever gave up walks. One had bat control, and the other had pitch control. At the very end of Young's career, he wound up on the Cleveland team that Lajoie managed.

Observing Lajoie's talent, Young pointed to the hitter's habit of hitting line drives up the middle that could do harm to a pitcher.

Sports writers wanted to know what went through Lajoie's head while facing pitchers like Young, but he revealed little about facing any pitchers. "I never care to anticipate the kind of a ball a pitcher is about to deliver," Lajoie said, "as I find a low ball no more difficult than a high one. The pitcher's thoughts are his own. I am no mind reader."[6]

This Americans overwhelmed the opposition over the summer of 1903. In the final tally, Boston won the pennant over the Philadelphia Athletics by 14½ games. It was no race at all down the stretch. Philadelphia finished 75–60. Connie Mack's crew was under construction, not quite there yet, but eventually emerged as the American League's best for a time. Coincidentally, some of the A's regulars were former Young teammates, including Ossee Schrecongost and Ollie Pickering. More important for that club's future was Mack's bit-by-bit assembling of a brilliant pitching staff. Already starters on that club in 1903 were Eddie Plank, Rude Waddell, and Chief Bender. They won 23, 21 and 17 games, respectively, and all three ended up in the Hall of Fame.

The Athletics and the Americans, led by Young and Waddell, were poised to become great rivals over the first years of the American League. Philadelphia won six pennants between 1902 and 1914. Boston won six pennants by 1918. The Chicago White Sox won four times between 1901 and 1919. And the Detroit Tigers won three straight pennants between 1907 and 1909. There were four other teams in the league, but one would hardly know it.

On days when it was known that Young and Waddell would pitch against one another, fans turned out in droves by early 1900s standards, crowds sometimes reaching nearly 20,000 people. But not all of Young's tensest, toughest games came against the Athletics. From June 13 through July 1, Young threw four straight shutouts, three of them by 1–0 scores, beating St. Louis, Detroit, St. Louis again, and Chicago. As evidence that relief pitchers were rarely used, in one game that season Young was clobbered for 18 runs and 15 hits, yet stayed in the game. That game, outweighed by more good turns, encapsulated the bad and the ugly in one outing for Young.

It was clearly overshadowed by the preponderance of the evidence on Young's side that season. Boston led the league in hitting, allowed the fewest runs, once again featured the best pitcher in the league, and won the most games. The 379,338 fans who attended home games would be awarded bonus games that were earmarked to be special for their team.

In a year that would write history, the Americans earned the right to compete in the first World Series against the Pittsburgh Pirates.

16

The World Series

Although perhaps recognized with less drama at the time, history appreciated the circumstances. Cy Young, the man destined to be the winningest pitcher of all time by far was the man standing by himself on the pitcher's mound of Boston's Huntington Avenue Grounds on October 1, 1903. When he went into his windup, Young became the first hurler to throw a pitch in the World Series.

Lovers of baseball history appreciate the symmetry of a pitcher of such magnificent achievement being the one to make that throw. How appropriate, the best kicking off a revered tradition. Of course, that viewpoint comes with the passage of time, but it is unlikely any baseball fan would not let a tiny smile crease his face when mulling the combination of the player who won 511 games being the anointed one on this special day for baseball.

It just so happened that the team Cy Young worked for was able to win the American League pennant at the same time baseball powers negotiated their peace and set the champions of the AL against the champions of the National League to determine a world's champion. Much later, social critics would argue that the World Series could not represent a true world champ when only American teams were involved. Still later, the big leagues welcomed the best players in the world onto rosters from all countries, giving more credibility to the world championship tag. Back in 1903, however, the naming of the championship post-season play as a World Series was not arrogant because all of the best players in baseball played in the United States. The rest of the world barely knew what the sport was as the clubs embarked on a best five-out-of-nine series.

The Boston Americans won their pennant and the Pittsburgh Pirates won their pennant, and for the first time the twain should meet, American League versus National League, to decide supremacy on the field. Each team won 91 games during the regular season, though Pittsburgh lost two more, 49 defeats in all. The climate of the times, with the leagues battling for the fan dollar, having battled for players over the two preceding seasons, did suggest that besides the winner's share of the loot, the players might well be adding pride to the mix for motivation, seeking to prove who was the best. Many of the players representing the teams from each league knew one another. There had been considerable team jumping between 1901 and 1903, individual players looking for the best financial deals. Beyond that, many of the players had been foes within the NL before the American League was formed in 1901.

On October 1, 1903, the *Boston Globe* headline related to that day's Series opener read: "Ready To Battle For the World's Championship." Tim Murnane, probably the best-known sports scribe of the period, wrote: "Both teams are in the pink of condition, and a battle royal may be looked for. For three years the friends of the National and American leagues have longed to see the champions come together, but it was reserved for Boston to have the honor and pleasure of witnessing the first game."[1]

Few players were asked for predictions about pending games in those days, partially because few were talked to, and with the regular schedule, game succeeded game swiftly. This one was different because it was a longer series. Pittsburgh third baseman Tommy Leach did let it be known how he felt about the Americans.

> I think we have it all over them. I don't see how we can lose. I know the Boston Americans are in the upper class as a ball team, and nobody but a lunatic would deny that. Still, we have been playing together for a long time and our pitchers are in shape. The Boston Americans will realize they are up against the toughest proposition yet when they stack up against Pittsburgh. It will be a fight from the drop of the hat, and no doubt the better team will win the Series.[2]

Even the best ballplayers now admit to some nerves when they step on the field amidst the hoopla and pageantry that turns up the notch with World Series atmosphere. Even Young, 36, who had more experience than anyone else, felt the pressure, was juiced for the occasion of choosing a title winner in a best five-out-of-nine series. "I thought I had to show all my stuff and I almost tore the boards off the grandstand with my fastball," Young said.[3]

Maybe Young was stoked on too much adrenaline. Contrary to Young's goal, he did not show the 16,242 fans in the park his sharpest stuff. Or maybe other distracting emotions went through his mind, like anger. Sometime before the game, Young was approached by two young men who began casually talking baseball to him. The general conversation shifted, and suddenly the men were offering a bribe to Cyclone.

"Young, we represent some operators who have a proposition for you," they said. "Proposition?" Young replied. "Well, a suggestion. If you will ease up a little bit in this game we are authorized to tell you that there will be a neat $20,000 in it for you. Our operators have a lot of money bet on Pittsburgh." Offended, but subdued in delivering his answer, Young said, "I suggest that if you fellows value your money you put your bets on me. I'm going in there to win that game."[4]

So even at the first World Series, gamblers sought to get their hooks into the action and sway the result. Was twisting the World Series result on gamblers' minds every year until the 1919 Black Sox scandal emerged into public light? Young did not tell anyone about the bribe attempt until years later, after gambling on baseball became such a public issue.

The Pirates lined up as a worthy foe for the Americans. The management, ownership and roster of the Pittsburgh franchise bulged with future Hall of Famers. That included owner Barney Dreyfuss, player-manager Fred Clarke, and shortstop Honus Wagner, regarded as one of the greatest all-around players ever. The pitching staff had no one to match Cy Young (as if anyone could) but did feature some big winners with talent. Deacon Phillippe (189–109) and Sam Leever (194–100 with a 2.47 ERA) each won 25 games during the 1909 season, although Leever got hurt at an inopportune time.

Rather unusually, Leever began his professional life as a teacher and was 26 before he pitched in his first big-league game. Before joining the Pirates, he pitched ball on Sundays while working full-time at schools. His No. 1 weapon was a curve, and that pitch lifted Leever to a .660 winning percentage in the majors. "Most spectators have an exaggerated idea of the curveball in pitching," Leever said. "They think the man in the box can send in all kinds of twists and thus fool the opposing batsman, but the control—emphasize the word—and knowledge of the batter's weaknesses, are much more important."[5]

One of Leever's hobbies was trap shooting, and somehow, as the end of the regular season approached, he suffered an injury to his pitching shoulder while firing away. That disability may well have cost the Pirates the championship. Leever was hurting but started Game 2 of the Series, only to ask to be removed after one inning. Was he finished for the season? Or would he be able to gut it out and return? For the time being, at least, it was a huge loss.

Honus Wagner's given name was Johannes Peter. He was born in Chartiers Township, Pennsylvania, in 1874. Wagner has endured as a great name in the sport, and he and Lajoie were just about equals with the bat. Lajoie hit higher at his finest, but "The Flying Dutchman" hit high more often, winning eight National League batting titles. Wagner was more the NL's Ty Cobb than Nap Lajoie, the Pittsburgh player also leading his league in stolen bases five times while amassing 3,420 hits. Wagner never batted .400, but over his 21-year career his average was .328. Wagner was the player the Americans feared the most.

He stood 5-foot-11 and weighed 200 pounds, was extremely strong, quick in the field, and was regarded as a fast runner. Widely respected as a nice guy within the sport and as a gentleman by the public, Wagner was still a very tough player. He had no greater admirer than John J. McGraw, the snarling, decades-long manager of the New York Giants. "You can have your [Ty] Cobbs, your [Larry] Lajoies, your [Hal] Chases, your [Home Run] Bakers, but I'll take Wagner as my pick of the greatest," said McGraw, who just could not stop gushing about Wagner. "He is not only a marvelous mechanical player, but he has the quickest baseball brain I have ever observed."

And more from McGraw: "I name Wagner first on my list, not only because he was a great batting champion and base runner, and also baseball's foremost shortstop, but because Honus could have been first at any other position, with the possible exception of pitcher. In all my career, I never saw such a versatile player."[6]

The Royal Rooters were thrilled to cheer their boys on at the Huntington Grounds, but despite being strong in numbers and still much very allied with the cause, in the Series, what could be called "just Bostonians," as opposed to the year-round legions of Rooters, dwarfed their turnout. Filled to overflowing, the Americans had become more than a sporting team, pretty much a civic cause.

However, the Royal Rooters did manufacture something special for the special occasion. So closely identified with the singing of "Tessie," members modified the words to make for a unique taunt of Wagner. Their word changes came out like this:

> *Honus, why do you hit so badly?*
> *Take a back seat and sit down*
> *Honus, at bat you look so sadly.*
> *Hey, why don't you get out of town?*

Tim Murnane, on the scene for the opening game of the Series, described what he saw: "The crowd, which encircled the field, was held well back by ropes, and a small army of policemen and the best of order prevailed. Both teams received liberal applause for good work. The Boston players evidently were a little nervous, as is usually the case with teams on the home grounds in an important series."[7]

When Game 1 began, the moundsmen were Cy Young for Boston and Deacon Phillippe for Pittsburgh. Phillippe, a right-hander from Rural Retreat, Virginia, did not pitch in the majors until he was 27 in 1899. He captured at least 20 victories in each of his first five seasons and topped 20 for a last time in 1905. Known as a marvelous control artist, Phillippe was one of the stingiest pitchers of his generation when it came to allowing walks. He and Young shared that trait.

Young had the honor of starting in the first World Series game and throwing the first pitch of a World Series to Pittsburgh center fielder Ginger Beaumont, but he was not in top form that day. He allowed four runs in the top of the first inning and surrendered the first home run in the history of the World Series.

Right fielder Jimmy Sebring, then 21, owned Young that day. Sebring, who played five Major League seasons and batted .277 with 20 stolen bases during the 1903 regular season, cracked three hits with four runs batted in. His long-distance swat off Young came in the seventh inning. Tommy Leach, who spent most of his 19-year career with Pittsburgh, smashed two triples and collected four hits. Fred Clarke, who played left, contributed two hits. All of them outdid Wagner that day, who did go one-for-three and scored a run, but was not the main man on offense.

The Pirates shook Young from the start with those four runs and sprinkled three one-run innings over the rest of the game as they took the contest, 7–3. Phillippe gave up three runs on six hits, but shut Boston out until the seventh inning. Buck Freeman and Freddy Parent each hit safely twice for the Americans, but Young allowed 12 hits.

This fairly thorough beating kept the crowd more subdued than it had been at the start, when many fans surged against the ropes holding them back from the playing field. Once the Pirates gained a solid lead and built it on the back of the people's hero, the Boston supporters did as much muttering as cheering. Often one game will diminish fan ardor and turn them into doom-and-gloom soothsayers almost instantly. A phrase that would become a cliché of baseball, basketball, and hockey post-season series played with the champion needing four wins applied in this case: Fans needed to be reminded that it was a long series.

When the Boston players retreated from the field, that was exactly the talk manager Jimmy Collins delivered. Rather than dwell on the defeat, he almost seemed to erase it from his mind instantly and wanted his guys to do the same. "We've rid ourselves of a lot of bad baseball," Collins told his men. "Now let's get out there and win."[8]

This was indeed a must-win outlook. There was no time to mope around. Game 2 was scheduled for the next day in Boston. Unlike the modern World Series schedule in which longer distances are usually involved and rest days are budgeted into the overall plan, breaks were at a premium during the early Series. The Americans and Pirates were due to meet again almost immediately.

Although the Americans had counted on Cy Young giving them the lead in the Series, the one flawed game wasn't cause for Collins to give up on him. Up to nine games could be played to determine the champion. Of course he was going to turn back to Young as soon as he judged the old-timer was ready. "Cy won't give us another game like that one," Collins said."[9]

The schedule may have allowed for a long series, but any team that loses the first two games of a playoff at home has to be demoralized, and whether players admit it or, they feel doubts. Boston needed the Game 2 win by any yardstick. This was the game when Sam Leever gave it his best to ignore injury and pain in his shoulder, but lasted just one inning. It was not a pretty inning, either. Leever allowed Boston three hits and two runs before Clarke removed him and put in what was probably thought of as a "substitute" pitcher rather than a relief pitcher.

Bucky Veil was just 21 years old and in the first of only two seasons in the majors. He went 5–3 in the regular season and did not know he was closer to the end of his career than the beginning. His biggest moment of glory in baseball before going 0–0 in 1904 was his use right here in the Series. Veil, who went to Bucknell University in Pennsylvania with Jimmy Sebring, was scouted by Pirates owner Dreyfuss personally. But that didn't seem to help Veil in the long run. It was too late to save Pittsburgh after Leever's shaky start, but Veil performed admirably over seven innings, allowing only five hits and one run.

Attendance at Huntington Avenue Grounds was 9,415 for Game 2. Either the loss dampened Boston fans' enthusiasm, or more people turned out for Game 1 because it was an event as much as a game. Veil did his job, but the Pirates could not catch up. Patsy Dougherty hit a home run off each Pittsburgh pitcher, and Boston won, 3–0.

The real story for the Americans was righty Bill Dinneen, who was almost untouchable. He allowed just three hits in a complete-game shutout that took just 1:47 to complete. Dinneen struck out 11 Pittsburgh hitters. Wagner did not even get a hit. This was the beginning of the Bill Dinneen Show, the man who would have been given the Most Valuable Player Award if there had been a Most Valuable Player Award in 1903.

The two runs in the bottom of the first inning were telling, as sharp as Dinneen was, and Boston added a single run in the sixth. As reliable as Patsy Dougherty was all season, he was also the right man on this day with three hits, two home runs and a single. He was the offensive complement to Dinneen's first-class work. "Dinneen had a real good day," Young said later.[10]

It was a life-saver of a day for the Americans, giving them the 1–1 tie in the Series.

It is possible that if this were still the 1890s and Cy Young was in his

20s, Jimmy Collins might have rushed him back to the mound for Game 3. Maybe Collins toyed with the idea and maybe he didn't, but when the next game began October 3, again at the Huntington Grounds, Tom Hughes was on the mound for Boston. It was theoretically the smart choice. Hughes had his 20 wins in the bank from the regular season and earned the start. Having three 20-game winners in the rotation wasn't going to do the Americans much good if any of them stayed on the bench.

The circumstances surrounding play were a bit of a mess when too many fans showed up and constituted a near-riot on the field as Huntington Avenue Grounds ran well over capacity. Large swarms of policemen sought to control the fans, sometimes using clubs (apparently even baseball bats) to subdue the unruly fans. While attendance was announced at more than 18,000 in a ballpark built for 9,000 or so, many speculated that 25,000, or even 30,000, people came out.

For Boston, Hughes pitched poorly, and the Pirates took Game 3, 4–2. It was Pittsburgh that had the problem of a shortage of starters, so Phillippe went again on two days' rest. That was a necessity for Fred Clarke. Phillippe was magnificent again. He shouldered the work load and came through in a time of need. This was shaping up as the Deacon Phillippe series after he held Boston down again with two runs on four hits.

Not only did Phillippe show that a good pitcher could come back quickly, Collins was quick with the hook on Hughes, pulling him after he surrendered three runs in two-plus innings. In the absence of a deep staff as teams carry today, and in the absence of a regular reliever, whom did Collins turn to? Cy Young entered the game and threw seven innings of relief, permitting just one run. Though Young was pitching with a deficit when he came in, it was almost like a second start over three days. In the era when starting pitchers endured all kinds of shellings and remained in the game, Collins was impatient with Hughes.

It might be that even in 1903, Collins was utilizing the strategy often seen in World Series since roughly 2015; when a starter seems to be even slightly off, he is yanked and sent to the showers early rather than giving him time to work into a groove. Also, it may be that Collins was in a hurry to get Young back on the field, make him focus on what he did best, and erase his poor start from memory. Either way, though, the Americans' bats could not overcome the early Pirates runs, so the Series game count was 2–1 Pittsburgh. Now the World Series was shifting to Pennsylvania, with the Pirates holding the high cards in the rich poker game.

In 2020, Pittsburgh is considered to be one of the most livable cities in the United States, heavily involved in the high-tech world. In 1903, Pittsburgh was a city of smokestacks, the symbol of a more rugged economy, and was often casually referred to in remarks as "the smoky city" and in similar derogatory ways. In those days, the Pirates played in Exposition Park, though it should be noted that there were three Exposition Parks. Following the first two stadiums, beginning in 1879, the city was up to the third one by the 1903 World Series. The Exposition name stemmed from the fact that all kinds of entertainment was hosted there, including the circus and horse racing, as well as early football and baseball. Capacity was 16,000 people. Forbes Field opened in 1909 and became the Pirates' next home, replacing Exposition Park III.

One of the biggest gambles of the 1903 Series was Clarke's reliance on Phillippe day in and day out. If Joe McGinnity didn't already possess the nickname "Iron Man," it may have fallen to Phillippe. After the first three games in Boston, however, there was a two-day gap before Game 4, one extra empty day in the schedule because of rain. Once more, Phillippe got the call. These were the days of his life, whether he knew it or not.

The afternoon contest began at 1:30 p.m. for the entertainment of 7,600 spectators. This loomed as a pivotal game in the Series with Pittsburgh leading, 2–1. Boston needed the win more desperately than the Pirates, but Phillippe kept things rolling, going against Dinneen.

Pittsburgh clipped Dinneen for one run in the first inning, and after the Americans tied it with a run in the top of the fifth, the Pirates quickly retook the lead with a retaliatory run in the bottom of the fifth. That's where things stayed until the home half of the seventh, when the Pirates touched Dinneen for three runs and a 5–1 lead. This was one game where Wagner was a major factor, striking three hits, equal to the production of leadoff man Ginger Beaumont. Phillippe did not overpower Americans hitters—he totaled just two strikeouts—but he kept fooling them.

Until he faltered in the visitors' top of the ninth. The Americans pushed across three runs to threaten. First baseman Candy LaChance and outfielder Chick Stahl cracked their second hits, Boston closed to within 5–4, and then Phillippe shut off the spigot. Phillippe was 3–0 in the Series, hero of all three Pirates wins. Pittsburgh was inching towards clinching the title.

Young was well-rested, and Phillippe was not super-human, so Young started Game 5 knowing his team's chances of overall victory in the nine-game series were minuscule if he could not attain victory. His assignment was to top William Park "Brickyard" Kennedy, starting in lieu of the injured Leever. Kennedy, who turned 36 the day after the game, was a reasonable choice for the start.

Earlier in Kennedy's career, he won at least 20 games four times for Brooklyn, including 25 one campaign. He went 9–6 during the regular season for the Pirates with a 3.45 earned run average after recovering from arm injuries before he transferred teams. Whether he knew this would be the case or not, this day represented the final game of Kennedy's 12-year, big-league career.

Not for Cy Young, though. He was aging but still potent, and he showed it in this game. Boston's bats were alive and the Americans pummeled the Pirates, 11–2. Kennedy held Boston scoreless through five innings, but then the Americans exploded for six runs in the sixth inning. By the time Kennedy was lifted for reliever Gus Thompson, he had been clobbered for 10 runs. The Americans' final run came off of Thompson.

Cy was the Young of his relief showing, not his opening-game off-day. He went the distance, allowed six hits and two runs, neither of them earned, struck out four, and didn't walk a man. It was a big win for Boston, who collected 13 hits, three by Dougherty and two each off the bats of Collins, Freeman, and Parent. This was one of the most important wins in the short history of the Boston team. The Americans now trailed in the Series, 3–2, which felt considerably better than the alternative. "How could I lose?" Young said. "The Pittsburgh players and fans became just a little too cocky."[11]

Only Leach had two hits, and Wagner was 0-for-4. Young beat the cockiness out of the Pirates with the strength of his right arm. The real issue was what was next. Pittsburgh still had the upper hand and could once again open a daunting lead by taking Game 6. It was Dinneen's turn to pitch for Boston, and the Pirates, whether they wanted to or not, came back with Sam Leever, healthy or not. This was definitely a resurrection, a ghost returning with the hope he could haunt the opposing team at a critical point in the Series.

Leever gave it a noble whirl. He went the nine-inning distance, a feat in itself for someone less than 100 percent, and he kept the game close for a few innings. The Americans reached Leever and teed off on him in the third inning when they compiled a 3–0 lead. Going into the bottom of the seventh inning, Boston led, 6–0. Dinneen was hittable—he gave up 10 safeties in all—but the Pirates clustered them together to push runs across only once. For a time, it seemed Dinneen would walk off with a shutout. But in the bottom of the seventh, the Pirates rallied for three runs. That tightened things up, but that was the end of the day's scoring. Dinneen notched his second victory of the Series, and that Series was now a 3–3 affair.

Game 7 was lined up for October 10, still in Exposition Park. In the future, much of the drama of World Series would play out in Game 7s, the deciding event of the championships. Not this year because the teams were embroiled in the original, best-of-nine version. Whichever team won Game 7 would have the lead, but would not clinch the title. At this point, Jimmy Collins was not about to start any pitcher not named either Young or Dinneen. Young was the man for this start. Similarly, after limping through a couple of games, Fred Clarke was ready to send Deacon Phillippe out for another stab at it.

Phillippe was already 3–0 in the Series, establishing a record for wins that has never been broken, only tied. If he had won this game, he would have been the only pitcher in history with four wins in a single World Series. Others who have won three times in the same Series include Christy Mathewson, "Smoky" Joe Wood, Bob Gibson, Mickey Lolich, and Randy Johnson, among others. If it happens again the way the modern game is played, it will be because a closer, not a starter, got the job done in late or extra innings each time.

The Americans gave Young help from the start, scoring two runs in the top of the first inning. That was an obvious confidence booster for Boston versus Phillippe, making him appear vulnerable. Two more runs in the fourth inning, two in the sixth, and a solo run in the eighth gave Young a comfortable lead to work with. He pitched a complete game. While permitting 10 hits, he allowed just three runs for the 7–3 margin. Young struck out six. This time, Phillippe was more reachable, giving up 11 hits and seven runs, five of them earned. Four Boston players chipped in with two hits each, Chick Stahl, Freddy Parent, Hobe Ferris, and Lou Criger.

After the long vacation in Pittsburgh, the teams took trains back to Boston to conclude the Series. Boston hosted Game 8 on October 13, three days later. That even allowed the Pirates to throw Phillippe out there for a fifth time in the playoffs. Bill Dinneen was the starter for Boston. If there was a ninth game to settle matters, Young would pitch. It was not necessary for him to warm up again, though. Dinneen won for the third time, dominant as he went the distance with a four-hit shutout. Dinneen struck out seven, including Wagner to end the game and the Series. Although he would have other series opportunities in his career, the great Wagner batted just .222 this time.

Although Phillippe took two losses, he was an imposing figure in the showdown, working nobly and hard as his team relied heavily on him. Later, Young said of Phillippe, "He was one of the greatest pitchers of his time."[12] Many times that was said of Young, of course, only changing the description to "of all time."

Boston officials were slow to organize a dinner to honor the city's champions, so the event never came off. These days it is routine for big-league communities to throw a parade in celebration of a championship performance. While crowds are estimated, not counted individually, often the number mentioned is that one million or more people came out to cheer and clap as their favorite athletes rolled past on floats. Such a figure would have astounded the early ballplayers since no team drew even close to that amount of fans across an entire season in the early 1900s.

Seventeen Boston players went home for the off-season with winner's shares of the booty from the Series of $1,182, a healthy bonus for the eight games. Back in Ohio as usual, Young expressed his feelings about how things had turned out for him since departing Cleveland for Boston. "I am very glad, indeed, to be with the American League," he said.[13]

This World Series experiment, sanctioned by both the American and National Leagues, was a success. There was suspense in evenly matched games, there was an undisputed champ, and people made money. What was not to like?

It was Jimmy Collins, the Boston-player manager, who looked ahead and foresaw a World Series being played at the conclusion of every season in the future. "I should not be surprised to see post-season games each fall as long as there are two big leagues," Collins said.[14]

Never mind a million fans lining streets for the biggest street party most of those title-winning cities have ever experienced. Another major development never foreseen by those who played the game in 1903 was the craze for possessing sports memorabilia a century-plus later.

In the autumn of 2018, shortly after the Boston Red Sox, descendants of the Americans, won another World Series, a rare object from 1903 came onto the auction market. It was announced that one of three known surviving five-cent copies of the scorecards sold to the public in Pittsburgh during that year's Series was being put up for sale. It was predicted the scorecard would fetch between $150,000 and $250,000 at auction because it originated at the first World Series. In 2011, one of the two others did sell for $241,500 in an auction. The third is in the possession of the National Baseball Hall of Fame in Cooperstown, New York.

At the time, it was said the program card had been residing in a safe deposit box for 40 years and was one of only three known copies in existence. The scorecard, which had been filled in by a fan with a pencil as Game 7 was played, was the one where Cy Young won the big game for Boston. This is the only scorecard known to exist from that particular game.

"'Holy Grail' is a term that gets bandied about and overused on the auction block," an auction house called Huggins & Scott commented at the time, "But nowhere does it ring more than true with the fabled 1903 World Series program at Pittsburgh. Up to now, there were only two such treasures extant."[15]

In the end, less than three weeks after the announcement that the program would go up for sale, this new-to-the-market item was purchased for $228,780. Imagine the astonishment of Cy Young, Honus Wagner, Deacon Phillippe, and Bill Dinneen if they were told such a thing could occur.

17

Another Pennant

The second thought championship teams have as soon as the first celebration passes is, "We want to do it again." Title-winning teams always believe they should be able to repeat their success. Over the decades since the Boston Americans won baseball's first World Series, probably every single American professional sports team thinks it has the capability of doing it all over again. Turns out repeating is often more challenging than winning the first time.

Similarly, players who enjoy great individual seasons come to think their star-studded statistics are a floor, not a ceiling, that what they accomplished one year will translate into what they will do the next, that they will keep improving, as if there is no such thing as a best season over the horizon, just another like it.

The Cy Young of 1903, with his American League-leading 28 wins, was magnificent. But he was also 36, already the oldest player in the league. In the eyes of many, he had already defied time. So many other early great pitchers were already retired as Young trucked on. During the 1904 season, Young would be 37. The question was how long could he keep going at such a high level of achievement?

While Young was an approved candidate to take some spring training time on his own in Hot Springs, Arkansas, because he enjoyed the place for workouts, the fall-out from the AL-NL peace treaty hit some other players. As was predicted, the owners wished to hold the line on salaries, and negotiations with some key players did not go well. Two top Boston players, Bill Dinneen and Buck Freeman, were holdouts, though rather than vegetate at home, they joined Young in Hot Springs. They made the effort to stay in shape even while not under contract. Young did not have that problem. He was set to make $6,000 for the 1904 season.

Young may have gained a little weight in the off-season as he stuck to the farm in Peoli, Ohio, as usual, but if he had lost any sharpness on the mound, it was not evident in 1904. Young, like many other pitchers, benefited from the change in the foul strike rule. Batters definitely were feeling the pinch with averages dropping. Those super-high averages of a few years earlier were disappearing, and the pitcher advantage, coupled with the Deadball Era ball itself, meant that slugging opportunities had not increased either.

The Americans were one of the teams that was capable of repeating its run to an American League pennant—and did so. Boston finished 95–59 to take first place. The runner-up was the New York Highlanders, the former Baltimore Orioles who within the decade would change their nickname to Yankees. New York chased Boston to the finish line, but ended up 92–59. Playing three fewer games in the modern era that could change the outcome of a pennant race would not be acceptable, but not all rained out games were made up in the past, and it cost New York dearly.

Many of the cast members were the same in the Boston lineup, but not many players hit as well as they had before. As a team, the pennant-winners batted just .247 and hit only 26 home runs all season. This was no bludgeoning group. No one on the team hit .300—and this was the best team in the league. Freddy Parent hit .291 at shortstop, and Chick Stahl .290 in the outfield, with Freeman at .280 and Jimmy Collins at .271. Freeman knocked in a team-high 84 runs. Offense seemed to be a forgotten art in the 1904 season.

Young's partner, Lou Criger, was still catching, but he hit only .211. Patsy Dougherty, so terrific the year before, was reduced to 49 games and batted .272.

Ah, but the pitching. That was something extraordinary. Boston fielded four hurlers who won at least 17 games. Only one other pitcher, George Winter, even received a decision, and he went 8–4. This was obviously a dominant group, compiling a 2.12 earned run average. One needed to read that figure with a microscope. Boston pitchers were a threat to pitch a shutout just about every game, it seemed.

First up was Young. His win total was slightly down, but his performance wasn't. He went 26–16 with a 1.97 earned run average, 40 complete games over 380 innings, and 10 shutouts. This guy never got tired. He seemed as if he could pitch forever. That phrase was later applied to Satchel Paige as the name of his autobiography, but it really seemed as if Young could maintain his high place as the league's best pitcher forever.

It was comforting to know that Dinneen was still right there in the rotation in the No. 2 slot and was still pitching great with a 23–14 record and a 2.20 earned run average. Norwood Gibson was still around and won 17 games with a 2.21 ERA. Most years, that kind of pitching depth would be enough. But the Americans had added another great pitcher to the roster by trading Tom Hughes to New York for Jesse Tannehill, 29, who won 21 games with a 2.04 earned run average. It was almost ridiculous how little chance batters had to score runs off this bunch.

Before Tannehill flamed out early, the southpaw won 197 games, at least 20 in a season six times. Tannehill also compiled a .255 lifetime batting average in 15 seasons and was good enough with his club to periodically play the outfield on days he was not throwing, or to pinch-hit. What a bonus acquisition for Boston.

This was a risky trade for Boston because Hughes seemed to be blossoming. Instead, Tannehill far eclipsed Hughes' showings over the next couple of years. Hughes was just 7–11 with the Highlanders before being moved again the same season to Washington. His combined mark was 10–23 in 1904, roughly the reverse of Tannehill's. Even before the action played out that season, Collins said he was quite satisfied with the deal, even if Hughes was four years younger. "I am more pleased than ever with my trade for Tannehill," Collins said. "We need a left-hander and I don't know a better one in the business. He is in great shape and will be Johnny-on-the-spot with that stick of his and that helps a team wonderfully, I tell you."[1]

Jake Wells, one of Tannehill's minor league managers, saw that Tannehill was well-equipped for major league success and echoed some of Collins' later observations. "I think Tannehill [is] the greatest of living pitchers for the good reason that he was never rattled in his life," Wells said. "No matter how hard his delivery may be [hit], he never loses his head. I like a pitcher who can take punishment and pull himself together at a critical moment. Then, don't forget that Tannehill is a good batsman."[2]

Not that anyone else who wasn't related to Tannehill would have called him the greatest living pitcher with Cy Young not only still around, but a teammate as well.

Tannehill, who died of a stroke at 82, was in the mix of pitchers considered to be the best in the game during his career. He just did not have the longevity of some of the others. Tannehill twirled one of the highlight games of the year for the 1904 Americans. The 5-foot-8, 150-pound Tannehill was never crisper than on August 17 against the Chicago White Sox when he became the first left-handed pitcher in Americans/Red Sox history to throw a no-hitter.[3]

This game came not long after Cy Young's memorable perfect game on May 5 over the Philadelphia Athletics by a 3–0 score. Considered the finest of the hundreds of games Young pitched, the first perfect game of the modern era could not be topped by Tannehill, but it did provide for juicy comparison to have two such hurlers throw landmark games in the same season for one team.

For a guy who was not very big and played the shortstop position where not much was expected from him at the bat, Freddy Parent always seemed to make big hits at important moments, whether it was aiding Tannehill as he chased his no-hitter or in the World Series. All of his best hitting seasons were in the early years of his career, and Parent was still hitting well in 1904. With the overall hitting down in the league and the Americans' lineup behaving in similar fashion, it was a good year for Parent to hit .291.

Parent, who lived into his 90s, was the last living ballplayer who participated in the first World Series of 1903, and he played in the Boston back-to-back flag years of 1903 and 1904. That certainly gave him the last say on anything and everything. Late in life, when Parent was being attended by a nurse, sports writers used to visit him. Mostly, more than the 1904 pennant, they wanted to hear what he remembered about the 1903 World Series. Although respectful of Honus Wagner's stature in the sport, Parent had a better Series than the Pirates' shortstop. "He wasn't in very good shape for the Series," Parent said, "and he didn't do too good. But he was one of the great players."[4]

Parent was still talking baseball in 1970, and he had a long-view perspective on the changes that came to the World Series, then being played in large, football-type stadiums, in front of national television audiences of millions, heard by national radio audiences. The Series was little when it started and kept growing, but Parent also remembered the enthusiasm of fans for the new playoff, even if there were fewer of them in attendance or paying attention.

"It must have been," Parent said of the level of interest being high right away. "They had to make special ground rules for a two-base hit that went into the crowd because the crowd broke down the fences and the gate in Boston. They didn't do as bad as that in Pittsburgh because they were losing. People in those days, they liked the Series because it was something new. I can remember the most when we were in Pittsburgh and they had us three to one in games and we finished it up in Boston."[5]

Of course those interviewers would have been eager to extend their inquiries to discussions of the 1904 World Series as well, since the Americans followed up their triumphs of 1903 by winning another American League pennant in 1904. But there was no World Series of 1904. Jimmy Collins' forecasting that the World Series was such a special event it was probably here for good, was proven wrong a year later due to the intransigence of two men.

Thank you, John J. McGraw and John Brush. McGraw, the manager of the New York Giants, led that team to a phenomenal season. The Giants won the National League pennant by 13 games over the Chicago Cubs with a record of 106–47. The Giants would have been favored over the

Americans, but throwing a tantrum, McGraw did not want to play Boston. He thought his team's .693 winning percentage spoke for itself, and the Giants already showed they were the best club in the world. Phooey, was his attitude, who needs the American League? Ditto from Brush, the Giants owner.

In fact, the Giants clinched the pennant early enough that they seemed to be going through the motions over the final days of the regular season, acting as if it was mission accomplished. Some days McGraw didn't even show up at the Polo Grounds and let the guys play on. This indifference seemed so prevalent that New York newspapers criticized the club. Even super pitcher Christy Mathewson, the emblem of purity and goodwill, came under assault. The *New York Times* said that Matty "just seemed to toss the ball to the batsmen."[6]

These are the kinds of obvious behaviors a commissioner of baseball would fine a team for doing. But there was no commissioner, no central commander, of the game in 1904. Those writers had in common the perspective that the Giants were acting as if the season was already over when not only were there regular season games to be played, but the upcoming World Series facing the American League champ.

The announcement that the Giants had no intention of playing in such a high-profile and lucrative Series was made on September 25 by team owner John Brush. Brush was not the most beloved of baseball magnates, and McGraw was pretty much viewed as Mr. Grumpy outside New York. They clearly had conspired to avoid Series participation with the outlook that their Giants were champions of all they surveyed.

McGraw was not as vocal as Brush, but it came out later that he held a grudge against Ban Johnson from run-ins when McGraw played for the Baltimore Orioles in their first year in the American League in 1901. "I know the American League and its methods," McGraw said. "I ought to, for I paid for my privilege. They still have my money." He said he would not play "a box-office game with Ban Johnson & Company. No one, not even my bitterest enemy, ever accused me of being a fool."[7]

Brush first issued a statement praising his own team and his own manager and then infuriated the rest of the baseball world with an arrogant statement of declared superiority. The Giants, he said, had won "the championship of the United States in the National League of Professional Base Ball Clubs" and owed much of their success to McGraw, who as "a manager of a base ball club stands alone and is without a rival." So far, so good. Then Brush let loose. "There is nothing in the constitution or playing rules of the National League which requires its victorious club to submit its championship honors to a contest with a victorious club of a minor league."[8]

"A minor league." Ban Johnson had to sputter when he heard Brush's words. There was more. "There may be those who think the winner in the Eastern or in the Southern, or some other league, is superior to the winner in the National. That is their privilege to so believe and there can be no criticism for such opinions, but that furnishes no reason why the champion of the National League should enter into a contest with them."[9]

How to make friends and influence people. The Giants did not fare well in the court of public opinion, nor did Brush individually. Newspaper editorials and columnists inveighed against his decision and word choice, as did baseball fans. Most of the baseball universe wanted to see the Series played. Johnson said he thought there was a deal in place before the season began to pit the pennant winners against one another.

The *New York World* said Brush had no right to deprive baseball fans of this special event.

> He gets his money from the sports-loving public of this city and should consider their wishes. The document sent out by Brush giving his alleged reasons for not going after the world's championship is the weakest statement of the kind I ever read or heard. In the first place, Brush's hidden slur placing the American League in the minor league class is so stupid it will not even deceive the bat boys at the Polo Grounds, to say nothing of any grown person that follows the game.[10]

A writer for *The Sporting News* let Brush have it, calling his action "so internally selfish that it chills the blood of every true sportsman. He may say he is not afraid of the outcome, but his acts give the lie to such an assertion."[11]

Since the Giants had made their declarations before the regular season ended, when the American League pennant race wasn't settled yet, they did so without knowing what team they might have faced in a World Series. The Highlanders were still pursuing the Americans and were in the hunt with just a few days to go. This was the season when righty Jack Chesbro nearly single-handedly pitched the Highlanders to the pennant with a let-me-carry-you-home performance. Chesbro finished 41–12 with a .774 winning percentage in 51 starts, while completing 48 games. His earned run average was 1.82, and he threw 454⅔ innings. Most of those statistics led the AL that year. Manager Clark Griffith may have worn Chesbro out for all time, but the Highlanders still could not catch the Americans.

So after Griffith and other New York American League figures bombastically reacted to the Brush-McGraw bombshell, it ended up that the Americans were the ones who were hurt by the cancellation of the World Series.

The Highlanders had their chance on October 8 after moving to within a half-game of the Americans the day before. A doubleheader was scheduled for the Huntington Avenue Grounds. Boston won the first game, 13–2, when Chesbro tired mid-game. The second game matched New York's Jack Powell against Cy Young. Powell had once been a Young teammate with the Cleveland Spiders and through an up-and-down career managed 245 wins. The one problem not foreseen was how to squeeze two games in before darkness fell. That ended up being costly to the Highlanders. As Young mowed down New York batters, Boston hitters barely touched Powell either.

In the fifth inning, Hobe Ferris reached base on a slowly hit grounder to the outfield. Criger sacrificed him along, and Young himself scored Ferris with an outfield fly. Boston led 1–0, and that was the game's only run when umpires halted the game because of darkness. The Americans led in the standings by one-and-a-half games.

The teams adjourned to New York by train for another doubleheader on October 10. Some 200 members of the Royal Rooters followed the Americans for the road games. Chesbro got the call against Bill Dinneen in the first game. Exhibiting the confidence he had earned with such a spectacular season, Chesbro said, "I am willing to bet my last dollar that I trim Collins' boys."[12]

He did and he didn't. The game turned into a suspenseful, low-scoring encounter, but Boston eked out the win, 3–2, by holding off a Highlanders rally in the bottom of the ninth inning. The victory gave the Americans an insurmountable lead in the standings. The teams played out the second game and New York won, reducing the final margin back to one-and-a-half games. Boston had repeated as the AL pennant-winner.

After all of the talk, it was not the Highlanders, but the Americans whom the Giants snubbed with their refusal to participate in a World Series. The Royal Rooters sent Brush a message, imploring him to give in and play. "Mr. Brush, we're on plush. Where are you? Don't be vain. Give us a game."[13] No games followed.

The Giants may have believed themselves world champions in their own heads, but others differed. The previously crowned world champs were the Americans in 1903. In the absence of a legitimate challenger, the *New York World*, in the Giants' own backyard, analyzed the situation with this headline: "The Bostons Still Hold Title Of World Champions, Giants Refusing To Play."[14]

As he always did, Cy Young delivered in the clutch with his pennant-winning game to beat the Highlanders. He would have loved to pitch in another World Series, but at 37 he was still showing the world he could dial it up when called upon. *Sporting Life* took note of that when Young polished off New York, saying, "nothing finer has been chronicled than the work of our 'grand old man' who keeps on pitching famous ball, despite the attempts to write him out of it."[15]

While no one expected the Cy Young they knew to deliver stand-up comedy routines or spout one-liners like a budding vaudevillian, sometimes Young could be too self-effacing. "I do the best I can with the ball up till the time it leaves my hand," Young said, "and after that it is up to the batter."[16]

Well, sure. The same could be said of any pitcher on any pitch. But it wasn't as if Young's fastballs and curveballs were not being propelled the 60 feet, 6 inches without intent. Young had a little something to do with where they headed.

18

Middle Age
and Middling Play

When the Americans' bats died, so did the 1905 season. Weak hitting dragged the team down in the American League standings and even reduced the great Cy Young's ability to win. Boston finished fourth at 78–74, and Young finished 18–19, the first time in his 16 big-league seasons that he ended the campaign with a losing record.

At 38, there was always the matter of slippage, and baseball people were on the lookout for even the most established of stars faltering, the end of their careers looming. Young did not think he was fading out, and one argument in his favor as evidence this losing mark was not really his fault was his earned average. Over 320⅔ innings, Young's ERA was 1.82, the second-lowest of his 22-year career.

The rest of the American League still could not hit Young's fastball, but his teammates simply could not hit. Coming off two straight AL pennants and a World Series championship, it appeared the whole team got old in a hurry. No one, it seemed, had a strong year at the plate—not even close—not even past greats. The team batting average was just .234, and none of the regulars hit .300. This squad had Jesse Burkett, a previous .400 hitter, and he batted only .257. Buck Freeman managed to hit .240. Catcher Lou Criger couldn't break .200. Freddy Parent's mark was .234. Player-manager Jimmy Collins did reach a respectable .276, but his 65 runs batted in led Boston—not enough.

The one indisputable star, who had the stats to show it, was pitcher Jesse Tannehill, who finished 22–9 with a 2.48 ERA. Bill Dinneen was 12–14, like Young not nearly at his best. How much of his losing record was truly Young's fault? An earned average such as he recorded shined from a distance. But he did not have the necessary luck to make more out of it.

During the 1905 season, Young hurled one of the finest games of his career—and lost it. It was a wish-I-had-been-there game, for sure. And you couldn't make up for being anywhere other than the Huntington Avenue Grounds on July 4, 1905, because there were no highlights shown on video that night through any kind of technology.

Boston hosted the Philadelphia Athletics in a holiday doubleheader that brought 12,666 fans through the turnstiles. After Boston dropped the first game, 5–2, the second game was the crowd-pleaser. Young Rube Waddell's fun-loving antics had made him a popular draw in ballparks, and he could back up much of his boastful talk with excellent mound results. In the eight-team American League, Waddell and Young ran into one another often, going head-to-head as the aces of their teams.

The year before, on May 4, Young pitched his perfect game at Waddell's expense. Nothing got the southpaw down for long, and he looked at this match-up with Young as part of a continuing saga, an episodic show for the fans. After a break, the teams lined up again for the second round of the day's action. Waddell had appeared in relief in the opener. If he wasn't tired, at least he was loose. Hungry to make up for the first-game loss, the Americans jumped to a 2–0 lead in the first inning. Young worked in his usual manner, mixing fastballs, curveballs, and change-ups with superb results, until the sixth inning, when Philadelphia tied the game at 2–2.

And then nothing. No damage done to the Rube by the Boston swatters. No harm done to Cy by the Philly swingers. No more runs. The game ran its course through the ninth inning, still tied. Extra frames followed. Neither man allowed a run as the game continued through the 10th, 11th, 12th, and 13th. The afternoon wore on, and the pitchers pitched on. Waddell was 28 years old that season and won 27 regular-season games with an absurdly low 1.48 earned run average, tops on a staff that saw four pitchers win at least 18 games. Young was a decade older. Surely, if someone wore out, it would be Young. But on they went, completing the 14th, 15th, 16th, 17th, and 18th innings. Once the duo of hurlers finished the 18th still tied, the game went into the record books as the longest-to-date in American League play.

But the contest wasn't over yet. Waddell wasn't helping himself at the plate, going 0-for-8 against Young. It got to the 20th inning, still 2–2, when Boston's defense, as much as Young's pitching, faltered. Revered for his control, Young hit a batter and, combined with two Americans errors, Philadelphia scored twice and won the game, 4–2. Both starters pitched complete games. No one kept track of the number of pitches a pitcher threw in a game back then, but it was guessed that Waddell threw 250 times, and Young's workload was nearly his equal, maybe a few fewer. That would seem like almost a month's work for the 2020 starting pitcher.

Waddell insisted he was not even tired at the conclusion of the outing despite its three-and-a-half-hour duration. "That 20-inning game was the

best game I ever pitched," he said. "But it did not take a feather out of me. I
felt just as good after the game was over as I did during the contest. I can't
claim that I did better work than Young. I had the luck. The fact that it was
the Fourth of July kept me going, and I guess the shooting of revolvers, the
fireworks, and the yelling made me pitch better."[17] Waddell always did like
a commotion.

Although it would be difficult to choose this event over his year-old
perfect game, for Young it was a notable achievement to complete 20 innings, win or lose. Perhaps that was Young's reasoning when he said this
game was "the greatest game of ball I ever took part in."[18] Certainly there
have not been many games like it.

Young did make another point about it being somewhat amazing
that he came out as a loser with such an effort. "I don't walk anyone in
20 innings and I still lose," Young said.[19] Unlike Waddell, the older hurler
admitted that he was fatigued after the long afternoon's work. "I all but
keeled over," Young said. "When I tried to take off my shoes, I hardly had
the strength to untie the laces."[20]

If both pitchers go the distance, one of them has to lose. Perhaps one
percent of baseball fans have seen a game as long as 20 innings, but assuredly no one who is living has seen two pitchers throw that many innings in
the game. In the modern era, if a game lasts 20 innings, it is about as likely
there will be 20 pitchers, 10 per side.

Young was a good judge of his own work. He knew he pitched well
enough to win without anyone else telling him so. He knew on which trips
to the mound he was fortunate to emerge a winner and on which trips he
was unlucky to be a loser. Young was a seasoned veteran who had been
through just about every situation a pitcher can face. He comprehended
that on some days the breaks would go the other way. He was not a com-
plainer on the field, in the dugout, or on the team train. He was a calm
man in general and did not let developments eat away at him. As a pitcher
of many years' duration, and with a track record jammed with impressive
statistics, it was difficult to shake up Young during a game. He showed the
opposition respect, but he did not fret much over their capabilities. "There
never was a pitcher in the box that has the confidence that Cy has," said
Billy Hamilton, a Hall of Fame outfielder with a .344 lifetime average and
917 stolen bases, who played 14 seasons overlapping with Young.[21]

While Young's earned run average of 1905, and the kind of stamina
shown by throwing 20 innings in one game, offered testimony that he was
still the same pitcher, that one-game-under-.500 record was bothersome.
Was this the beginning of the end for Cy Young, or was it a mere reflec-
tion of being part of a poorer team? That season did signal the end of the
Americans' run as a top-tier team. This was a season that rose only slightly

above mediocrity following two stellar years. The question facing the club was whether the team could reinvent itself and move back up, or was destined to fall.

Young was not pleased by his losing record, but he did not feel slowed physically. He was still an able fielder and, unlike so many of his contemporaries who threw their arms out by absorbing so many innings, Young seemed unaffected by the volume of innings hurled. He never held back on the mound, but he was not foolish in training. Most of the tricks pitchers acquire to soothe post-game swelling or aches were adopted later, one by one as the decades passed. And, of course, the serious injuries of the early years could sometimes be fixed a century later by surgery.

For a player of his time, Young was prudent in the way he protected his right arm, his money arm, from danger. He tossed a minimum number of warm-up pitches before each game, about 10, did not throw hard when back on the farm in the winter, and seemed well aware that careless treatment could halt his baseball career.

Young was likely the type of man who didn't trust doctors who operated on baseball arms anyway, at least not at first. He once said, "I was never on a rubbing table in my life. I wouldn't let them monkey around with [the] old soup bone." The player who did not smoke, drink, or keep late hours believed it was the individual player's job to stay fit, saying an athlete "must take good care of himself. This is absolutely essential. A man's constitution is his stock in trade."[22]

Still, athletes in all four major American sports leagues show diminished skills as they approach 40 years of age, or exceed it. Hawk-eyed sports observers seem hot on the trail of any indications of decline. Modern medicine, a close eye on nutrition, a room full of team doctors and trainers ready to pounce on the first sign of a blister, a cold, or a twisted muscle, lay in the future. Young was right. A player had to take care of himself if he wanted to last. Eventually, naturally, age would creep up on everyone, whether they got to play their sport until they were 40 or not.

After the 1905 season ended, when the Americans played the Beaneaters in a meaningless post-season exhibition series, basically for money, fans and sports writers wanted to know if Young had any intention of retiring. Nope, he said, not him. He fully planned to play in 1906. "Good for another season," Young said.[23]

At least he was of sound body and mind. As for the good part, that remained up in the air, many wondering whether Young would be down-graded from great to merely good, or if a more depressing scenario waited with the first pitch of the next season.

The announcement that Young had signed with Boston again for the 1906 season came from owner John Taylor. Young's deal was worth

$4,000. He was no longer in the $6,000 class. Taylor said Young wrote to him making his commitment. "I am pleased to be with the Boston Americans once more and hope to be in shape to do my full share of the work necessary to land another pennant for Boston."[24]

It made sense that Young would harbor such optimism. Although it had been two seasons since the Americans won the 1904 pennant, they were okay in 1905. Good players always want to think good thoughts. In this case, however, Young may have been as shocked as the Boston fans at the way things turned out. That season the Americans were terrible, far worse than they had been since joining the major league ranks in 1901 and as bad as they would not be again for almost 20 years.

A pennant wasn't at issue. Neither was a .500 record. The Americans were so awful they didn't seem capable of finishing the season. Field leader Jimmy Collins did not make it through the year. As Boston sank to a 49–105 record, last in the standings and 45½ games out of first place, Collins departed with a 35–79 record in favor of new manager Chick Stahl, who finished 14–26.

The White Sox won the AL pennant with a 93–58 record, three games ahead of the New York Highlanders. With the sizzling Cubs setting a National League wins record with a 116–36 mark, it was an all-Chicago World Series. The White Sox were known as the Hitless Wonders yet somehow won the championship. That year, Mordecai "Three-Finger" Brown, the right-hander who lost some of his fingers in a farm accident as a youth, recorded a mind-boggling 1.04 earned run average. The Cubs' win total remains an NL record and has been equaled only once, by the Seattle Mariners of 2001 in the American League. No pitcher has had a lower ERA in the National League since 1900, with only Tim Keefe's 0.86 in 1880 bettering it. Boston's Dutch Leonard 0.96 in 1914 in the American League is the only other lower figure.

To some degree, Americans fans hung in there with support the team was not worthy of, turning up 410,209 strong, fourth-best in the league. That was only a decline of about 58,000 fans from 1905. It took longer for the fans to become mortified than Collins. He appeared in just 37 games that season, partially because of a sprained knee. He was under such pressure as manager because of the lost season some said he was literally losing his mind due to depression. Yet this was not the end of Collins in Boston, as might be surmised. He did return to play in 1907 and then completed his on-field days with the Philadelphia Athletics.

A glance at the statistics produced on the field by the 1906 team would have driven any sane man wild, though despite his woes, Collins still batted .275. That was better than almost all his teammates, however. Chick Stahl hit .286, which was robust compared to the others. Backup second baseman Heinie Wagner was not to be confused with Honus Wagner, the Hall of Famer who was sometimes also referred to as Heinie. Heinie's lifetime average was .250, and he hit .281 in nine games for Boston that season.

Moose Grimshaw, the first baseman in the middle of his three-year Boston and Major League career, was the best batsman, hitting .290. He did not hit a single home run and drove across just 48 runs. Grimshaw, whose given name was Myron, was from upstate New York and did not reach the majors until he was 29. He played in 110 games in 1906, though in one of them he banged up a knee. It looked like a serious injury initially, but he finished the game. That was the kind of bravado the Americans could have used every day that season.

This was a pathetic hitting team with a team average of .237, but even more tellingly, a club that could not regularly push across runs by any means. The total runs scored for the season was 463. That was down from 579 the year before. In the World Series-winning year of 1903, the team scored 708 runs. With the downturn in scoring and a final record carrying more than 100 losses, the pitching staff suffered. Some pitchers contributed to the disastrous season, like Joe Harris, whose record was 2–21 and whose lifetime mark in three years with the team was 3–30. Bill Dinneen finished 8–19, George Winter, 6–18. The staff survivor was Jesse Tannehill, who managed to go 13–11.

Ralph Glaze, a rookie right-hander from Denver, went 4–6. He was previously an All-American football end from Dartmouth, despite playing at 5-foot-8 and 153 pounds. He pitched for Dartmouth and threw a no-hitter against Columbia, an Ivy League rival. Glaze spent just three years in the majors and later became a college football coach. But in 1906, Glaze tossed a memorable game for the Americans. On August 31, he edged the Philadelphia A's and Rube Waddell, an unknown beating a star on that given day.

The 1906 debacle even ensnared Cy. His record was 13–21, his earned run average 3.19, not horrible, but not as good as usual. When a 39-year-old pitcher who has been both indestructible and dominating for so long finds himself staring at numbers like that at the end of the year, he must question himself. Others will certainly do it for him. Once again the question must be asked was how much of the bruising record was Young's fault and how much of that losing season should be pinned on the teammates who didn't hit and the disarray the club found itself in. It was also said that Young did pitch through a sore elbow at one point of the season, and that inhibited the number of curveballs he threw. If that semi-injury made him more vulnerable to hitters, that was not a good sign either.

Young's regular catcher, Lou Criger, was hurt for most of the season and appeared in just seven games. The team's top receiver that year was Charlie Ambruster. Bob Peterson, 39 games, and Bill Carrigan, 37, also saw action. The two catchers who were Young's battery mates for the bulk of his career were Chief Zimmer and Criger. As Criger aged, his batting average kept declining, and it would not be long before his and Young's partnership ended. How much did the absence of Criger influence Young's down season? Not an easy thing to measure, but since they were deemed virtually inseparable and spoke of one another as if they sent telepathic signals between mound and plate, it is a possibility.

Criger, whose strength on the field was always as a glove man, displaying a strong arm when players tried to steal, and in his smarts calling pitchers, was definitely losing it at the plate. In his limited appearances, Criger batted .176, and he never hit .200 again.

By 1906, Young was not as thin as he was when he was younger. If there was a time in his career when he was encroaching on 230 pounds, as some have written, it had to be showing by 1906. But he refused to believe he was done, that his baseball career was over. He was determined to show the baseball world that what he believed was also true. He went around telling sports writers that not only would he back for the 1907 season, he would be as good as new, and he planned to play for four or five more years.

More than a century later, another Boston superstar athlete, New England Patriots quarterback Tom Brady, who at 41 helped win the team's sixth Super Bowl, said the same thing when anyone brought up his age. Coincidentally, both men, Brady as a quarterback, and Young as a pitcher, have both been described as the G.O.A.T. of their positions, or Greatest Of All Time.

Grantland Rice, a legendary sports writer born in 1880, was old enough to witness Young pitching. A gifted wordsmith with a knack for colorful phrasing applied to sporting figures, Rice was the one who wrote a poem which extolled the talents of Notre Dame's football Four Horsemen. Rice also wrote a poem about Young when he was reaching athletic old age, praising him for being the old war horse that he was.

> Fame may be fleeting and glory may fade –
> Life at its best is a breath on the glade.
> One hero passes, another is made.
> New stars arise as the old ones pale.
> So when a stalwart steps out from the throng
> On with the tribute, let garlands be flung –
> Here's to the king of them all, Denton True Young.[25]

Not even after the dismaying 1906 season was Cy Young prepared to become yesterday's hero.

19

1907–1908

Cy Young refused to believe that his second straight losing season in 1906 meant that he should retire, even if he was turning 40. His body and arm felt too good after another winter on the farm in Peoli. It was stunning enough that the Americans had played so poorly, had endured the worst season in 1906 in the young history of the franchise. But Young was caught up in the collapse, not one of the causes of it. He was determined to show he was still one of the best pitchers in the game.

The team was a mess in 1906, as if felled by the plague. Players who previously were leaders and top players were either gone or failed to play up to their past standards. It began with Jimmy Collins, the player-manager who basically had a nervous breakdown and was through as manager, barely up to playing third base.

Yet while Chick Stahl had taken control as manager, surprisingly, Collins was prepared to make a comeback as a player. Team management welcomed the thought. After all, any club that loses 105 games is open to suggestions for ways to improve. Collins, always a sharp fielder, could still play, even if he was 37.

Most professional athletes in the big four sports across the spectrum in the United States are mulling retirement by Collins' age. Young was about three years older, and the percentage of 40-year-old big-league athletes is a tiny one. It takes a special athlete to keep up the conditioning required to stay at the top of his game, as younger players come along and challenge him for his roster spot. Young may have been gaining weight, but he still had faith in his right arm, and his standard off-season routine of hard labor on his farm over the winter had long paid dividends.

Young had never before gone through the frustration he experienced in 1906. Only during his rookie season of 1890 were the results of his season pitching won-loss record as limited. That year he was 9–7 in less than a full season and one in which he was getting his bearings. After that, Cy Young was Cy Young, winning 30 or more games regularly and

20 or more the rest of the time. The 1906 campaign just had to be an aberration.

When Young arrived at spring training, he whispered an aside to his friend and catcher Lou Criger reflecting his mindset heading into the regular season. "I believe I will have a good year," Young confided in Criger.

The Americans' outlook was not terribly rosy, but the feeling passing through players' minds was that the team had to be better. A season of 49–105 can leave scars on those who played through it. It is demoralizing to suffer so many bruising defeats, so it is natural to think the next season will be better. Based on his lifetime body of work, Young was capable of thinking that way. As for the others, at least spring is the time of optimism, of blooming flowers, when it seems all things are possible.

Owner John Taylor named outfielder Chick Stahl the permanent manager after he finished the 1906 season. At 33, Stahl played in 155 games the previous season and batted. 286. While respectable, that was a decline for a man who in 10 big-league campaigns batted .305. Stahl stood 5-foot-10 and weighed 160 pounds, an average-sized person for the era. Stahl was born in Avilla, Indiana, and still made his home in Fort Wayne, Indiana. While a ballplayer without power (except for a league-leading 19 triples in 1904), he was always a reliable hitter, twice shining with averages higher than .350.

It seemed Taylor had made a secure choice following the revolving door manager situation of 1906. It was Stahl who selected the spring training site of Little Rock, Arkansas, as a twist for the team to begin a fresh start to 1907 right away.

Young had no intention of staying home after the grim 1906 season, but he endured some other setbacks. He and Robba had never had children, but in 1906 she was pregnant and due to give birth in September. A baby girl was born to the couple but died within hours after a difficult pregnancy for the mother. There is little known record of Young speaking publicly following the loss.

After his high salaries of $6,000 for a few recent years, he signed for 1907 to play for $4,000. The club broke camp and, as it always had, started a series of exhibition games, working its way north. On March 25, however, Stahl suddenly resigned the manager's job. The Americans were in West Baden, Indiana, for a March 28 game when stunningly, Stahl committed suicide.[1]

There were slightly varying versions reported in newspapers about how his deed played out. Stahl, as a team leader, visited in the morning with the owner of the hotel where the team was staying, requesting bath house tickets for the players. He then adjourned to his room. It was not 100 percent clear if Stahl was sharing a suite with Collins or staying in his own room, but there was a door between the bedrooms of the two men.

Alone, Stahl drank a three-ounce bottle of carbolic acid, then half-dressed and stumbled in on Collins, who was pulling on his uniform for the game. Gazing at Stahl's instability, Collins immediately realized something was amiss. "What is the matter with you?" Collins said. One account said Stahl replied, "Nothing," then fell over onto a bed.[2]

Another story, reported much later after considerable investigation, relayed that Stahl said, "I couldn't help it. I did it, Jim. It was killing me and I couldn't stand it."[3] Then he pitched forward.

Collins yelled for help, and other teammates poured into the room as a doctor pushed his way in. It was too late to assist Stahl, though, and he perished there at age 34. He was gone approximately 15 minutes after ingesting the poisonous substance.

This event was widely reported. The multi-deck headlines in the Cincinnati Enquirer, atop a report filed by a special correspondent, read this way: "Drained Bottle of Carbolic Acid As Means to End His Earthly Troubles. 'Chick' Stahl, Famous Ball Player a Suicide. His Death at West Baden a Great Shock to Fans—Career of a Great Outfielder Is Brief."[4]

Despite these final words, it was not positively certain what drove Stahl to the drastic decision. It was initially assumed in the baseball world that he could not handle the pressure of being manager.

About a century later, a member of the Society for American Baseball Research reported a possible cause other than professional pressure driving Stahl to his death. Stahl had been a playboy of sorts during team travels, a woman-in-every-port kind of guy. It was suggested that a woman appeared from his dalliances and threatened to blackmail him. A good Catholic observer for the most part, Stahl had married in 1906, and it may be that he feared the shame resulting from the blackmail attempt. Or perhaps the combination of a blackmail threat, declining batting skills, and the prospect of a bleak season at the helm of what had been the worst team in baseball the year before, contorted Stahl's mind.

The Americans may have been shocked Stahl did himself in, but Stahl's acquaintances back home in Indiana apparently were not. They seemed to be aware that he suffered from long-term depression. A headline of an Indiana paper's story of the time revealed this truth. "Meditated Self-Slaying, Chick Stahl Had Often Talked About Suicide. Base Ball Player Had Entertained Dangerous Ideas About Self-Destruction."[5]

It was all very confusing. When he stepped down from the manager's slot without managing a 1907 regular-season game, Stahl said, "This handling of a baseball team both on and off the field is not what it is cracked up to be. Releasing players grated on my nerves, and they come so frequently at

this time of the year that it made me sick at heart." In explaining his res-
ignation from authority to his wife by telegram, Stahl sounded relieved of
a burden when he wrote, "Cheer up little girl and be happy. I am all right
now and able to play the game of my life."[6] That did not sound like a man
poised to take his own life.

The start of the regular season lay shortly ahead, and the grieving
Americans were without a manager. Young's 40th birthday was March 29,
and originally the team had planned a party. Stahl's death benched that
idea. However, Taylor approached Cy Young and asked him to become
manager. Young had never aspired to be a major-league manager, and he
really had little interest in assuming the role then. After discussions with
the boss, Young agreed to take the job temporarily, only on the condition
that Taylor find someone as swiftly as possible to replace him. Then Young
addressed the reeling team.

"It's mighty tough, boys," Young said. "I never dreamed such a thing
could happen." He expressed his admiration for Stahl, whom he may not
have known for long as a manager, but who had been a several-year teammate. "Players may come and go, but there are few Chick Stahls," Young
said.[7]

Young was much more focused on redeeming himself as a pitcher
in the eyes of the sport than managing, to prove himself again to any of
the doubters who felt he might be obligated to quit after the sketchy 1906
season. "Judging from the way I have been going this spring," Young told
Taylor, "I believe I will have one of my best seasons this year and I would
not have anything worrying me. I also believe I do not have the ability to
manage the team. I feel highly honored, but I could not do justice to both
positions."[8]

Young did okay during his brief tenure. The Americans went 3–3
under his leadership, but then began a revolving door series of field bosses,
a few others learning managing was not for them, or Taylor learning they
were not for him. Boston finished 59–90, a 10-win improvement from
1906, but still not a record worth more than seventh place in an eight-team
league. George Huff succeeded Young and went 2–6. First baseman Bob
Unglaub came next and went 9–20. Then Deacon McGuire concluded the
season with a 45–61 record, which was deemed good enough for him to
carry over into 1908.

Unglaub was a peculiar choice. He was just 26 and while playing
full-time, he was not shaking up the world, hitting just .254. A Baltimore
native, he spent six years total in the majors with a .258 average. Although
he did not commit suicide, less than 10 years later, at 35, Unglaub was
dead, as well, the victim of an accident at work while employed in a rail-
road job.

Runs were very scarce again for the Americans this season, with the club accumulating just 466 of them. Unglaub's 62 RBIs was the most on the team. Hitting all around was weak, with Collins, appearing in 41 games, the top batsman with a .291 mark. Outfielder Bunk Congalton, who began his season in Cleveland and was wrapping up his career, hit .286. Freddy Parent came through with a .276 average.

The pitching produced some bizarre statistics. Never have so many hurlers who allowed so few runs been so penalized by lack of run support. Cy Young was right about how he felt in the pre-season, and he delivered. Back from the brink, he was a cyclone once more. Young's record for the poorly achieving team was 21–15, his earned average a stingy 1.99. He was very much his old self.

Boston had little behind Young on the mound as far as records went, but it was hard to blame this staff for not pulling its weight. No one else had a winning mark. George Winter finished 12–15, but his earned run average was a sparkling 2.07. Ralph Glaze went 9–13, 2.32. Jesse Tannehill, in the final season of his career, went 6–7, 2.47. Cy Morgan, who soon would record some fine years for the Philadelphia Athletics, finished 6–6, 1.97.

Glaze was an interesting figure. Later in life he coached college sports, but in between, for three seasons in 1906, 1907 and 1908, he pitched for Boston, with a lifetime 15–21 record and a 2.89 earned run average. Between 1908 and 1924, Glaze coached college football, basketball, and baseball.

A couple of guys strayed over the 3.00 mark in earned run average, though not much so, but they paid the price. Tex Pruiett went 3–11, and Joe Harris was 0–7. No pitcher can be expected to pitch a shutout every time out, not even Cy Young, but that's basically what it took to win a game for Boston that year.

The "old man" wowed the baseball world in 1907 with his recovery. It turned out that Buck Congalton, who played just this one season with Boston, had harbored some questions about Young's likelihood of success at this advanced age, but realized swiftly that Young still had the goods. "Play behind him a few weeks and you can see why he is so good," Congalton said. "That old fast ball of his is about as effective as it ever was. He uses his head, too, and has the faculty of making men play behind him. He has as much ability as anyone in the business."[9]

Although this happened a little bit later, John Taylor took on a partner in ownership of the Boston ball club in 1911. It was a former teammate of Young's, outfielder Jimmy McAleer. McAleer also managed a few clubs and made enough money to make a major investment in the Americans. After two years, he and Taylor had a falling out, and he severed ties with the team. In 1931, suffering from cancer, McAleer committed suicide.

There was little to be surveyed on the Boston roster of 1907 that would lead an Americans fan (though with attendance at 436,777, third-best in the league, there were still a surprising number of them) to look towards 1908 and think, "We're going to be OK next year."

The biggest single reason for optimism was probably not even apparent to the average fan. A 19-year-old outfielder from Texas, who appeared in just seven games and batted only .158, represented the future. Tris Speaker, one of the finest all-around players ever, who became renowned as a center fielder and batted .345 lifetime, was a year or two away, but was getting his first taste of Major League life.

One of the first to recognize Speaker's potential was Cy Young. He befriended the young player, offered advice and instruction, and encouraged him. "I was by no means a finished outfielder when I started in the American League," Speaker said years later. "I give Cy Young all the credit. I learned to watch batters by watching Cy pitch. I didn't start with the crack of the bat. I started before the ball was hit. Another thing about old Cy—he had great patience with me and believed in me and he would hit fungoes to me for 30 minutes a day. A wonderful pitcher and a wonderful man."[10]

Young raised sheep on his Peoli, Ohio, farm during his playing days and after retiring in 1911.

Speaker's style was to play hitters in shallow center, then dart back and catch up to the ball. During the first half of the 20th century, he was considered the best ever to field the position, though that was before Willie Mays joined the Giants.

Cy Young's September 9 outing put an exclamation point on his season even though he did not earn a win. He employed all his weapons and all of his old stamina and durability by going 13 innings without allowing a run against rival Rube Waddell and the Athletics. The score was 0–0, with Young permitting six hits and striking out eight men. The game was called on account of darkness before it could be decided.

In 1907, although Boston continued to struggle, Cy Young lived up to his own expectations. There were no indications that he was slowing down. Why couldn't he keep on winning 20 games each year?

Between the end of the 1907 season and the start of the 1908 season, the Boston American League club made an historic change. Henceforth, the team nickname would be the Red Sox, thus beginning a tradition that has lasted more than a century. Taylor said he made the permanent change by harkening back to an earlier time when Boston's team was called the Red Stockings. Team uniforms were altered for the 1908 season, reflecting the change. The new jerseys displayed the word "Boston" superimposed across a red stocking.

Not so many people quizzed Young about retirement during the off-season between 1907 and 1908. In one of Major League baseball's wildest seasons, the Red Sox were not part of the thrills of the 1908 pennant races. Boston improved again, this time to a 75–79 record, inching towards .500. But that was pretty much a sideshow of interest only to Bostonians. The rest of the nation's baseball fans were riveted to the suspense on display in both the American League and National League pennant competitions.

The Red Sox crept up to fifth place, but that was essentially inconsequential. During the closing weeks of the season, four teams had a shot at the AL pennant, and going into the last few days, three teams were still alive. The standings ended this way: 1) Detroit Tigers, 90–63; 2) Cleveland, 90–64, one-half game back; 3) Chicago White Sox, 88–64, one-and-a-half games back; and 4) St. Louis Browns, 83–69, six-and-a-half games out.

In the National League, the Chicago Cubs prevailed with a 99–53 record. Tied for second place were the Pittsburgh Pirates and the New York Giants, with records of 98–54.

Boston won more games because run production was up. It was not like the days of yesteryear in 1903, but there was an intriguing mix of players passing through. Criger, at 36, still caught more games, 84, than

anyone else despite a dismal batting average of .190. The first baseman
was Jake Stahl, who hit .244. For decades, Jake was referred to as the
brother of Chick Stahl, but that was not true. It is not certain where the
confusion began, though both were born in Indiana. Speaker made it into
31 games at age 20 that season, but he still wasn't ready for full-time play,
hitting .224.

The 1908 season was pretty much a cameo for Gavvy Cravath, who
was a 27-year-old rookie from California and the epitome of a late bloomer.
During his single season with Boston, Cravath appeared in 94 games and
batted .256. Since he hit exactly one home run in 340 plate appearances, it
was hard to tell that he would soon emerge as one of the National League's
top power hitters.

It took another four years, when he was 31, for Cravath to reach his
potential. In 1912, Cravath hit 11 homers for the Philadelphia Phillies.
Then, pretty much to the astonishment of all, in 1913, Cravath led the National League in hits, home runs (19) and RBIs (128). That year was the
first of three straight years of Cravath topping the NL in home runs, and
by 1919 he had done so six times. His high year of 24 homers came in 1915,
when no one else was hitting nearly that many. How could Boston have
known so many years earlier what Cravath would become?

While Tannehill pitched in just one game, heading towards the exit,
buried in the shuffle of many players coming and going was a young hurler
who not too far in the future became something special on the mound
for Boston. The equivalent of a young Tris Speaker in the field, "Smoky"
Joe Wood was just 18 and went 1–1 in six appearances. In 1912, Wood
would put together the best pitching season ever by a Red Sox player, even
eclipsing Young's best, with a 34–5 mark. Cy Morgan was still around and
finished 14–13, again with a first-rate earned run average of 2.46.

From the perspective of history, and a fact often overlooked, was another starting pitcher on the roster in 1908. Eddie Cicotte, who might well
have been famous for inventing the knuckleball, but instead became infa-
mous for being a key villain when the White Sox threw the World Series
in 1919, was just trying to make his way. Cicotte finished 11–12 with a 2.43
ERA while hurling 17 complete games.

Pitching as if he meant it—pitching as if still trying to prove himself—
Cy Young again won 21 games. This was the 16th time Young won at least
20 games in a season. If a modern-day pitcher wonders what it takes to
accumulate more than 500 wins, that is a road map. Even more amazing,
Young's ERA in 1908 was 1.26, the sixth time he allowed fewer than two
earned runs per game over the course of a season, and the lowest mark of
his 22-year career. The man was 41 at the time.

Young simply overpowered the league in a rather efficient 299 innings, low for him. He tossed 30 complete games and on any given day threw high-quality baseball as excellent as just about any day of his life.

On May 30, Young's complete-game, 6–0 victory over the Washington Senators was a one-hitter with zero walks. On June 30, in an 8–0 win over the New York Highlanders, Young was even better. This was the third no-hitter of his career, and Young came close to pitching another perfect game.

New York's leadoff man was second baseman Harry Niles, and he worked Young for a rare walk. Young led his league in fewest walks per nine innings every season between 1893 and 1906 except 1902, so any base on balls off him was worth discussion. Pretty soon, Niles was back on the bench discussing the walk because when he attempted to steal second base, Criger threw him out.

Young retired the next 26 batters in order to claim another no-hitter. He was the first big-league pitcher to record three such gems.

The boys wearing the red socks helped Young out with some offense that day. Second baseman Amby McConnell, first baseman Unglaub, and third baseman Frank LaPorte each contributed two hits. Remarkably, Young swatted three hits and drove in four runs on one of his finest days as a hitter.

Later that season, the team scheduled a special day to honor Young. It was "Cy Young Day" in Boston on August 13, 1908. The festivities included an exhibition game between the Red Sox and other American League players. Sox players dressed in silly outfits as if it were Halloween, and paraded onto the field. There was presentation of a unique trophy for Young, as well as gifts, and speeches were made praising him. Management decreed that all gate receipts, which turned out to be about $6,000, were for Young. The

At the end of his career, Cy Young returned to Cleveland to pitch once more. This time, however, Young was a member of the Naps, named for manager-star player Napoleon "Larry" Lajoie. Later, the team changed its name to the Indians.

loot from that day was said to exceed any single salary year of his, something which surprised and delighted Robba.

Eben Draper, the lieutenant governor of Massachusetts, was given the task of speaking about Young while handing over the silver trophy. "I know very few boys and men in this country who are not much interested in our great national sport," Draper said, "and they feel pleasure and pride when any man connected with one of our great baseball teams acquits himself particularly well, as you certainly have done for many years."[11]

Young was expected to deliver his own speech to the crowd. Whether he was too timid to do so, or for whatever other reason, that day Young was no orator, talking as briefly as possible. He merely said, "Thank you." However, Young did tip his baseball cap to the cheering throng, a second thank-you.

What neither Young nor those Boston baseball fans realized at the time, near the end of that 1908 campaign, was that his gesture was also a goodbye wave.

20

The End of the Line

The unthinkable occurred over the winter before the 1909 baseball season began. Cy Young, the greatest pitcher in history, feted near the end of the 1908 season by his adoring fans in Boston, was traded.

Basically, the Red Sox ditched him. Unconvinced by Young's two superb recent seasons of 21 wins each, the club shipped him to Cleveland. At least it was Cleveland, his other big-league home. The deal brought Boston right-handed pitcher Charlie Chech, lefty pitcher Jack Ryan, and $12,500.

The trade was made in February, and Young found out he was leaving his most recent team for his old playing city when a sports writer visited him at the farm in Ohio. The way the tale was told, Young was actually milking a cow when he learned of his upcoming change of scenery. A few months earlier, Boston had traded catcher Lou Criger to the St. Louis Browns. Young and Criger had almost been twins in the Boston lineup. But Criger, in his late 30s, had not hit well for some time. So it was much less surprising that the Red Sox parted ways with him. Less understandable was the deal severing ties with the iconic pitcher.

The split from Criger left Young melancholy when he shared the information about the trade with Robba. When his wife asked him why, Young said, "Don't know." But it was obvious that Criger's trail of sub-.200 batting averages had caught up to him. That left Young with a premonition Boston might discard him. He was turning 42 in late March, before the 1909 season began, and with the departure of Criger his antennae were up. "I almost expected this," Young told the bearer of the news of his trade. "I didn't know why, but it had seemed to me for the last week or 10 days as if something of this kind was going to happen. I have been packing up, little by little, preparatory to the trip to Hot Springs to join the Boston team, but something told me all the time that I was to go to some other club."[1]

Young launched into a valedictory address of sorts about his years spent in Boston, praising the experience. "I'm sorry to leave Boston," he said, "but if I am to leave that good, old city I'm glad to be going back to Cleveland where I made my start in major league society 19 years ago. I would have been satisfied to end my baseball career in Boston, and I'll be satisfied to end it in Cleveland where I have always been received like a king."[2]

Yes, this was a return to Cleveland, near his home, but it was not a return to the Spiders. That franchise was defunct. The American League team that replaced it went through some nickname changes. At that moment it was called the Naps in honor of manager and star Napoleon "Larry" Lajoie, the veteran star who helped build the AL along with Young back in 1901.

Cleveland was in the mix of that heady pennant race of 1908, finishing just a half-game shy of a first-place tie. Cleveland, with Lajoie quite certain Young could still be of value, wanted to make the trade. "Cy Young will be one of our mainstays for several seasons," Lajoie said. "The beauty about Cy is that he can work in any kind of weather."[3]

The Naps of 1908 won 90 games, and the club believed the addition of someone of Young's ability could take the team to the pennant. The Naps already had the brilliant Addie Joss, who won 24 games the previous season with a 1.16 earned run average, a player who bested Young's 1.26. At 28, Joss was in his prime and was coming off a fourth straight 20-victory season.

Possessing a blazing fastball, Joss was both highly respected and well-liked around the league, and he was viewed by some as close to the best active pitcher in the league. On October 2, 1908, Joss pitched the second perfect game of the 20th century, following Young's of 1904. Joss defeated the Chicago White Sox, 1–0. The opposition pitcher was "Big" Ed Walsh, who allowed four hits and one unearned run while striking out 15 batters and lost the game. Walsh could only express admiration for what he witnessed. "That was surely a great pitching performance Addie Joss treated Cleveland fans to Friday," Walsh said afterwards. "I was almost as much pleased with his feat as if it had been I who had equaled the world's record instead of Addie. Joss' fadeaway ball was working to perfection. He is a wonderful pitcher."[4]

In an aside, Walsh recorded the lowest career earned run average in baseball history at 1.81. Joss is second at 1.89.

This trade of Young did not pan out as well for either side as expected. Chech went 7–5 and Ryan went 3–3 for Boston, even though the rebuilding Sox were moving up and finished third in the league at 88–63.

Young went out of his way to sound grateful to Boston upon departure from the Red Sox's rotation.

Boston is by all odds the best baseball city in the world. I say that without reservation. In what other city could a special day be arranged, as was arranged for me last fall, with nothing at stake on the game and box receipts over $6,300 realized for the player in whose honor the day was set aside? Nowhere, not even in New York or Chicago. Yes, Boston is the best baseball city in the world. Its fans are the most loyal and the most forgiving. I shall leave that city with the greatest regret and I am only glad that I am going to another first-class city where I have always been treated with the utmost kindness.[5]

Cy Young was no politician, but he was a diplomat. Young knew his own body better than the Red Sox and gave the Naps exactly what they sought when they made the trade. Unfortunately for Cleveland, the team coming off the high of the great pennant race faltered in many ways. Yes, Cleveland added a new weapon, but alas, the holdover players did not match their usual output.

Lajoie, the fabulous player, was, at 34, still a .324 hitter. Otherwise, his batting order let him down, and surprisingly, even Addie Joss slumped. Joss went 14–13, although that was probably a casualty of the hitting since his earned run average was 1.71.

The great pitcher grew up on an Ohio farm and remained a farmer his entire life. Young, with Robba sitting in their newfangled mode of transportation, displays some of his baseball trophies on the running board of the vehicle.

In spring training, the Naps threw a birthday party for Young when he turned 42. He was the only one who didn't care how many candles were on the cake, and he also seemed to be one of the few players immune from whatever disease afflicted the other Naps. Cleveland took the big fall, rather than adding to its win total, dropping to a 71–82 record while scoring just 492 runs. No pennant contender, Cleveland placed sixth in the standings. Lajoie did not even last the season as manager. He lost his authority when the club was 57–57. Deacon McGuire, who had managed in Boston during some of the recent bad days there, closed things out at 14–25.

But Young, impervious to age, was the best pitcher on the team, going 19–15 with a 2.26 ERA in 294⅓ innings. There was a reason Cleveland treated Young as a king—he was still royalty. Once again he had proven himself, though before that sports writer had departed his property, Young had grown reflective, revealing some of his innermost thoughts. This trade, as well as the numbers on his birth certificate, still seemed to signal the approaching end of his big-league career.

It was Young's turn to pitch on July 19, in the first half of a double-header against his old Boston mates. Young scattered eight hits and beat the Red Sox, 6–1. The loser, as fate would have it, was Chech, who was hit hard by Cleveland. While it was logical for Young to be the man of the hour, he was only runner-up for attention that day.

That is because Cleveland shortstop Neal Ball, who stroked two hits, including a home run, made the play of the century in the field. At least it was at the time, although the century was just a decade old. For the first time in Major League history, a player achieved an unassisted triple play, putting out the other side on just one hit ball.

Ball, who was from Michigan, was small for a professional athlete. He stood 5-foot-7 and weighed 145 pounds. He was 28 at the time and had come over from the New York Highlanders, who used him little. This was one of the 96 games Ball played for Cleveland that year. There were about 11,000 fans in house at League Park when Ball made his miraculous play.

It was the second inning of the first game. Boston's Heinie Wagner singled. Jake Stahl beat out a bunt, putting two men on. Next up was Amby McConnell, who responded to a hit-and-run sign to try and move the runners along.

"Cy Young was pitching for us when McConnell fouled off the first pitch," Ball said.

> On the next pitch, McConnell shot one right over Young's head. It was on the rise and I didn't think I had any chance of getting it. But I gave it a try. There was the ball, traveling over second. I jumped, and sure enough, it stuck in my glove. After that, there was no trouble. Wagner had already rounded third and all I had to do

to get him was step on second. Stahl was racing to second when I caught the ball. He couldn't stop and ran right into my hands. I actually waited for him.[6]

Young was one of the people on the field who did not immediately grasp what had happened. When Ball started jogging to the dugout, the pitcher asked his shortstop, "Where are you going, Neal?" Ball said, "That's three outs."[7] Many years later, Ball's glove was donated to the Baseball Hall of Fame. The feat was such a shock, Ball later posed for a picture with the three Boston players he got out on that single play.

To date, 15 players have made unassisted major league triple plays. There was not another one in the big leagues after Ball's until 1920. The last one was performed by Eric Bruntlett, second baseman for the Philadelphia Phillies against the New York Mets on August 23, 2009.

It was not as if Young was prepared to retire, but he was reading the tea leaves. "I don't expect I'll be leaving the farm many seasons more," he said. "When a farmer gets to be 42, he begins to long for home and begins to dread the long bumps and the long days in the hotels that are part of a ballplayer's life. I shan't be sorry when the time comes for me to settle down here, but as long as I'm in the game, I'm going to do my best for the club that employs me."[8]

For all of that admission, Young was going to be much like most other stars. He would not voluntarily remove himself from the game he loved until he was told he had to go. While he had dropped hints about the nearness of retirement before the 1909 season, winning 19 more games (darn, he would have liked to pick off that 20th one more time), his showing convinced team officials that it was worth investing in Young for another season. Once the team expressed interest, Young was on board. "I'll be back," he said.[9]

Young did come back for another round in 1910 with the Naps. But this time, at 43, he didn't work into shape as quickly, and when the games began for real, he had problems putting up victories. His weight had become a factor in his spryness leaving the mound to field balls hit in front of the plate or bounding towards the base lines. He had difficulty closing teams out. His workload dropped to 163⅓ innings. Yet for all of that, Young's earned run average was still an excellent 2.53. The why behind his 7–10 record was a little bit confounding.

The 1910 campaign brought with it big problems for Cleveland. Addie Joss tore a ligament in his right elbow, and he finished 5–5 in 107⅓ innings of pitching. Hopes for a pennant went down the drain with the sidelining of Joss, and the team finished 71–81. Even though he was no longer manager, Lajoie was still his usual self at bat, hitting .383. But he had no help to speak of on offense. The team was outscored by 109 runs. A new face

Cy Young (left) spotted the talent of Tris Speaker (right) when Speaker was a teenager and helped him develop his fielding before the newcomer emerged as a Red Sox star. They remained lifelong friends.

showed up in the Cleveland lineup, if only for 20 games, a player who could be a savior. "Shoeless" Joe Jackson batted .387 in his limited play a year before he became a full-timer in 1911 and batted .408.

As Young struggled on the mound as he rarely had since being dubbed Cyclone so many years earlier, there was one indisputable highlight—a game to last forever in his mind and in the record books. It was a place Young traveled that no other pitcher ever had, or ever would.

On July 19, 1901, Cy Young took the mound for Cleveland in the second game of a doubleheader against the Washington Senators on the road. There were 7,132 paid customers for the games. Young was at low ebb, plagued by a 2–7 record when the contest began. When the game ended in a 5–2 Cleveland victory, Young had won his 500th career game.

The game lasted 11 innings and Young, naturally, went the distance, as he always set out to do. He surrendered five hits and two runs, just one of them earned, while walking three men. The opposing pitcher was Doc Reisling, who stuck around through nine innings and kept the Senators in the tie before extra innings. Reisling pitched four seasons in the majors with a lifetime 15–19 record. He was relieved for the last two innings by Bob Groom, a 10-year player, who fell to 8–10 when he took the loss that day. During his career, Groom lost 26 games in a season and won 24 games in a season.

The Senators nicked Young for a run in the first inning, and he trailed until the Naps came up with two runs in the top of the ninth. Young could not hold the Senators off, though, as they pushed across the tying run in the bottom of the inning. Cleveland's salvaging inning came in the top of the 11th with three runs. It took two hours and 12 minutes to make history that day.

The *Cleveland Plain-Dealer* heralded the milestone victory this way: "Cy Young Takes 500th Game—Cleveland Boats Win; Five Hundredth Game Is Finally Won By the Great Veteran, Cy Young." The story, attributed as "Special to the *Plain-Dealer*," began with the words, "Uncle Cy Young breezed home a winner today, his 500th big-league victory, and was as happy over the triumph as a child with a new toy." It was added—even in the moment—"that it is a mark that probably will never be equaled."[10]

When asked how he had lasted so long as a big-league hurler and won so many games, Young was brief. "I just keep good care of myself, in season and out of season," he said.[11]

After an 0–4 start, Young reached 7–7. But then he lost three decisions to end the season. There was reason for worry, but not enough to make a drastic decision about calling it a career. "Quit the game?" was Young's answer to a sports writer about his future. "I am better now than I have been in years. I'd be awfully lonesome and you know this is a healthy game. I'll not quit until I have to."[12]

Whether it was a just-in-case scenario or not, in August, Cleveland gave Young another special day to honor his career. This occasion wasn't as spectacular as the Boston party, but the thought was there.

When the season ended, despite Young's poor win-loss record, Cleveland offered him a contract for 1911. He signed. Young would be 44 by the time the next season started, and for the first time in several years he went back to the farm with a losing record. Was there anything left to achieve? It was more so that a team of oxen couldn't have kept him away from spring training one more time.

The 1911 season began on a downer of a note for all of baseball, struck by a stunning tragedy when Addie Joss died at age 31 on April 14. Earlier in the month, Joss became ill, on April 3 passing out from heat prostration on the field in spring training. He was hospitalized and then sent home. Doctors ran through a variety of possible diagnoses, from ptomaine poisoning to nervous indigestion to pleurisy. As the season was about to begin, Joss passed away from tubercular meningitis. Joss' funeral was on April 17, the day of a scheduled game by his Cleveland team against the Detroit Tigers.

When initially the game was not postponed, Cleveland players revolted, saying they intended to attend the funeral. The team activities came to a standstill while officials and players grieved. Cy Young, who was Joss' road roommate the year before, publicly shed tears at the funeral. The Reverend Billy Sunday, a one-time big-league player who became a famous evangelist, presided over the service.

It was then agreed that on July 24, a benefit game to aid Joss' family would be played featuring top players from around the league. Joss' Naps team lined up against all-stars from the other seven teams, managed by Jimmy McAleer.

Among those who played for the all-stars were Ty Cobb, Frank "Home Run" Baker, Walter Johnson, Eddie Collins, Tris Speaker, and Sam Crawford, all eventually Hall of Famers, as Joss became as well. The all-stars won the game, 5–3, before 15,270 fans, with $13,000 raised for Joss' family to cover medical bills.

Young, who greatly respected and liked Joss, started the game and pitched the first three innings. "My baseball experience has thrown me with practically every man in the league for more than 20 years," Young said. "But I never met a fairer or more square man than Addie."[13]

When the 1911 season began for Young, he had 504 victories on the ledger. He dreamed of repeating how he had killed the rumors of his demise in recent seasons when he won 21, 21, and 19 games, all in his 40s.

Early in the season, Young took ill with a bronchial infection. He was slow to bounce back and did not start a game until June 9. He was sitting on a record of 3–4 with a 3.88 earned run average on August 16 when Cleveland released him. Surely, this was the conclusion of a glorious career. Since Peoli was only a couple of hours away by train, once Young packed up, he was home—he believed for good—in a short time.

Young seemed to acknowledge a failure to keep off excess weight, how it showed around his belly, and hindered him in his older athletic age. "The boys are taking unfair advantage of an old man," Young said, phrasing things in a half-joking manner. "They know this big stomach of mine makes it difficult for me to field bunts, so instead of swinging at my stuff, they are laying the ball down [for bunts]. When the third baseman has to start doing my work, it's time for me to quit."[14]

Young, who always was a man of the soil and embraced the farmer's lifestyle, went right back to work at home when he was cut, though there was an immediate rumor that he would be joining the New York American League franchise. That did not happen. But one of the best-known and most popular of ballplayers was not quite through with the game yet. Inside, he may have believed so, but he was defiant to sports writers who demanded to know if this truly was the end. "There is a lot of good pitching in me yet," Young said. "The public hasn't seen the last of me. I will be a good pitcher for a number of years."[15]

Such bravado was uncommon for Young. He never bragged when he was the best. Now he was bragging when he was no longer the best. At the least, he was trying to display a tone of confidence.

Soon after being dropped by Cleveland, Young received an offer he couldn't refuse. The Boston Rustlers, aka the Braves eventually, were in the midst of a horrible season. The idea of bringing in a Cy Young who could draw fans to a team that would finish 44–107 was a little-risk gamble. For a man of pride, the arrangement of finishing the season back in Boston had appeal.

Young showed up, pitched 80 innings and went 4–5, albeit with a higher-than-norm 3.71 earned run average. It was not a half-bad showing for a 44-year-old athlete. The 511th and last win of Cy Young's baseball career was recorded on September 22, 1911. Boston defeated the Pittsburgh Pirates, 1–0, and yes, the Cyclone pitched a complete-game shutout.

He lost a few more games to complete the season, but that superb game emboldened Young to try to live up to his pledge to pitch even longer. Young did sign a contract with Boston for the 1912 season and went through spring training, looking trimmer from weight loss. But then Young was afflicted by one of the pitchers' nemesis injuries he had rarely endured. He came down with a sore arm and never got off the Braves' bench. "It's no use, I'm not going on," Young said. "My best days were spent on the diamond. I hate to leave the game."[16]

So the most amazing big-league pitching career of them all finally came to an end. Denton True "Cy" Young retired with 511 victories and 315 defeats, both records, and 815 starts and 749 complete games, also records. Plus 7,356 innings pitched, another record. He was known throughout the country, and even though he still had half his life to live, it was agreed that this man's pitching marks would live forever.

21

The Farmer Comes Home

When Cy Young returned to his Peoli, Ohio, farm and wife Robba to stay, he returned to the lifestyle he knew best. For all of his 22 years as a Major League pitcher, he had always spent his winters close to the land, the same land he grew up on. Farming and baseball were what made the man. One role was performed quietly, out of the limelight. The other made him a national celebrity. Denton True Young was always true to himself. He was not a man of pretense, even if he was a pitcher of prominence and self-assuredness.

Apparent even when Cy Young retired before the 1912 season was that his defining baseball statistic of 511 wins would last for eternity as a baseball record. Yes, he left behind other records, but he made the number 511 legendary. It seemed clear to the sporting press of his day that no one would ever eclipse such a mark. Every passing decade or generation since then, some sportswriter would bring it up all over again and reaffirm the thought.

The number is magic. The number is his. The number is closely identified with Cy Young, any which way someone wanted. As in, how many victories did Cy Young record in his big-league career? Or, what pitcher won 511 games in the majors?

Actually, the funny thing about that dazzling 511 total is that Young always claimed he was cheated out of one more win by errant scorekeeping. He told sportswriter Grantland Rice and informed others of the same thing periodically. Maybe so, but 511 is what is written.

It is not as if Young cornered the market on pitching greatness. Many of his contemporaries were great. Many of those who played immediately after he retired were great. Future generations of pitchers came along and were great. But not a one of them could come close to winning as many games as Cy Young, nor could they sustain such a level of greatness for so long.

In 1973, the renowned St. Louis sportswriter Bob Broeg said of Young, "Trying to keep up with Cy's accomplishments, much less comprehend them in the light of modern measurements, is as difficult as trying to pry a ball out of the old man's iron grip. What feats those ancient eyes had seen and tireless right arm achieved make Cy Young seem in the '70s as both its most amazing physical specimen and its link between the game's primitive infancy and its modern maturity."[1]

Young leads the list of the winningest pitchers of all time, a mark never challenged following his retirement. Walter Johnson is second with 417 victories, Grover Cleveland Alexander and Christy Mathewson are tied for third with 373 apiece, followed by Pud Galvin, 365, and Warren Spahn, 363, who is the winningest lefty.

Young either pitched against or saw all of them pitch during his lifetime. Johnson is just about the only one in the group who is ever favorably compared to Young, despite their disparity in victories. Johnson, who played for many bad Washington Senators teams, broke into the majors in 1907, 17 years after Young, and their meetings were few. Near the end of Young's career in 1911, he lost a game to Alexander, who was just getting started with the Philadelphia Phillies. There was no shame in that, since Alexander was about to become one of the all-time greats himself, but that's not how it looked to Young at the time. "I always said I would quit when the kids could beat me," Young said.[2]

Addie Joss, who by comparison to the others was a shooting star, dying early, believed Young was the best pitcher he ever saw, but when he got a glimpse of Johnson's stuff, it made him exclaim, "That young fellow is another Cy Young. I never saw a kid with more than he displayed. Of course, he is still green, but when he has a little experience he should be one of the greatest pitchers that ever broke into the game."[3]

Young went hard into retirement, grudgingly giving up the game, though he did continue to throw some local ball in between the chores on the farm. He made a goodly sum from the sport at a time when a goodly sum was minuscule compared to what it is now, but he was able to live comfortably with Robba. He rose early and milked cows. He hayed and grew crops and raised sheep. He also hunted in the fall, another serious pastime. "I'll farm, hunt, help some of the young fellows, and maybe play in a game now and then," Young informed his wife after he retired.[4]

A generation later, Young was described as having gray encroaching in his dark hair, but still possessing a twinkle in his blue eyes. He set the record clear that he was aware he was indeed closing in on his 500th victory at the time and grew frustrated with the wait after he failed to obtain it in several tries.

I had lost seven or eight games straight after chalking up my 499th victory, and I couldn't seem to break my losing streak. Then I broke the spell in the game with

**After World War II, when Little League ramped up, Young was an avid sup-
porter of kids playing ball.**

> Washington. So I decided to keep the ball I used in that game as a souvenir. You
> will probably run across several balls around the country which are said to be the
> one I used in the 500th win, as my dad used to like to give away souvenirs to the
> friends and relatives when they visited us. He would tell them all that the ball was
> the one used in hitting the 500 mark. But this is the original one.[5]

In an era when it was common for players to become player-managers
or swiftly jump to the helm of a big-league club to stay in the game as soon
as they lay down their gloves or bats, Young had regularly said he had
no interest in running a team or coaching full-time. His only stint as an
American or National League manager was that 3–3 stretch with Boston
as an emergency fill-in when Chick Stahl killed himself.

Young did not purposely distance himself from the game, but he liked
being a farmer. He was not about to live in a big city that he wasn't playing
in. He was courtly if sports writers came around to pump him for thoughts
of the old days. He enjoyed telling baseball stories from the time period
when many of his inquisitors had not yet been born.

These were not the sportswriters who wrote stories about the games
he pitched. They were from a later generation, newcomers speaking to a

gradually aging man whose right arm had spewed flames when he needed them. He made comparisons about the players he saw up close and those he played against. Young was a living shrine. Many came to kneel at his feet to hear his words of wisdom about pitching as if he were a Buddhist wise man perched upon a mountain-top.

During one of those sessions, Young named "Wee" Willie Keeler and Ty Cobb as the two toughest players for him to get out. He picked Keeler

Cy Young threw out the first pitch at many Ohio Little League events, and signed autographs for the young players, too.

first, though both men were outstanding batsmen and tough outs for everyone. "Keeler was harder to fool than Cobb," Young said. "Cobb could pull, or push, a pitch, and he was a great bunter. I never saw a batter who could drag a bunt like Cobb.[6]

Much later in life, Young chose a personal All-Star squad representing the best players he saw compete in person. He did not include himself on the list, even though he did mention a decent-sized pitching staff. In many ways, Young's selections mirrored the choices of the Baseball Hall of Fame, though others may well have been named by a prejudiced mind in that he knew the guys and liked them.

Young's pitching staff included Walter Johnson. The remainder are men of distinction, but not the biggest winners of them all. He made room for Addie Joss, Rube Waddell, with whom he had several tight confrontations, and Ed Walsh. Walsh's arm wore out before he could top 195 wins, though he and Joss had the two lowest earned run averages of all time. Walsh won 40 games in one season for the Chicago White Sox.

Young picked three catchers, and it is here where his personal preferences came into play the loudest. He named Lou Criger and Chief Zimmer, the two men who meant the most to him as battery mates, were close friends and helped guide him to his success. The other catcher was Hall of Famer Bill Dickey of the New York Yankees.

The rest of Young's starting line-up consisted of Lou Gehrig at first base, Eddie Collins at second base, Jimmy Collins at third base, and an outfield of Babe Ruth, Ty Cobb, and Tris Speaker. Only Collins, who did make the Hall of Fame, stands out as someone who was close to Young in his life. Young's list of substitutes (keeping it limited since he was used to playing on small-roster teams long before clubs were permitted to carry 25 players) included outfielders Harry Hooper, Hugh Duffy, Fred Clarke, and Jimmy McAleer, and shortstop Fred Parent.

More often when Young's thoughts were probed, he was asked about pitching, his forte. However, the questions posed more or less came down to the same thing: How did you do it? How did you win 511 games?

> I could throw a tobacco ball, a pitch that was dirtied and a ball that wasn't so lively. I had excellent control [something he repeated throughout the years], throwing with four different deliveries and wheeling on the batter to hide the ball. I had the benefit of a larger strike zone—from the top of the shoulders to the bottom of the knees—and I admit some of my cut-plug tobacco would get on the ball, but there were disadvantages other than the obvious financial ones.[7]

For those who played pre–1900 and during the early days of the 21st century, the game was very different. Ballpark seating was smaller, the structures were flimsier, the same ball was used inning after inning, the uniforms were hot and baggy. "I'm thinking of the poorer fields, poorer equipment, bad food, bad traveling conditions, no shower baths, sooty trains, noisy rooming houses, some of them full of bedbugs that'd keep you up all night," he said.[8]

Cy Young did not make playing big-league ball at the time sound very glamorous.

Playing a game with a single umpire handling all of the calls from behind the plate was no treat either, Young said. He recalled an occasion when the home ump was looking in another direction and John J. Mc-Graw, then playing for the Baltimore Orioles, cut right across the pitcher's mound to go from first to third, dashing past Young. The howls of Young's Cleveland Spiders calling for an automatic out on McGraw did not result in the play being overturned.

As someone who was a believer first in control and nicking the corners to make batters reach for a pitch, Young said he always tried to steer away from hurling the ball over the main hunk of the plate, but reserved the right to go by feel at other times. "But I defend pitchers who throw the ball into the strike zone at times with a count of two strikes and none," Young said. "I don't think the pitcher can permit the batter ever to type him or take him for granted. Every now and then on an 0-and-2 count I'd bring the ball right to the hitter, hoping to surprise him."[9]

Those young lads seeking advice from the old pro likely never followed the type of off-season workout regimen Young recommended. Besides the basic farm work, he said chopping wood with an axe was good for the body. And long before the running movement, Young integrated long-distance running into his pre-spring training trips, for at least a solid three weeks.

One other thing was made clear in retirement. Yes, Young said, "True" was his real middle name, not "Tecumseh" which somehow got attached to him by Robert Unglaub along his journey. Tecumseh really did stick for a long time, too, even appearing on Young's Hall of Fame plaque initially.

Young had always been happy as a stay-at-home guy on the farm with his wife for company, but his life was severely disrupted in 1933 when Robba passed away. Cy was left alone at the once-comforting farm house and grew disenchanted and lonely. A close friend, John Benedum, and his wife, moved in and for two years brightened Young's days. Still, Young couldn't bear to spend so much time in the place that had produced so many good memories.

In 1935, Young sold his farm and much of his other personal property and went on the road as a barnstorming baseball player for an old-timers team, returning to his favorite game at 68. In Young's case, he really was an old-timer. The Benedums bought the farm next door and stayed in the

When Cy Young (right) was 86, an Akron, Ohio, rubber company planned to build a factory not far from Newcomerstown, the largest town near his farm. The company happened to employ another man named Cy Young (left) and sent him to chat with the old pitcher for a story in the company newspaper.

neighborhood. When the 1935 season ended, though, and Young returned to Ohio, he was still melancholy.

Back in Peoli, this time the Benedums made Young the same offer he had made to them. They asked if he would like to live with them, and he moved in, taking up residence in the farm next to the former Miller-Young place. He resumed working the land, helping out his new landlord. The Benedums considered Young to be a member of the family. When they had a baby girl named Jane, she became Young's de facto granddaughter. The relationship was a delight and a long-lasting one.

At one point during his long, close relationship with the Benedums, Young did disembark for Boston again and became a hotel greeter for an old friend, though that was not a permanent deal. In 1905, baseball executives decided to explore the roots of their sport. Albert G. Spalding, the one-time pitcher and sporting goods magnate, was the one who urged Major League leaders to get to the bottom of the sport.

Although what the Mills Commission announced was incorrect, its findings were embraced for many years. The committee spent three years investigating and concluded, based on flimsy evidence, that the sport was invented in Cooperstown, New York, in 1839 by a young soldier named Abner Doubleday, who went on to become a general in the Union army during the Civil War. This fiction was swallowed whole, and it was not for many years that the story was debunked and replaced with the more believable tale that baseball's similar antecedents, rounders and cricket in England, represented the genuine origins.

However, it was far too late for a do-over when it was proposed that a Baseball Hall of Fame be based in upstate New York. Well before the brick and mortar building was constructed, the Hall of Fame had been created on paper. Stephen Carlton Clark, a Cooperstown hotel owner, is credited with the idea of establishing a Hall and for it to be constructed in Cooperstown. From the beginning, the voters were members of the Baseball Writers' Association of America, players could only be considered if they had played 10 seasons in the majors, and to be chosen they had to receive 75 percent of the ballots cast. Voters could check off only 10 players for consideration. In one difference at the time, only players who competed in the 20th century could receive votes. A separate category was created for old-timers, but originally, it wasn't completely clear how it was defined.

The results of the first voting for the Hall were announced on February 2, 1936. Although there was to be no induction ceremony since there was no Hall of Fame building, the first class receiving the great honor consisted of Ty Cobb, Walter Johnson, Christy Mathewson, Honus Wagner and Babe Ruth. Left out because he did not receive 75 percent of the tally was Cy Young, who surprisingly only received 49.11 percent support that year.

It seems inconceivable that Young was not chosen while two other pitchers, though clearly great ones themselves, were elected ahead of him. This was the man who won 511 games. Perhaps some voters skipped Young because he played the first decade of his career in the 19th century. Whether the veterans designation hurt Young's chances or not, this was a bit embarrassing.

The snub was soon rectified. Although the building housing the Hall of Fame was nowhere close to completion, the voting continued each year. The group was expanded by eight in 1937. Cy Young was selected in that vote. Other top players added were Napoleon Lajoie and Tris Speaker. Connie Mack and John McGraw were included as the first managers, and Ban Johnson, founder of the American League, Morgan Bulkeley, the first president of the National League, and George Wright, who organized the start-up of the Cincinnati Red Stockings, the first professional club, were elected as the first executives.

These were tricky times, going back to the roots of the game, the real pioneers of baseball being measured against more recent players. That was the task to get right as the fledgling organization sought its footing. The three individuals added to the Hall in 1938 by the voters were pitcher Grover Cleveland Alexander, Alexander Cartwright, founder of the 1800s New York Knickerbockers and believed at the time to be the architect of some primary rules of the game, and Henry Chadwick, who invented the box score, the statistical mechanism by which baseball history is recorded.

The next year, 1939, a large class was named. This group of 10 included the great New York Yankees first baseman Lou Gehrig, who was forced to retire at 36 due to a debilitating illness after playing eight games that year (and died just shy of his 38th birthday in 1941). A special exception from the rules was adopted to allow Gehrig to be inducted immediately.

Adrian "Cap" Anson, the early star who initially misjudged Cy Young's talent, Eddie Collins, Buck Ewing, Willie Keeler, George Sisler, and Charles "Hoss" Radbourn were other players honored. Charles Comiskey, owner of the Chicago White Sox following his playing career, Albert G. Spalding, the pitcher-sporting goods manufacturer, and Candy Cummings, a 145-game winner as a pitcher, but most significantly regarded as the inventor of the curveball, joined the list.

Cummings and some friends were playing on a beach when the curve was born as an offshoot of him throwing seashells. "I get a great deal of pleasure now in my old age out of going to games and watching the curves, thinking that it was through my blind efforts that all this was made possible," Cummings said later in life.[10]

Following the election of the 1939 class (Gehrig was not chosen until a little bit later in the year) an induction ceremony was scheduled. At last the building had caught up with the paperwork. The event was scheduled for June 12, 1939, on Main Street in Cooperstown, right outside the front door of the new building.

Some 25 men besides Gehrig were honored with induction, but they were not all present for the festivities. Of the first five, Christy Mathewson had already passed away. Bulkeley, Ban Johnson, McGraw, George Wright (whose brother Harry would be elected in 1953), Cartwright, Chadwick, Comiskey, Cummings, Ewing, Keeler, Radbourn, and Spalding were all dead and unable to respond to their invitations. That was a large percentage of the group.

A famous photograph was taken at Cooperstown on the day of the induction of those still living and present. The picture includes 10 men wearing suits and ties, not the uniforms by which they had become so well-identified. Six of the men are standing, and four are seated. The standing row features Wagner, Alexander, Speaker, Lajoie, Sisler, and Walter

Johnson. Seated are Collins, Ruth, Mack, and on the far right, Cy Young. Still with a thick head of hair (it is not possible to tell how much gray had taken over since it is a black-and-white photograph), in a light-colored suit, Young sits with his right leg is crossed over his left. His head is turned away from the photographer, and he is gazing to his left, as if someone distracted him at the wrong time.

Famously, Ty Cobb was late and missed posing for the picture and the historical record it represented. While some intimated that Cobb, who was accompanied by his son, planned this maneuver to make a splashy entrance for the event, he was actually late to Cooperstown because his train to Albany ran behind schedule. It does make one wonder why another shot was not taken after Cobb got there. Sisler referred to the ceremony as "rather simple, but dignified" and added that being part of it was "a great honor."[11]

Cy Young's visit to Cooperstown was a treat of a trip for him. He began giving much of his personal memorabilia to the Hall of Fame, and the hall's museum always displays some of it. Young enjoyed seeing other old-time players and reminiscing with them about their days in the big leagues.

Cy Young's acceptance speech was not terribly long, but it was heartfelt. "I'm very glad to be here," he said in part. "Nothing pleases me better than to be about and see and know that the young generation today is following our footsteps going along throughout our land. One of the greatest games on earth.... I do hope and wish that 100 years from now the game will still be greater."[12]

A century has not passed since Young uttered those words, although more than a century has passed since he retired from active play. Young lived half of his life beyond the days when he traveled to either Cleveland or Boston for most of his professional ballplaying. The game has rolled on with some variations, but everyone who follows the sport knows that Cy Young won more games than anyone else in history.

22

Grand Tributes

Cy Young was 72 years old when he was inducted into the Baseball Hall of Fame. Since retiring as an active big-league pitcher 28 years earlier, he had been out and about on the baseball scene when invited, open to visits by baseball writers to chat about his days in the game, and a regular visitor to Cleveland Indians home games, taking the short drive north.

He stayed up on current baseball events, watched with admiration as Babe Ruth came along and revolutionized the game with his home run power, and appreciated the speed and form of Indians star pitcher Bob Feller. Feller was a fastball specialist and a strikeout king, and Young liked to watch him work. "The best pitcher I've seen among the modern boys," Young said of Feller.[1]

Feller, another farm boy, from Iowa, actually made his Major League debut at 17. He won 266 games but would have likely won many more if he had not volunteered to serve in World War II and missed nearly four full seasons. Feller led the American League in strikeouts seven times, and his 348 Ks in 1946 was a landmark achievement at the time.

Young was an astute baseball man, and while he kept demurring about any desire to manage a big-league team, he broke his vow never to do so in 1913, when the Federal League formed as a competitor to the American and National Leagues. Before staking its claim as a major league for the 1914–1915 seasons, the Federal League started as a minor league. A team was placed in Cleveland, one of Young's major haunts, and the Green Sox surprisingly convinced Young to run the squad.

Playing in Luna Park, the Green Sox went 63–54 (some say 64–54), about 10 wins shy of first place. This was Young's only other managing job besides filling in with the Red Sox briefly. He made himself available for this work due to its convenience and because after being out of the game as a pitcher, he was already beginning to miss the sport's summer rhythms.

The Federal League lasted, but the Green Sox did not. They played that single season in Cleveland and then became a Toronto minor-league franchise. Young did not accompany the team north.

In 1921, during a celebration in Cleveland, Young took the mound as a pitcher for fun. He was 54 years old, and his appearance was for show, not designed to showcase his stuff.

A year after Young was inducted into the Hall of Fame, he announced that he would ship many of his precious big-league souvenirs, described as loving cups, to the Hall of Fame. There was a passing mention that they might be worth something like $700 in value. That would be a ludicrously low estimate today. Although there was no inventory noted, they surely would be valued at hundreds of thousands of dollars in the modern sports memorabilia world. "I don't need them," Young said.[2] But the baseball world appreciated them being preserved and transferred to a safe place.

The older Young got, the more people seemed to take note of his passing birthdays, especially the milestone numbers. In 1942, when he was about to turn 75, a drive was begun to send him happy birthday postcards from all around the country. E. R. "Turk" Reilly, who was Wilson Sporting Goods' major league representative out of Columbus, Ohio, came up with the idea. "I know it would be a source of great pleasure to Cy up in the lonely hills of Eastern Ohio," Reilly said.[3]

The thought was kind, but Young's birthday was amply celebrated by local people. Although Peoli, Ohio, may have had a mere dozen residents, nearby Newcomerstown was the hub of Tuscarawas County, and a testimonial dinner was thrown for Young as a birthday party that year.

The Sporting News checked in with Cy Young on his birthday, noting that he rose at 6 a.m., as usual, and completed several farm chores. Young recounted his perfect game of May 1904, when his superstitious teammates on the Boston Americans ignored him in the dugout as the game progressed. "Funny thing," Young said. "Between innings on the bench, the boys wouldn't speak to me. No one even offered me a chew. I was puzzled. Then, after the game ended, I realized they had worried for fear they would break my luck. They sure pounded me then."[4]

In 1944, when Young was 77, World War II was raging and many baseball stars, including Ted Williams, Joe DiMaggio, Bob Feller, were out of the game, serving their country. Young took a tour of minor league and Major League parks and viewed games to see how the sport was faring. He paused in Philadelphia at Shibe Park to visit with Connie Mack, then 81 and still the manager of the Athletics. Young said he thought the sport was doing okay despite the disadvantages of the nation being at war and so many big names missing from lineups. "It doesn't look as if the war or manpower shortage has seriously affected baseball," Young said. "While many of the game's headliners are in the service, there are plenty of promising youngsters filling their places and doing a right smart job, too."[5] That was overly optimistic testimony, but it was achievement enough that big-league ball continued to be played during the war, thanks to the blessing of President Franklin Delano Roosevelt.

Mack even asked Young to throw a few pitches from the mound at his advanced age, and Cy obliged. "By golly, if he was only 40 years younger I'd sign him on the spot," Mack said. Young responded, "And maybe you don't think I'd like nothing better to be pitching right now. Especially this night stuff. They tell me all you need is a fastball kept around the batter's legs."[6]

At 79, Young was visiting New York, mostly to watch big-league games, when he encountered a *New York Times* sports columnist, who tackled him for an interview. Young mentioned that not so long ago, his wood chopping produced 3,000 rail posts. He was still attempting to maintain some kind of condition.

The biggest celebrations for Young occurred when he turned 80 in 1947. Newcomerstown threw a big bash, and Bill Veeck, the future Hall of Famer who was probably the most fan-friendly baseball owner in history and who then operated the Cleveland Indians, joined in to add to the scope of the event.

The Newcomerstown party brought out 800 people to honor Young on March 29. A banquet was conducted with a menu that included roast beef, mashed potatoes and gravy, a lettuce salad, baked corn, a relish plate, rolls and butter, tomato juice, coffee, ice cream, and cake. Storefronts all over the town of 5,000 people displayed happy birthday signs for Young. Young received a new car. Some former big-leaguers, such as pitchers Sam Jones and Waite Hoyt, journeyed to the affair. The entire crowd sang "Happy Birthday" to Young. A beaming Young called the tribute "the greatest day of my life."[7]

Connie Mack sent a telegram to Young wishing him a happy birthday. "My sincerest congratulations on your 80th birthday," it read. "And I hope you'll make it at least 100. You should feel highly honored in having the citizens of your hometown pay you such a fine tribute. You have left a record in baseball that will not be excelled by any individual."[8]

At that time, the Cy Young victory count had been registered at 510, not 511, before additional research picked up another win. (Maybe that was the one Young thought was missing.) Waite Hoyt, who was inducted into the Hall of Fame in 1969, won 237 games. "Sad" Sam Jones, who was also present, won 239 games. "Sam and I know better than any person present just what it means to have won 510 games," Hoyt said.[9]

Young, much thinner and with age lines on his face, posed for innumerable photographs that day. He had become a pipe smoker, and one of the pictures showed him puffing on a pipe that resembled Sherlock Holmes. One of Young's gifts was a lifetime supply of Granger Rough Cut, his favorite tobacco for the pipe.

During the birthday party, Veeck, president of the Indians, in a grand gesture, invited Young and the entire town to an Indians game of his choosing later in the summer. Indeed, Veeck was the man who presented Young with the key to his new sedan. But as part of passing along the key, Veeck obtained Young's autograph—on a new contract with the Indians, 57 years after he first signed to play ball for the old Cleveland Spiders. "In the jam I'm in for pitchers, I can't let any talent like this get away from me," Veeck said.[10]

It was said that Veeck made 5,000 tickets available—to all of Young's good friends—and a special train picked up fans in Newcomerstown and then scooped up others on the way to Cleveland.

At 80, Young still held his opinions about the sport and freely compared his era to the current one. "In the old days, we used to play a game with one or two baseballs," Young said. "Today they use dozens. You really worked, too, as a pitcher. If you were relieved, the game was lost. And you went in right from the bench, not from the bullpen. The key to my success was that I was never wild. I could put the ball where I wanted to, inside or outside, high or low."[11]

A year later, a year after the big party, Cy Young's 81st birthday was a lot more low-key. That didn't stop sportswriters from checking in with him about his plans. That day was more typical. Up early, helping friend John Benedum with the farm work, as usual. "I can still do my work," Young said. "I feel good and I sleep good. But I'm slipping a little, for I can't see very well."[12] That was an unfortunate development because it meant Young didn't trust himself behind the wheel to drive the car he was presented with for his 80th birthday.

In 1953, when he was 86 years old, Cy Young was invited to dine with President Dwight Eisenhower at the White House. U.S. Rep. Frank Bow, the Congressman who represented Tuscarawas County, was going to accompany him to a Washington Senators game. However, Young was not feeling well enough and had to decline what would have been a special trip. "I don't feel quite up to it," Young said, as quoted in the *Congressional Record* by Bow.[13]

The plan was for Young to be present in the gallery while Bow read remarks into the *Record* about his fabulous career. Bow proceeded without Young's presence, something he lamented. Bow said, "I regret this very much, for Cy Young is a wonderful example of a young American who gained great fame entirely through his own efforts and I had hoped to pay fitting tribute to him here today.[14] Instead, Bow read into the

Cy Young always did the chores around his farm, whether it was milking cows, pitching hay or tilling soil.

Congressional Record a lengthy article about the Young of then-vintage which appeared in an Akron newspaper.

While Young's stay-at-home choice due to the demands of travel to Washington garnered this special attention, he did celebrate that same birthday in his home area with a few friends and did chime in with a few comments about baseball. "Where youngsters are still interested in baseball, there is still hope for the world," Young said.[15]

The youth of America in connection with baseball were never far from Young's thoughts. On October 31, 1948, Young made a speech in Alliance, Ohio, as part of an effort to bring more youths into the game. Little League Baseball was founded in 1938 in Williamsport, Pennsylvania, by Carl Stotz. It was not until 1948 that the first Little League outside of Pennsylvania was created, when New Jersey joined in. Now, Little League is played in all 50 states and 80 countries. But these were embryonic days, and Young wanted to give the plan a push. "Boys, I want to congratulate you on your plans ... but I want to give you some advice, too," Young said. "Get the kids the equipment, the uniforms and balls and bats, but make them earn it. Even if the kids you sponsor are only 10 years old, get a program for them that will make them hustle every minute."[16]

When Cy Young died in 1955, his beloved wife Robba had been dead for 22 years. He was buried next to her. Although the stone monument spelling of her name reads "Roba," all written references to her spell it Robba.

This was actually what the Ohio benefactors called a "Hot Stove League." The first Little League play in Ohio was officially conducted in 1949, and Young threw out the first pitch.

What was noted in a local article in 1953 was that Young had dwindled to 150 pounds. Recalling that Young was 210 pounds in his prime pitching days and up to perhaps 230 pounds when he pronounced himself too large to field his position, this was considerable shrinkage.

Arthur Daley, a 1956 Pulitzer Prize-winning *New York Times* columnist, knew Young for many years and wrote that in the final years of his life, he had indeed taken on the appearance of a very old man. "Cy Young was bent and gnarled and shriveled in his later years," Daley wrote. "But the broad sweep of his shoulders betrayed the former athlete. Wherever he went he was treated with reverent respect and even hard-bitten big leaguers, men without any stardust in their eyes, gathered around him like unashamed yokels."[17]

Denton True Young, Cy, or Cyclone, was 88 years old when he died on November 4, 1955, ending an extraordinary life begun in the shadow of the Civil War and spanning World War I, World War II, the Korean War, the earliest days of professional baseball, and entrée into the modern era of the game he adored.

Young passed away while sitting in an armchair in the family home of his friend John Benedum in Peoli, where he previously tended his own farm and lived for decades with his beloved wife Robba. Young had been slowed and lost much of his eyesight, but was not incapacitated in his last days, and the cause of death was given as a heart attack. The death certificate issued by the Ohio Department of Health called it a "coronary occlusion." The place of death was referred to as Newcomerstown, perhaps because Peoli was too small to be counted as an independent village.

Young had been failing gradually, though he continued to adhere to all of his old habits, despite some doctors' suggestions that he change some of them. He had some chest pains the day before he died, but before that he had meticulously spelled out the details for his own funeral, services, and the like. He even had a premonition he was about to die and was proven right.

The most popular man in the region, as much because of his personality and being "one of them," as much as being a star ballplayer, Young was surrounded by friends in the nearby communities. His wake might

On August 13, 1908, the Boston Red Sox (who had adopted their nickname that season), honored their star pitcher with "Cy Young Day." Young (left), his long-time catcher, Lou Criger (right) and their teammates dressed in oddball costumes for the day before playing.

have been termed lying in state, as if in the U.S. Capitol, and an estimated 2,000 people paid their respects. Young's funeral took place on November 7 at a Methodist Church, which gave many of his fellow players and teammates the chance to attend. Some of those baseball personages in attendance were Tris Speaker, Bob Feller, Billy Southworth, Sam Jones, and Steve O'Neill.

Young's estate was valued at $20,000 in shares of stock, and his will split the value between John Benedum and his wife, Ruth, and their daughter, Jane. Young was never a rich man, although he did well financially when he was a player. But he did not rake in money over the years that followed retirement, once saying he was nothing special as a businessman.

"Big" Ed Walsh called Young "the greatest pitcher of all times." Ty Cobb referred to Young as "a wonderful guy."[18] No one thought Cy Young was a more wonderful guy than Jane Benedum, whose married name was Meuhlen, Young's surrogate granddaughter. She said she remembered Young every day of the year, especially on March 29, when his birthday came around.

"Because that was our special day," said Benedum Meuhlen, who in her professional career became a nurse and died in 2011. "I don't remember it, but I was told often enough that Cy used to tend me while mother was busy. When I was still a baby, he'd sit in his big chair and she'd put me on a pillow on his lap. He was just Cy to me, and I was Little Jane to him. He was a big man, in heart as well as in size. He was proud, yet humble."[19]

Benedum Meuhlen had a lifetime's worth of memories from time spent with Young. When she was older, she accompanied him to big-league games and on visits to Honus Wagner an hour away, and through Young she met Connie Mack and Tris Speaker. She said Young helped her with her homework by using a magnifying glass when his vision declined, and taught her how to milk cows and shuck wheat. They were a tight pair. "He raised me," she said, giving Young credit alongside her parents. "He helped on the farm. He called me 'the kid.' He always said 'Bring the kid over to me.' I was always happy when I was around him."[20]

Not long after Cy Young passed away, Ford Frick, the Commissioner of baseball, announced a special way to honor the pitcher and his accomplishments. Some 44 years after his retirement, few baseball experts could be found to declare that Young's mark of 511 victories would ever be approached, never mind broken.

Frick, the one-time baseball writer, served as president of the National League from 1934 to 1951 and was baseball's head man from 1951 to 1965. During his previous league executive stint, Ford contributed to the establishment of the Baseball Hall of Fame. Now Frick spearheaded the establishment of the Cy Young Award. Beginning in 1956, the trophy was presented to the best pitcher each year. Between 1956 and 1966, just one award-winner was selected annually, covering both leagues. Starting in 1967, and ever since, the National League and American League have honored one pitcher from each league at the end of the season.

The first winner of the Cy Young Award was the Brooklyn Dodgers' Don Newcombe. Newcombe, then 30 years old, was a 6-foot-4, 220-pound fastball specialist who went 27–7 in 1956 with a 3.06 earned run average. Newcombe also won the NL Most Valuable Player Award that season. Newcombe previously had won Rookie of the Year honors, too. "It was very gratifying," Newcombe said of winning the first Cy Young Award. He did not know that much about the man, but he was aware of one salient factor, that Young had won more than 500 games. "That seems to be two baseball careers. It's pretty hard to get to 300."[21]

Newcombe showed some signs of being an old-time pitcher, one who could work on short rest if he had to do so. During one doubleheader, Newcombe threw a nine-inning complete game against the Philadelphia Phillies in the opener, and then threw seven innings in the second game. Speaking in 1992, Newcombe said he could not imagine pitchers of that era trying that. "Guys today don't want to pitch seven innings," Newcombe said. "Never mind a doubleheader."[22]

The Hall of Famers who have won the Cy Young Award are Warren Spahn, Early Wynn, Whitey Ford, Don Drysdale, Sandy Koufax, Gaylord Perry, Jim Palmer, Jim Hunter, Rollie Fingers, Randy Johnson, Dennis Eckersley, Pedro Martinez, Roy Halladay, Tom Glavine, Ferguson Jenkins, Greg Maddux, Steve Carlton, Tom Seaver, John Smoltz, Bruce Sutter, and Bob Gibson.

Roger Clemens has won a record seven times in both leagues. Also, Jim Perry, Gaylord's brother, captured the honor once. On nine occasions a relief pitcher has earned the prize, something that would have been an alien concept to Young. Oh, and Jane Benedum Meuhlen owned a replica Cy Young Award trophy.

A museum was opened in Newcomerstown, primarily to commemorate Young's life and career. Many of the exhibits were items owned by Young, or by his neighbors and friends (including the pitcher's old axe), and illustrate his career and connection to the community. It has variously been referred to as "Ohio's Baseball Museum and Hall of Fame," "Cy Young Museum" or "Cy Young's Hometown Museum."

"We are not trying to compete with Cooperstown," said Thomas Eakin, the main founder, at the museum's 1975 dedication. "We just want to establish a fitting tribute to Cy Young and Ohio baseball."[23] Eakin was a vested-interest Cy Young memorabilia collector and transferred many objects from his own collection to the museum. "I used to have a lot of this stuff in my attic," Eakin said.[24]

Newcomerstown is the site of a mini-baseball field with a large Cy Young monument placed on the pitcher's mound. Young is actually buried in Port Washington, about 10 miles away, and an impressive headstone is upon his grave. There is a Cy Young Memorial Park in Newcomerstown, home to a Cy Young Days Festival.

Not only was Young born in the immediate area and grew up there, but he returned to his farm every off-season when he was playing, and then settled back in his original area. That made Young even more special to the local residents. Young was always clear this was home to him even though the local citizens always thought his fame would take him away for good. "But he never changed," said Newcomerstown businessman Gary King in the 1970s. "All his life he remained a quiet, humble man. Even when he was in his 80s, he took an interest in Little League. He was always throwing out first balls."[25]

Peoli, Ohio, was always a tiny place. Cy Young was the only roadside attraction. In the early 1950s, there was a plan to close the post office. Then the decision was more closely examined, and it was realized that Young alone received enough mail to keep it going. Only after his death did that office shut down.

Cy Young was more deeply imbedded in Ohio than anywhere else in the world. But his second home was Boston, where he did great things and was revered for a large portion of his career. Nearly 40 years after his death, a movement grew to commemorate the famous pitcher's connection to the city. Tied in to a 90th anniversary celebration of the first World Series of 1903, which involved Young and his Boston Americans, a statue honoring Young was unveiled.

The location was fitting for the extra-large bronze that the Boston Red Sox and the Yawkey Foundation helped bring to fruition. Placement was on the Northeastern University campus because that's where the old Huntington Avenue Grounds stood and where Young so magnificently toiled. Indeed, the old home plate was situated 60 feet, 6 inches away and is marked by a plaque.

The statue is even bigger in real life than Cy Young was, weighing 1,000 pounds and measured at 6-foot-8. In the work by sculptor Bob Shure, Young is leaning forward towards his catcher, left hand (wearing a glove) resting on his left knee as he peers in for the sign. His right arm is draped across his backside, a baseball nestled in his palm. Young's socks go high up his leg, to just below the knee.

George Kimball, one of Boston's renowned sports columnists, trotted out an old, but not-so-well-recalled tribute to Cy Young by quoting clever poet Ogden Nash, who put into verse what ran through the minds of many during Young's prime. "Y is for Young," Nash wrote, "The Magnificent Cy; People batted against him; But I never knew why."[26]

After all, what was the use of carrying those clubs to the plate when the man of 511 victories was at his finest on the mound?

Jane Benedum Meuhlen was 58 at the time and made the journey from Ohio—her first airplane flight—for the ceremony. It was old home week, far from home for her, as she gazed upon the sculpture. "I was startled when I saw that," she said of Young's hand on the ball in the statue. "I can't tell you how many children Cy taught to throw a baseball using that very grip. Back on the farm, Cy always talked about Boston. He was always saying what a wonderful place it was and how he'd never forget it."[27]

The bronze statue of the winningest pitcher of all time demonstrated that Boston still remembered Cy Young, 82 years after his Major League career ended and 38 years after his death. Maybe that's what they mean when they say those elected to the Baseball Hall of Fame are immortals.

Chapter Notes

Introduction

1. https://www.baseball-almanac.com/quotes/quoyung.shtml. "Cy Young Quotes" (quote from August 3, 1948).

Chapter 1

1. Alan H. Levy, *Rube Waddell: The Zany, Brilliant Life of a Strikeout Artist* (Jefferson, NC: McFarland, 2000), 156.
2. *Ibid.*
3. *Ibid.*, 158.
4. Reed Browning, *Cy Young: A Baseball Life* (Amherst: University of Massachusetts Press, 2000), 143.
5. David Southwick, "Cy Young," Society for American Baseball Research, no date, Cy Young file, Baseball Hall of Fame Library Archives. https://sabr.org/bioproj/person/dae2fb8a.
6. Browning, 144.
7. Al Hirshberg, "Cy Young, Hurler Of 3 No-Hitters," *Boston Herald-Traveler*, date missing, second part of series, Cy Young file, Baseball Hall of Fame Library Archives.
8. Southwick, *ibid.*
9. Norman L. Macht, *Connie Mack and the Early Years Of Baseball* (Lincoln: University of Nebraska Press, 2007), 328.
10. John Carmichael and Francis J. Powers, *My Greatest Day in Baseball* (Lincoln: University of Nebraska Press, 1945/1996 reprint), 103.
11. *Ibid.*
12. *Ibid.*
13. Browning, 143.

Chapter 2

1. Reed Browning, *Cy Young: A Baseball Life* (Amherst: University of Massachusetts Press, 2000), 4.
2. Ralph H. Romig, *Cy Young: Baseball's Legendary Giant* (Philadelphia: Dorrance, 1964), 8.
3. *Ibid.*, 4.
4. *Ibid.*, 5.
5. Browning, 8.
6. Romig, 12.
7. *Ibid.*, 13.
8. Browning, 10.

Chapter 3

1. Reed Browning, *Cy Young: A Baseball Life* (Amherst: University of Massachusetts Press, 2000), 13.
2. Hal Lebovitz, "Used Beefsteak Padding in Light Mitt Behind Plate," *The Sporting News*, January 12, 1949.
3. Ralph H. Romig, *Cy Young: Baseball's Legendary Giant* (Philadelphia: Dorrance, 1964), 17.
4. Browning, 35.
5. Romig, 19.
6. *Ibid.*, 21.

Chapter 4

1. Romig, 26.
2. Browning, 16.
3. Ira Smith, *Baseball's Finest Outfielders* (New York: A.S. Barnes, 1954), 38.
4. Browning, 17.
5. Sid Keener, "On the Sideline," *St.*

Louis Star-Times (date missing), National Baseball Hall of Fame Library.

Chapter 5

1. Browning, 22.
2. (No byline) "Worried and Worked Batsman," *Cleveland Press*, November 17, 1906, Cy Young file, Baseball Hall of Fame Library Archives.
3. Romig, 30.
4. Cy Young, "How I Learned to Pitch," *Baseball Magazine*, September 1908, Cy Young file, Baseball Hall of Fame Library Archives.
5. *Ibid.*
6. *Ibid.*
7. *Ibid.*
8. *Ibid.*
9. *Ibid.*
10. *Ibid.*

Chapter 6

1. (No byline), "Clarkson's Position" (Headline, publication cut off, Clarkson file, National Baseball Hall of Fame Library Archives, January 22, 1890. Sub-head, "The Boston Pitcher Explains Just Why He Signed with the League and Why He Acted as an Agent."
2. *Ibid.*
3. David Nemec, "Buck Ewing," Society for American Baseball Research (no date). https://sabr.org/bioproj/person/d60ea3ca.
4. Lawrence Feid, "Chat with Jesse Burkett," *Worcester Sunday Telegram*, January 11, 1953.
5. *Ibid.*
6. *Ibid.*
7. *Ibid.*
8. Browning, 36.
9. *Ibid.*, 44.
10. *Ibid.*, 39.
11. *Ibid.*, 41.

Chapter 7

1. Browning, 40.
2. *Ibid.*, 44.
3. Mark Twain, "Top 80 Famous Mark Twain Quotes," www.quoteambition.com, July 18, 2017.
4. *Ibid.*
5. *Ibid.*
6. Dave Condon, "In the Wake of the News," *Chicago Tribune*, November 7, 1955.
7. "How Old Cy Young Keeps Up the Pace," *Cleveland Press*, February 27, 1907.
8. *Ibid.*
9. *Ibid.*
10. J.G.T. Spink, "Looping the Loops," *The Sporting News*, June 22, 1944.
11. Turkin, Hy, "Cy, Oldtimer," *New York Daily News* (no date available), Baseball Hall of Fame Research Library.
12. Browning, 50.
13. Lawrence Feid, "Chat with Jesse Burkett," *Worcester Sunday Telegram*, January 11, 1953.
14. Lyle Spatz, *Willie Keeler: From the Playgrounds of Brooklyn to the Hall of Fame* (Lanham, MD: Rowman & Littlefield, 2015), 57.
15. *Ibid.*, 59.
16. Browning, 56.
17. (No byline), *Sporting Life*, October 19, 1895/Spalding's Official Baseball Guide.

Chapter 8

1. Browning, 59.
2. *Ibid.*, 61.
3. Mike Sowell, *July 2, 1903: The Mysterious Death of Hall of Famer Big Ed Delahanty* (New York: Macmillan, 1992), 102.
4. Browning, 62.
5. Cy Young, "How I Learned to Pitch," *Baseball Magazine*, September 1908.
6. Spatz, *Keeler*, 80.
7. National Baseball Hall of Fame archives summary on Cy Young. Baseballhall.org/hall-of-famers.
8. Young, "How I Learned to Pitch."

Chapter 9

1. Ralph Berger, "Dummy Hoy," Society for American Baseball Research, no date. https://sabr.org/bioproj/person/763405ef.

2. Romig, 37.
3. Browning, 67.
4. *Ibid.*
5. Romig, 37.
6. Brian McDonald, *Indian Summer* (Emmaus, PA: Rodale Press, 2003), 101.
7. *Ibid.*, 71.
8. *Ibid.*, 83.
9. *Ibid.*, 94.
10. *Ibid.*, 101.
11. David Fleitz, "Louis Sockalexis," Society for American Baseball Research, no date. https://sabr.org/bioproj/person/2b1aea0a.

Chapter 10

1. Arthur Daley, "Sports of the *Times*: Birthday Greetings to Cy Young," *New York Times*, March 29, 1943.
2. Bob Broeg, "Cy Young a Legend for Durability, Skill," *The Sporting News*, May 27, 1978.
3. *Ibid.*
4. Browning, 72.
5. *Ibid.*, 74.
6. Brian McDonald, *Indian Summer* (Emmaus, PA: Rodale Press, 2003), 200.
7. *Ibid.*, 203.
8. *Ibid.*, 205.
9. *Ibid.*, 205.
10. *Ibid.*, 205.
11. *Ibid.*, 207.
12. Mark S. Halfon, *Tales from the Deadball Era* (Lincoln, NE: Potomac, 2014), 43.
13. Bob Broeg, "Durable Ace Cy Young—A 511-Game Winner," *The Sporting News*, April 17, 1971.

Chapter 11

1. Browning, 76.
2. McDonald, 218.
3. Romig, 40.
4. Browning, 78.
5. Browning, 78.
6. *Ibid.*, 80.
7. Dan Coughlin, "No Question, Spiders Are Worst Ever," *Chronicle-Telegram* (Elyria, OH), September 28, 2003.
8. Jim Ingraham, "The 2003 Tribe Has Nothing on the 1899 Spiders, the Worst Team in Baseball History," *Morning Journal* (Lorain, OH), May 6, 2003.
9. *Ibid.*
10. Steve Krah, "Lou Criger," Society for American Baseball Research, no date. https://sabr.org/bioproj/person/95e23fdd.
11. Norman L. Macht, *Cy Young* (Philadelphia: Chelsea House, 1992), 29.
12. "Two Great Deals," no newspaper name, December 17, 1908, National Baseball Hall of Fame Library Archives.
13. Krah, "Lou Criger."
14. Cy Young, "How I Learned to Pitch," *Baseball Magazine*, September 1908.
15. Hype Igoe, "Donlin Own Press Agent in Turkey Trot to Top," *The Sporting News*, January 25, 1945.

Chapter 12

1. Romig, 44.
2. *Ibid.*
3. *Ibid.*, 45.
4. Browning, 87.
5. *Ibid.*, 91.
6. Baseball Hall of Fame biography of Ban Johnson. Baseballhall.org/hall-of-famers.
7. "Buck Freeman Acknowledges Babe Ruth's Batting Superiority," *Los Angeles Times*, September 19, 1919.
8. *Ibid.*
9. *Ibid.*
10. *Ibid.*

Chapter 13

1. Browning, 97.
2. *Ibid.*, 99.
3. *Ibid.*
4. *Ibid.*, 98.
5. Norman L. Macht, *Cy Young* (Philadelphia: Chelsea House, 1992), 33.
6. "Takes the Crowd, American League Opens with Boom in Baltimore," *Boston Globe*, April 27, 1901.
7. Browning, 105.
8. C. J. Kritzer, "Late Jimmy Collins, the King of Third Sackers Became Hot Corner Star by Ability to Handle Bunts," *Buffalo Evening News*, date missing, Jimmy Collins file, Baseball Hall of Fame Library Archives.

9. Browning, 107.
10. Hy Turkin, "Cy Young's Strategy on 2–0 Count," *New York Daily News*, June 21, 1945.
11. Browning, 111.

Chapter 14

1. Browning, 113.
2. Hy Turkin, "Cy Young's Strategy on 2–0 Count," *New York Daily News*, June 21, 1945.
3. Cy Young, "How I Learned to Pitch," *Baseball Magazine*, September 1908.
4. Turkin.
5. Browning, 113.
6. *Ibid.*, 114.
7. Stan Baumgartner, "Lajoie's Drives Made Infield Duck," *The Sporting News*, August 23, 1950.

Chapter 15

1. Browning, 122.
2. Jack Durkin, "Notables Laud Retiring A. L. Arbiter, Guest of Honor at Testimonial Dinner," *Syracuse Herald-Journal*, date missing, Baseball Hall of Fame Library Archives.
3. Bill Fleischman, "At 95, Freddie Digs Yaz, Hails Lajoie," *The Sporting News*, November 28, 1970.
4. *Ibid.*
5. *Ibid.*
6. Fleitz, David L., *Napoleon Lajoie: King of Ballplayers* (Jefferson, NC: McFarland, 2013), 108.

Chapter 16

1. Bob Ryan, *When Boston Won the World Series* (Philadelphia: Running Press, 2002), 93.
2. *Ibid.*, 94.
3. www.baseballalmanac.com, Baseball Almanac, "1903 World Series," (no date).
4. Romig, 62.
5. Mark Armour, "Sam Leever," Society for American Baseball Research, no date.
6. From www.baseballalmanac.com,

with citation from *The Sporting News*, December 6, 1955.
7. Bill Littlefield and Richard Johnson, editors, *Fall Classics: The Best Writing About the World Series' First 100 Years* (New York: Crown, 2003), 5–6.
8. Romig, 57.
9. *Ibid.*
10. Browning, 135.
11. *Ibid.*, 136.
12. *Ibid.*, 140.
13. *Ibid.*
14. *Ibid.*
15. David Seideman, "For Sale: Rare $250,000 First World Series Program Kept in Safe Deposit Box for 40 Years," *Personal Finance*, October 31, 2018.

Chapter 17

1. Nathaniel Staley, "Jesse Tannehill," Society for American Baseball Research, no date.
2. *Ibid.*
3. "Jesse Tannehill," National Baseball Hall of Fame Library clipping (no newspaper), September 22, 1954.
4. Ira Berkow, "The Lone Survivor of the First World Series," *Newspaper Enterprise Association*, October 6, 1970.
5. *Ibid.*
6. Benton Stark, *The Year They Called Off the World Series* (Garden City, NY: Avery, 1991), 159.
7. Charles Alexander, *John McGraw* (New York: Penguin, 1988), 109.
8. Stark, 160.
9. *Ibid.*
10. *Ibid.*, 163.
11. *Ibid.*, 164.
12. *Ibid.*, 182.
13. *Ibid.*, 188.
14. *Ibid.*
15. *Ibid.*, 180–181.
16. Macht, *Cy Young*, 36.

Chapter 18

17. "'It Didn't Take a Feather Out of Me,'" *The Baseball Bloggess*, July 4, 2014.
18. *Ibid.*
19. Romig, 72.
20. Browning, 165.
21. *Ibid.*, 158.

22. *Ibid.*, 160.
23. *Ibid.*, 165.
24. *Ibid.*
25. Benton Stark, *The Year They Called Off the World Series* (Garden City, NY: Avery, 1991), 181.

Chapter 19

1. Romig, 73.
2. "Drained," *Cincinnati Enquirer*, March 29, 1907.
3. Dick Thompson, "And in an Unrelated Development.... The 'Brothers' Stahl Weren't," (date and publication name missing), National Baseball Hall of Fame Library Archives.
4. *Ibid.*
5. Dennis Auger, "Chick Stahl: A Rainbow in the Dark," Society for American Baseball Research, *Deadball Era Research Committee Newsletter: The Inside Game* (November 2013).
6. *Ibid.*
7. Romig, 74.
8. Norman L. Macht, *Cy Young* (Philadelphia: Chelsea House, 1992), 42.
9. Browning, 171.
10. Ward Morehouse, "Tris Speaker Roams Field of Former Glories," *The Sporting News*, January 6, 1944.
11. Romig, 79.

Chapter 20

1. Romig, 80.
2. *Ibid.*, 82.
3. *Ibid.*, 83.
4. Browning, 184.
5. Ed Walsh, "Joss Is Best Ever," *Cleveland News*, October 3, 1908.
6. Romig, 83.
7. Kathia Miller, "Unassisted Triple Play Was One for the Record Books," naplesnews.com, July 10, 2009.
8. *Ibid.*
9. Romig, 83–84.
10. *Ibid.*, 86.
11. "Cy Young Takes 500th Game—Cleveland Boats Win," *Cleveland Plain-Dealer*, July 20, 1910.
12. Marc Bona, "Cleveland Pitcher Beats Senators to Make History," *Cleveland Plain-Dealer*, July 19, 2010.

13. Browning, 188.
14. *Ibid.*, 190.
15. Macht, *Cy Young*, 51.
16. Browning, 191.

Chapter 21

1. Bob Broeg, "Durable Ace Cy Young—A 511-Game Winner," *The Sporting News*, April 17, 1971.
2. *Ibid.*
3. Jack Kavanaugh, *Walter Johnson: A Life* (South Bend, IN: Diamond Communications, 1995), 42.
4. Romig, 91.
5. Bert Stoll, "Cy Young, Comfortable and Contented on Small Farm in Hills of Ohio, Recalls Days of Former Triumphs," (name of publication missing) National Baseball Hall of Fame Library Archives, February 4, 1932.
6. Jack Ledden, "Keeler Was Harder to Fool Than Cobb, Cy Young Claims," *Cleveland News*, no date, Baseball Hall of Fame Library Archives.
7. Broeg, "Durable Ace."
8. *Ibid.*
9. *Ibid.*
10. National Baseball Hall of Fame biography.
11. Rick Huhn, *The Sizzler* (Columbia: University of Missouri Press), 252.
12. Browning, 188.

Chapter 22

1. Browning, 205.
2. "Cy Young, One of 'Immortals,' Gives Trophies," *Associated Press*, May 1, 1940.
3. "Cy Young 75 on March 29," (publication missing), National Baseball Hall of Fame Library Archives, February 26, 1942.
4. Taylor Spink, "Young's 75th Natal Day," *The Sporting News*, April 2, 1942.
5. Don Basenfelder, "Cy Young Sees Close Pennant Races with Armed Forces Taking Stars," *Philadelphia Record*, May 22, 1944.
6. *Ibid.*
7. C. W. Phillips, "80th Birthday Party 'Greatest Day of All,' for Denton (Cy) Young," *The Sporting News*, April 9, 1947.
8. *Ibid.*
9. *Ibid.*

10. Gordon Cobbledick, "Old Cy Gets Car and Tribe Contract at Birthday Party," *Cleveland Plain-Dealer*, March 30, 1947.

11. Walter L. Jones, "Old Cy Young: Now 80 Years Old, One of Baseball's Great Pitchers Reminisces on His Farm," *Sportfolio*, June 1947.

12. "Cy Young, 81 Years Old, Will Help Do Farm Chores Today," *Associated Press*, March 29, 1948.

13. *Congressional Record*, June 6, 1953.

14. *Ibid.*

15. Dick Durling, "86th Birthday for Young," *Somerset Daily American* (Ohio), March 29, 1953.

16. Romig, 111.

17. Arthur Daley, "Sports of the Times: The No. 1 Pitcher," *New York Times*, November 6, 1955.

18. Browning, 210.

19. Richard Ellers, "Cy Young Was Little Jane's Papa," *Tribune-Chronicle* (Ohio) (date missing), National Baseball Hall of Fame Archives.

20. Mel Antonen, "To Friends, Cy Young's Legacy About More Than a Trophy," *USA Today*, November 4, 2002.

21. Lew Freedman, *Anchorage Daily News*, November 11, 1992.

22. *Ibid.*

23. Bob Stewart, "Cy Young Museum Dedication Set Friday," *Canton Repository* (Ohio), June 30, 1975.

24. Dan Coughlin, "The Paul Bunyan of Newcomerstown," *Cleveland Plain-Dealer*, July 2, 1975.

25. *Ibid.*

26. George Kimball, "Forever Young," *Boston Herald*, September 29, 1993.

27. Bill Parillo, "Hub Finally Delivers Honor to Cy Young," *Providence Journal-Bulletin*, September 30, 1993.

Bibliography

Books

Alexander, Charles. *John McGraw*. New York: Penguin Books, 1988.

Browning, Reed. *Cy Young: A Baseball Life*. Amherst: University of Massachusetts Press, 2000.

Carmichael, John P., and Francis J. Powers. *My Greatest Day in Baseball*. Lincoln: University of Nebraska Press, 1945/1996 reprint.

Fleitz, David L. *Napoleon Lajoie: King of Ballplayers*. Jefferson, NC: McFarland, 2013.

Halfon, Mark S. *Tales From the Deadball Era*. Lincoln, NE: Potomac Books, 2014.

Huhn, Rick. *The Sizzler: George Sisler, Baseball's Forgotten Great*. Columbia: University of Missouri Press, 2013.

Kavanaugh, Jack. *Walter Johnson: A Life*. South Bend, IN: Diamond Communications, 1995.

Levy, Alan H. *Rube Waddell: The Zany, Brilliant Life of a Strikeout Artist*. Jefferson, NC: McFarland, 2000.

Littlefield, Bill, and Richard Johnson, editors. *Fall Classics: The Best Writing About the World Series' First 100 Years*. NY: Crown, 2003.

Macht, Norman L. *Connie Mack and the Early Years of Baseball*. Lincoln: University of Nebraska Press, 2007.

McDonald, Brian. *Indian Summer*. Emmaus, PA: Rodale Press, 2003.

Romig, Ralph H. *Cy Young: Baseball's Legendary Giant*. (Philadelphia: Dorrance, 1964.

Ryan, Bob. *When Boston Won the World Series*. Philadelphia: Running Press, 2002.

Smith, Ira. *Baseball's Finest Outfielders*. New York: A. S. Barnes, 1954.

Sowell, Mike. *July 2, 1903: The Mysterious Death of Hall-of-Famer Big Ed Delahanty*. New York: Macmillan, 1992.

Spatz, Lyle. *Willie Keeler: From the Playgrounds of Brooklyn to the Hall of Fame*. Lanham, MD: Rowman & Littlefield, 2015.

Stark, Benton. *The Year They Called Off the World Series*. Garden City, NY: Avery, 1991.

Magazines

Baseball Magazine
Sportfolio
The Sporting News

News Services

Associated Press
Newspaper Enterprise Association

Newspapers

Anchorage (AK) *Daily News*
Boston Globe
Buffalo Evening News
Canton (OH) *Repository*
Chicago Tribune
Chronicle Telegram (Elyria, OH)
Cincinnati Enquirer
Cleveland News
Cleveland Plain-Dealer
Cleveland Press
Los Angeles Times
Morning Journal (Lorain, OH)
Naples (FL) *News*
New York Daily News
New York Times
Philadelphia Record
Providence Journal
St. Louis Star-Times
USA Today
Worcester (MA) *Star-Telegram*

Other Sources

Baseball Almanac, www.baseball-almanac.com
Congressional Record
National Baseball Hall of Fame Library Archives
Society for American Baseball Research

Index